365 DAYS

# Good Morning

## A journal, a cup of coffee, and Jesus

**Jim DuBro**

Follow Jim's continuing
journal writings
at James DuBro on facebook



ISBN 978-0-578-51163-4

Scripture quotations from the NIV
New International Version Bible

Printed in the USA
Ingram Spark

# ACKNOWLEDGEMENTS

I could never have accomplished this book without the continued encouragement and support of The Write Touch Inspirational Writers, the editing of Janice Lockert, the advice of my good friend Don Kenne (a proficient writer of a series of books) and most importantly the urging, support and encouragement of my wife Karen.

Special thanks to Karen DuBro and Sandra Fischer for their art enhancing my words, and for the design cover ideas and titles provided by Janice Lockert.

Here, from my collection of journal writing for the past two decades and more, are selections that represent my conversations with Jesus, my thoughts and my prayers. I still begin nearly every morning in conversation with him. He is the inspiration for my life and for my words.

So here it is: *Good Morning: A journal, a cup of coffee and Jesus.* Maybe in some small way, it will make a difference.

Jim DuBro

Thy Word is a lamp unto my feet
and a light unto my path.

Psalm 119:105

# GOOD MORNING
## INTRODUCTION

My journal journey began in the early nineties, though I didn't know it at the time. I was busy as the owner of a wholesale food business in Dayton, Ohio. I was a very one direction kind of guy, but God had something else in mind for me. It began innocently enough with a simple chapter from the book of Matthew chapter twenty-five. The gist of it all was "feed my children." Then I heard it at a Sunday church sermon. When I turned on my car radio, "feed my children" came over the air. The clincher was a "street angel" I shall refer to as "Sister Willa." She visited my wholesale food business often to purchase food for $100 or whatever cash she could collect. She was providing free meals for the homeless and poverty stricken. I couldn't help myself, the Lord was calling, counting on me to help. From feeding those under bridges and along the river bank to churches offering kitchens, and finally to taking possession of the Holt Street Miracle Center, an abandoned brick house where Sister would provide care for men recovering from addiction. We were "hooked" helping those who really understood that word. We broke bread together and each of us would respond on a weekly basis with some type of devotional. My turn, what could I offer? I decided to have the men begin "journaling," hoping it might offer new insights for them. Only one problem. I wasn't journaling, how could I ask them? I picked up my pen and began. There you have it, my book's beginning, what has now been well over twenty-three years ago. Eight thousand pages later, journaling has changed my life forever. Over the years, many of my blog readers and others have continued to ask, "Why don't you write a book?" Unsure I muttered "Ah, well, but, maybe, I don't know...." It took a nudge from the Lord to get it done. As I pondered how it all began, I located my first journal dating back to April 16, 1996. I was barely fifty years old and my life was at a critical juncture. I was experiencing deaths, marriages, financial crisis and business failure. Could this journey get any more difficult? Where was I to turn? What good could possibly come of all this? Thank God for the woman at my side! As God would have it, He had a plan for us. He placed Karen and me with the small group that would be charged to bring hope from despair for men whose life struggles made ours insignificant in comparison. They had lost everything! Theirs was of life and death as they struggled to overcome the deadly addictions of alcoholism and drug abuse and all their terrifying results. It was here that the Lord charged me to teach them how to journal that they might gain a new perspective for their lives. Little did I realize at the time that this was meant for me as well. What had seemed to me as the abyss, brought a new beginning; a closer encounter with the Lord, with my wife, with the world that I thought I knew. The Lord and I have shared a great many conversations since that Wednesday evening so many years ago. Now this is not to say that we haven't experienced suffering and trials at times along the way, but with the Lord we have never been alone. Last night and continuing this morning I spent some time looking back over the photos that I have taken with my cell phone since we have been in Tennessee. They number over two thousand. Along the way I have discarded a great many that lacked clarity or were inferior in quality. I never realized it, but they, like my journal, have become a story in themselves. In many instances I have sought to capture the wonders of God's creation in mountains, valleys, lakes and streams, flowers and pathways, waterfalls and the heavens above. I love the beauty that He has made known to us. There are also glimpses of who we are and where we've been. Like the movie starring Jimmy Stewart, It's A Wonderful Life, what a blessing! Can you go back to February 11, 2003 or June 12, 2012 and celebrate where you've been or what you may have been thinking? It is there that I am able to revisit the conversations and relive the places that God and I have traveled through together.

So with eternal optimism I shall begin a new chapter with God's Son who was never alone when He walked on Earth. As long as I have him in my life, neither will I ever be alone again. May your next chapter be filled with happiness and love knowing that you're never alone! No one may ever look at the two thousand pictures or read my six thousand pages, but to me they are priceless. With you, my many friends, I am honored to share a few of them.

HESED

GRACE

# DAY 1

Good morning. I believe I shall start with the first verse of "Amazing Grace." "Amazing grace how sweet the sound that saved a wretch like me. I once was lost but now am found, was blind but now I see." Do you have anything that you would consider priceless? I do not own a Rolls Royce or a Lear Jet. There is no Hope diamond or Mona Lisa in my care; no buildings rising into the sky nor islands in the South Pacific. Measuring by those standards I guess you could call me a poor man. Am I like the song by Tennessee Ernie Ford, "Sixteen Tons?" "You load sixteen tons, what do you get? Another day older and deeper in debt. Saint Peter don't you call me 'cause I can't go. I owe my soul to the company store." Actually there is so much else to life than diamonds, riches and more, more, more. If I was to select a song that I'd most like to be, it would be "Climb Every Mountain" from the movie Sound of Music. "Climb every mountain, search high and low, follow every byway, every path you know. Climb every mountain, ford every stream, follow every rainbow till you find your dream. A dream that will need all the love you can give, every day of your life for as long as you live."

*So I guess I would say that's the resolution that I choose to follow from here on in. Lord, they are your mountains and your streams, your paths and your byways that I choose to call priceless. Amen and Amen*

# DAY 2

Good morning. Every day there's a story there somewhere. I would say that's true with just about everything. Authors, song writers, producers and poets dedicate their lives to discerning just that, the story of life. Everything in life has a story to it, from Genesis to Heaven and beyond. Most of us never really get to tell our story. Just as everyone's life story is different, so too are others' stories we choose to know. For Katharine Hankey, who lived during the nineteenth century, her story was the beautiful Methodist hymn, "I Love to Tell the Story." She identifies it in her very first stanza. "I love to tell the story of unseen things above, of Jesus and his glory, of Jesus and his love. I love to tell the story because I know 'tis true, it satisfies my longings as nothing else can do." That was her story for the ages. We all want to know a story, whether it's a Bible story or the story of the universe as told by Carl Sagan. Maybe it's The Civil War as shared by Bruce Catton or The Shack by William Paul Young. Maybe you identified with Alex and Stephen Kendrick, the producers of the War Room movie. Perhaps you are searching for life's meaning, knowledge or purely enjoyment in Babe Ruth, John Kennedy, Jesus Christ, Quantum Physics, Martin Luther King or dandelions in the springtime. John Gresham, Max Lucado, Henri Nouwen have a story to tell. The real truth is that we all have a story, an unfinished one at that. What chapter are you in?

*You may be saying nobody cares about your story. God cares! I love to tell my story, but when all is said and done, I love best tell the story of Jesus and his love.  Amen and Amen*

# DAY 3

Good morning. Why do you suppose the Lord made you what you are? You could have been tall and handsome or maybe sleek and slim. What if He had made you black or brown or tan or perhaps the smartest of the clan? David was but a shepherd boy, Joseph a carpenter and I a teacher. Some were made to lead and many were made to follow, while others like Moses and Peter weren't quite sure just what the Lord had in store for them. What if we were all made to be sowers or philosophers? As I see it, God has a plan for each and every one of us. I so love the fact that He has given us the chance to accept the blessings of our gifts and talents. He made us in his own image because He loved us, and all He asks is that we would love him. He doesn't expect from us perfection or that we should all think the same. How amazing it is that He would construct us all the same, yet every last one of us is different! It is so wonderful to know that He has had a plan for me, and also for you, and yet He has given to us the authority to find that plan, or not. I know this to be true: I am glad to be alive and blessed to be just what He has made me to be.

*If you are not sure, I would recommend that you read Jeremiah 29:11-13. As God explained to the Israelites being held captive by the Babylonians, a long time ago, "For I know the plans I have for you, declares the Lord, plans to prosper you and not to harm you, plans to give you hope and a future. That you will call on me and come and pray to me, and I will listen to you. You will seek me and find me when you seek me with all your heart." Happy hunting my friends! Amen and Amen*

# DAY 4

Good morning. For the past two days Karen, and over one hundred ladies from our community, participated in a retreat that featured Laura West, a Christian comedienne and inspirational speaker. I happened there only because I had volunteered to help serve in the kitchen. Sometimes we receive some very unexpected blessings! Christian, comedienne, inspirational; they didn't seem to be very compatible. After all, being Christian is not a laughing matter. Or is it? Proverbs 17:22 says, "Laughter is good like medicine." Ecclesiastes 3:4 tells us there's "a time to weep and a time laugh." OK, OK, you've got my attention. Let's dissect this a little bit. "Laugh: a verb, gerund or present participle." I don't know what the heck that means. Go on, read the definition: "to make spontaneous sounds and movements of the face and body that are instructive expressions of lively amusement and sometimes also of contempt and derision." I would just as soon forget the last six words. There's all kinds: chuckles, chortles, guffaws, cackles, giggles, titters, twitters, sniggers, snickers, tee-hees and no doubt many more. Which one is yours? If you don't have one, shame on you. Did you know laughter decreases stress and increases immune cells and infection fighting antibodies, thus increasing resistance to disease? It releases endorphins, the body's natural feel-good chemicals. They provide a sense of well-being. And you don't even need a prescription.

*Let's laugh ourselves well. Perhaps you can even become a "doctor of laughter." It's a sure way to increase your lifespan. Did you hear the one about...? Amen and Amen*

# DAY 5

Good morning. Nobody would choose something that they did not like, would they? If that is true, then why do we find ourselves embroiled in those places and things that we find to be distasteful? Who would eat so much that they were uncomfortable? Who would eat foods that they know would cause distress? Who would smoke knowing that it might cause lung disease or cancer? Who would avoid physical or mental activity? Who would allow their home to become dirty or a health hazard? Who would avoid or deny their spiritual growth? Who would knowingly destroy healthy relationships? Who would work in a job that they did not like or even despised? Who would seek to be mistreated or abused? Who would take on more responsibilities than they could handle? Who would choose to become dependent on alcohol or drugs? We are an uncommon lot, aren't we? Do you want a good life? Start making the good choices. It's funny. We choose clean socks and underwear over health. We select wealth over happiness. We choose entertainment over faith and knowledge. Quit worrying over whether your shirt is green or blue or whether today it's briefs or boxers.

*And here is a little thought from Bobby McFerrin: "In every life we have some trouble, but when you worry, you make it double. Don't worry, be happy." Don't worry, be happy now! Amen and Amen*

# DAY 6

Good morning. Happy Birthday! Happy Anniversary! Happy New Year! Happiness should not have to be something brand new for us. Happiness should be an on-going goal for all, each and every day. Some of us will make bucket lists or plan a vacation or make resolutions, though I'm not sure of the differences, except that it has been my experience that New Year's resolutions are seldom kept. Why do you suppose that is? Is change really that difficult? I know of no one who claims that as of January 1 they were changed human beings. Some will lose weight, quit eating rutabagas or bananas, stop smoking or drinking; others will promise to be better fathers and a few will commit to be better Christians. Just how do you accomplish that? Will I pick up my Bible more often? Will I pray more every day? Will I join the church choir or attend every Sunday? Will I become more involved with anything of worth to mankind? What if I started by asking the Lord to forgive me of my trespasses and by forgiving those who have trespassed against me? What if I would not only believe in Jesus Christ, but I would also believe him completely? What if I would accept the knowledge that there is nothing on this earth that is more important than truly loving one another? Twelve pounds or a pack of cigarettes wouldn't mean so much then, would they?

*The only way to really enjoy God's promises is to obey him. Are we ready to accept that challenge? He promised to love us, accept us and to forgive us. Are we ready to do something for him? That's a resolution that is certainly worth keeping.*
*Amen and Amen*

# DAY 7

Good morning. Has your obedience to your God been tested? Did you pass the test? Abraham passed the test (Genesis Chapter 22). Moses passed the test. Peter and the Disciples passed the test as did Paul, Martin Luther King and Mother Teresa. But we are not talking about them right now, we're talking about you. (For clarity's sake, that's all of us, today, right now, tomorrow!) We say, "But Lord, I have prayed to you and I've been waiting for an answer." And He responds, "I offer you answers every day but you don't seem to be listening." Jesus spoke to the rich man (Matthew 19:23-24), "I'll say it again, it is easier for a camel to pass through the eye of a needle than for a rich man to enter the kingdom of God." What did He ask? "Give away all your possessions and give the money to the poor. Then come, and follow Me." Again in Matthew 25:44-45, "Then they will reply, 'Lord, when did we ever see you hungry or thirsty or a stranger or naked or sick or in prison and not help you?' And He will answer, 'I tell you the truth, when you refused to help the least of these, my brothers and sisters, you were refusing to help me.'" So how about our test, how are we doing? Can you watch the Wounded Warrior Project and not respond? How about the little children, the homeless, the hungry, the poor? Does your school need volunteers? How about the hospital, nursing home, or your neighbor, or your sisters or brothers?

*You say, "I pray for them." It's not enough! You can't be all things to all people, but you can be something to the one who needs you. The train ride to eternity is coming, will you be on it? Amen and Amen*

Shalom

Peace

# DAY 8

Good morning. "I'm doing all that I can." Is that you? "I pray every day. I volunteer every year at the church bazaar. I made a meal for my neighbor when she was ill. Why, I even serve on two boards and teach Sunday school." Is that all you can do? "You would not expect us to use our private time, would you? I've paid my dues, let someone else do it." Really? When we are called, it's not when we have "free" time that the hungry can wait. The starving children, the elderly man dying from cancer cannot wait. Serving the Lord, becoming His hands and feet cannot be done out of convenience. His hands and feet were bloodied on the cross. His feet were soiled on the dusty paths. His heart was broken for those who cried out to him. Is that a price that you are willing to pay? When He said follow me, it didn't mean when you have the time.

*How about you? Pray about it, are you doing enough? What is enough? God loved you enough to offer his only Son. Amen and Amen*

# DAY 9

Good morning. I can remember when I began playing football one of my coaches used to constantly tell us, "Pull till it hurts." Sweat was not enough! A lesson I learned from my high school wrestling coach was being all in was not 100%, but 110%. He said when you think you've reached your limit, your best requires even more. I believed it and bought into the thought hook, line and sinker. Guess what? I caught the fish I was trying to catch! Are you doing it all or are you just trolling? When I taught my "babies" (really my students, but how I loved them!) I expected their very best, nothing more, nothing less. One year I had a class where every one of them received an "A." Were they the smartest? Was I too easy, or did they give their very best? I expected from all the athletes that I coached, not necessarily to win the match or the game, but to win in life (so many of them did). Where can you do this? Why not start with your family, your church, your job; from there the rest will follow. Last night I watched Clemson win a national championship; Dabo Sweeney surely succeeded in passing along the idea of what "doing enough" is all about.

*Oh, by the way, this fits very nicely with one of my most favored beliefs (Mark 9:23): "If you can believe, all things are possible to him who believes." Amen and Amen*

# DAY 10

Good morning. Is anybody listening? When I began this exercise of writing my thoughts and prayers it was meant to be introspective. Who knew what I was to interpret from it all. It wasn't long (in God's time that is) before I began to realize that my writings were prayerful and meant to be directed by my Lord and maker and shared with others. Though somewhat of a stubborn soul and at times a slow learner, I began to recognize that this was not a one-sided venture, that the Lord was not only listening but sharing His thoughts with me. Shall I be so bold as to call it a conversation with the Lord? Finally, I understood that if my words were to have any lasting meaning and value they should be shared with any and all who choose to listen. No saint, no prophet, no priest or rabbi here, just a simple man seeking to find his way.

*If my search can offer any hope or enlightened understanding to another, then so be it. I pray that my thoughts and words are more than an echo reverberating through empty mountain valleys. I'll keep trying if you keep reading. Amen and Amen*

# DAY 11

Good morning. Beginnings. Aren't they great? We can start with "In the beginning." (Genesis 1:1) No better place than that! For each of us, it's every place that we start something new. Our first cry signals it all. Then first words, first steps, first friend, first school. That first whoopin' says it ain't all gonna be peaches and cream. There will be counting, alphabets, reading, writing and arithmetic and all the rest; first boyfriend or girlfriend, first date (scary), first communion and baptism, first job. Wow, I'm not yet sixteen and they are piling up, aren't they? First driver's license, musical instrument, football or soccer game and the lucky ones got to experience a first wrestling match, first win, first loss, first car, (careful now) did I say first beer or cigarette? Then the whoppers: first graduation, first serious love, first permanent job, first marriage (only one for me), first baby (awesome), first home...How'd I get to be thirty-three, wasn't I just a teen? We begin to say is that all there is? Not on your life, the fun has just begun! There are new firsts large and small: first move, promotion, grandchild, hole in one (still waiting), first family loss, first retirement.

*So what's left? That's all up to you, but one thing for sure, the greatest of all your firsts is that Jesus Christ will always remain first in your life. If He is not, it's never too late to make it so. I'm finally beginning to understand why on the sixth day the Lord saw all that He made, and it was very good (Genesis 1:31). Amen and Amen*

# DAY 12

Good morning. Where would you like to go? A very close friend and his wife shared with us their adventures to Australia and New Zealand. Another friend shared with me his desire to explore the Galapagos and yet another speaks of their anticipation of celebrating their anniversary in Hawaii. Two others shared their decisions to simply move to a smaller home. How about you? It seems that we are all going somewhere. Our daughter Kelli had to face the difficult decision to take her mother-in-law to a nursing home that cares for advanced Alzheimer's patients, at the same time her father-in-law readied himself for spending eternity with the Lord. Yes, some decisions are ours to make, while ultimately God knows full well where each of us has been and where we are going.

*Psalm 119:105 gives us this assurance, "Thy word is a lamp unto my feet and a light unto my path." What a great trip he has planned for us! Amen and Amen*

# DAY 13

Good morning. Some days ago I came across a story written by a close friend of mine from the distant past. It was his story. Though I had read it many years ago, the details had eluded me. I'm not really sure why I kept this ten page manuscript, but I had deposited it in the back of my mind, along with many other ordinary items that have made up my past. But it stayed on my computer table, too, challenging me to read it once again. This morning would be the day. The title, "The Test of Faith," is the reason I kept this glimpse into the life of a friend whom I admired. In the story he recounts a life-threatening event about being all alone in a sinking fishing boat—just Art, a cold winter's wind and the icy water. Was this how it would all end? "God, where are you?" he cried out. So the conversation between Art and God would begin. Another minute went by, maybe two, maybe an hour. Time had no meaning whatsoever. To this day he doesn't recall how long he lay motionless in the water before he said out loud, "God, if you're not real, it doesn't matter anyway." (Ironically, my friend would offer the same response several years later when friends asked if he was afraid while dying of cancer in a Florida hospital.) An hour or so later, he was lying on dry land in the warmth of the sun, and there it was again, the same soft voice.

*It was telling him "It's not the past, the present or the future that's your important test. It's your faith in Me that's important!" And he knew that's the truth! Amen and Amen*

# DAY 14

Good Morning. "Oh Lord, I have never been eloquent, neither in the past nor since you have spoken to your servant. I am slow of speech and tongue." (Exodus 4:10) You may well say that sounds much like me, but it was Moses. Growing up, my perception of Moses was that he was the one with a booming voice who was larger than life itself. Even as a young man I still thought of those I knew who were strong and bold as "Moses like." One of my close Emmaus Christian brothers recently shared his feeling of inadequacy when it came to praying out loud with others. How many of us, when God says, "Those whom I have chosen, step forward!" fall back cringing with fear or anxiety? Are you one of them? Read the advice below.

*Remember what the Lord's response was to Moses? "Who gave man his mantle? Who makes him deaf or mute? Who gives him sight or makes him blind? Is it not I, the Lord? Now go; I will help you speak and will teach you what to say." That very same God is also there for you. When He calls you, are you ready to wear the mantle He has offered? Amen and Amen*

Sim-ha

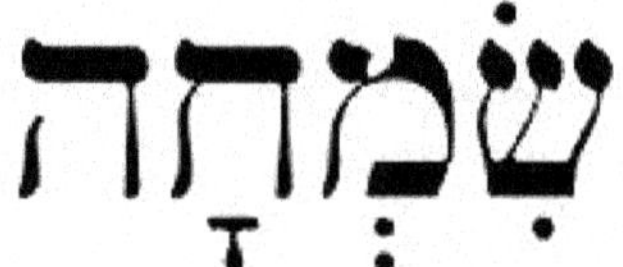

Joy

# DAY 15

Good morning. Did you ever wake up in the morning and stretch your arms to the heavens and exclaim, "What a wonderful world!" The song by the same name was written about fifty years ago. It was first sung by Louis Armstrong who so many have been blessed to know, and it was written by Bob Thiele and George Weiss. Never heard of them? Neither have I, but they sure had it right! Trees of green, skies so blue, rainbows so pretty and friends shaking hands saying how do you do—there is so much to see and do in this world, you don't want to miss any part of it. So what is it? Why, of course, it's God's magnificent creation, and that certainly includes you! Frank Sinatra and Barbra Streisand so strikingly made clear that "On a clear day you can see forever." See it, hear it, smell it, taste it and most importantly feel it. Don't ever allow it to be said, "I never noticed." If a painting or a picture is worth a thousand words, then what is the value of the real things? There are no substitutes for the blue waters of the ocean with whitecaps frothing on a windy day. Who could ignore a golden sun rising slowly just above the horizon, or a baby robin being fed by its mother? Have you ever watched the first snowflake falling or that first daffodil pushing its way toward Heaven above? Did you hear the owl, the chickadee or the crow calling its own? Have you looked deeply into the eyes of your one special love?

*You can hear and feel even with your eyes closed. Have you heard the Lord calling to you or felt yourself nestled in His loving arms? Believe me when I say, "What a wonderful world!"*
*Amen and Amen*

# DAY 16

Good morning. Now that's *important*! As we have gotten older (my wife and I) that word has entered into our lives more than once. I must tell you that "important" is not the same as it once was with us during earlier periods of our lives. Isn't it ironic that one thing that is often left out of our "Important List" is the determination of what is actually important? If we spend half of our waking hours watching television, offering our time to the Internet, Facebook, Twitter or hand-held gamesmanship, doesn't that describe what is really at the top of our lists? You may say, "Of course not, everybody knows that working is at the top." Really? Ok, keeping my house clean and in order or making sure my car runs perfectly; hobbies, collections, gardening, creative endeavors, reading, keeping fit, making sure that we get our fair share; aren't they all of considerable worth? It has been often said that where we put our time and money determines what we honestly consider to be important. Honestly? I haven't seen a word about faith, hope or love. How come? Is there a place at the top for husbands, wives, family, caring for others, learning, and good health? Do you think that you can squeeze in a little faith and Jesus, God, the Bible, prayer, mission; and didn't the Lord say something about the importance of love? Just wondering. Jesus said that only two commands are important to govern our lives: love of God and love of neighbor. Where do they fall on your compendium of what is important?

*Why not make knowing what is truly important the item highest on your list of what is important. Amen and Amen*

# DAY 17

Good morning. Have you ever asked, "Lord, do you really love me?" I'm sure that we have all at one time or another questioned that love. Why did this happen to me? Does this love have any limits? Where do I go to find proof of this love? Just how BIG is His love? We want assurance. It's deeper than the oceans, higher than the highest mountains, farther than the stars above! Seek out the Word, it's all there. I would tell you to read Romans 8:31-39, but instead allow me to print it here: "If God is for us, who can be against us? He who did not spare his Son, but gave him up for us all, how will He not also, along with himself, graciously give us all things? Who will bring any charge against those whom God has chosen? It is God who justifies. Who is he that condemns? Christ Jesus who died—more than that, who was raised to life—is at the right hand of God and is also interceding for us. Who shall separate us from the love of Christ? (Are you listening?) Shall trouble or hardship or persecution, or famine or nakedness or danger or sword? As it is written: 'For your sake we face death all day long, we are considered as sheep to be slaughtered.' (He is not finished with us yet.) No, in all things we are more than conquerors through him who loved (loves) us. For I am convinced that neither death nor life, neither angels nor demons, neither the present nor the future, nor any powers, neither height nor depth, nor anything else in all creation, will be able to separate us from the love of God that is in Christ Jesus our Lord."

*Jesus loves me, this I know. This indeed is our assurance!*
*Amen and Amen*

# DAY 18

Good morning. Have you ever felt totally lost? Some may be thinking "that's where I am right now." In Jeremiah 50:6 it says, "My people have been lost sheep, their shepherds have led them astray and caused them to roam the mountains. They wandered over mountain and hill and forgot their own resting place." Is that who you are? Or could it be as it says in that beautiful hymn, "Amazing Grace," "I once was lost, but now I'm found." Getting lost is not at all the same as being lost. I've been lost a few times, especially directionally. I remember being hopelessly lost in Arkansas, and once or twice in places like Washington, DC. I've been lost in a few classes like calculus and Latin II. Thankfully, I have never lost a job or a home, but I have lost many I would call friends, more than one family member and a number of beloved pets. There are times that I have felt lost at my job, with a health issue or two and fears about the future. It is when I truly found the Lord that the lost feeling began to dissipate.

*I may lose my glasses, my cell phone or my car keys, but I shall never lose my Lord, the One who saved a wretch like me. We may well all lose a battle or even many battles, but as long as we have the Lord in our lives we shall never be lost again.*
*Amen and Amen*

# DAY 19

Good morning. Once upon a time...sounds like a fairytale or a storybook to me. But it can also be our real life experiences. You know, those things you did at one time or maybe even those experiences that happened only once. That could make it extraordinary, special or possibly tragic. I only stood at the altar once, experienced a graduation, ate oysters on the half shell, coached a championship wrestling team once. I only owned a convertible once a long time ago. I only experienced the birth of a son once, had a fiftieth anniversary, was a CEO, went to Quebec City, Phoenix, Santa Fe, Key West and Hazard Kentucky once. I was only baptized once. I had major surgery only once and said a final goodbye to Mom and Dad once. I only owned one Irish Wolfhound, one Lhasa Apso and there was only one Stormy cat.

*Come to think about it, my real life experiences have indeed been a storybook and at times it has approached being a fairytale. Thank you, Lord, for all the "once upon a times" and all that are yet to come. Amen and Amen.*

# DAY 20

Good morning. I have been reading the Bible in its entirety for what now extends into my third consecutive year. You might ask if I tire of reading the same material over and over. To tell the truth it is much the opposite, though I still struggle with endless genealogies with names that only a linguist could pronounce. I find myself clarifying and understanding new thoughts, facts and meanings at every turn. Did I read that before? It's much like driving down a mountain road, every trip brings new landscapes and an increased awareness of God's handiwork. The seasons, time of day, weather and the location of the sun offer a multitude of options to explore. It's like Dr. Seuss's last book, Oh, the Places You'll Go. This is how it is when I am reading my way through Genesis, John and Revelations, to name just a few. "You'll get mixed up of course as you already know. You'll get mixed up with many strange birds as you go. So be sure when you stop, stop with care and great tact and remember that Life's a Great Balancing Act. Just never forget to be dexterous and deft and never mix up your right foot with your left. And will you succeed? Yes! You will indeed! (98 and 3/4 percent guaranteed.)" So Abraham, Noah, Rebekah, Job, Joseph, Matthew, Mark, Luke, John, Paul and Timothy, too, and of course my favorite of all, Jesus, especially you. It's great just getting to know you.

*I never seem to tire of finding my way, Lord, through your creation that extends from Alpha to Omega! Amen and Amen*

# DAY 21

Good morning. We humans are at the top of the food chain, or so we think. We have no overpowering enemy, except ourselves. We are not fearful of the lion or the bear, in fact we don't even think we need to fear God himself. If we truly did we would not kill and take advantage of one another. We scoff at the laws and the rules that God proclaimed in the Old Testament, particularly in the book of Leviticus. We tell ourselves that we are too advanced for all that. How is it that we have come to accept lying, stealing, cheating and even killing as just a part of life? Is the Sabbath really that important? Who ever heard of celebrations for the Lord and all that He has offered us? He only wants for us to be clean in mind, body and spirit; is that so bad? Were His laws about protecting the land "uncivilized?" Who among us offers our outer rows of food and grain, our olive oil and our grapes to the poor and the foreigners? Would it be so bad if we still abided by what is called Jubilee? I can't help but be reminded what God told his precious people about it when He brought them out of bondage from Egypt in Leviticus 23:13 "The land must never be sold on a permanent basis, for the land belongs to me. You are only foreigners and tenant farmers working for me."

*We should never forget, "For I am the Lord your God who takes hold of your right hand and says to you, 'I will help you.'" Isaiah 41:13. Are you listening to that still small voice deep within you that says, "I am your God?" Amen and Amen*

Nuach

Rest

# DAY 22

Good morning. Don't quote me on this, but I would suggest to you that nearly everyone has been quoted at one time or another. I was only four years old and I remember my brother running to Mom and blurting out. "Jimmy called me a poophead." There have been lots of “he saids” since that day a long time ago. There is a great difference between quoting and plagiarism (that is taking credit for another's thoughts or words). But it should be noted that being quoted is also one of man's greatest complements. Hopefully, if you are quoted, it will be for something a wee better than "poophead." Some great quotes have been recorded for mankind from the likes of Abraham Lincoln, John Kennedy, Martin Luther King, Mother Teresa, Franklin Roosevelt, Yogi Berra, and the greatest of all, Jesus Christ. Recently I was made aware of one of the most quoted men of the modern era, David Livingstone, famous African explorer.

*Allow me to share a couple of Livingstone’s sayings that have caught my attention: "I am prepared to go anywhere provided it be forward." "If you have men who will only come if they know there is a good road, I don't want them. I want men who will come if there is no road at all." And, "I will place no value on anything I have or may possess except in relation to the Kingdom of Christ." How would you like your words to be quoted? Amen and Amen*

# DAY 23

Good morning. There's an old saying, "It depends on which way the wind blows." The wind, how scary it can be; the wind, how refreshing it feels. Which will it be? King Solomon spoke of the wind over and over as he wrote Ecclesiastes 1:6: "The wind blows to the south and turns to the north, round and round it goes, ever returning on its course," and 1:17 "Then I applied myself to the understanding of wisdom, and also of madness and folly, but I learned that this, too, is chasing after the wind." Does that sound negative or disheartening? Then listen to what follows. "Moreover, when God gives any man wealth and possessions, and enables him to enjoy them, to accept his lot and be happy in his work—this is a gift of God." In more recent times we have reflected on the wind, when the Kingston Trio sang "They Call the Wind Maria" and Bob Dylan was reflective on life with his rendition of "Blowing in the Wind." As for me and my thoughts, you can just call me "Windy."

*Just know this, "He has made everything beautiful in its time." Ecclesiastes 3:11. Amen and Amen*

# DAY 24

Good morning. It is just that! Are you going to allow the "fly in the ointment" to ruin your day? How often we allow small matters to rule our lives. Why is it that such infinitesimal things as a spilled cup of coffee or socks thrown under the bed control our feelings and attitudes? After all, we are not talking about Armageddon. We argue with one another over matters that matter little or nothing at all. We allow a harsh word or a sour stomach to determine who we are. Is the "rain" of the day going to ruin your happiness? You do know that there is truth in the statement, "Into each life a little rain must fall." I for one am a proponent of turning lemons into lemonade. You may hate lemonade. No one says you have to drink it! If you begin your day thanking and praising the Lord for all the good things and the blessings you have received, it becomes much harder to let that fly ruin your day. Let's face it, there will be times when everything seems to go awry. That's exactly the time you need to remember that you're not trapped in an iron lung or that you have both hands and both feet. When your mud puddles seem too deep to cross, look to the Lord. Don't you recall, He carried an entire nation across the Red Sea?

*When all is said and done, you probably didn't need that ointment anyway, did you? If you offer me your glass of lemonade, I'll gladly share my tea with you! Amen and Amen*

# DAY 25

Good morning. When you look out your window what do you see? As the great singer and musician Louis Armstrong sang, we do have a choice. Was it, "Nobody Knows the Trouble I've Seen?" I personally would rather hear these words: "What A Wonderful World!" Everyone knows that in life we experience some of each, but which would you prefer to keep just outside your window sill? I'll take the latter. "I see trees of green, red roses too, I see them bloom for me and you And I think to myself what a wonderful world. I see skies of blue and clouds of white The bright blessed day, the dark sacred night And I think to myself what a wonderful world. The colors of the rainbow so pretty in the sky Are also on the faces of people going by, I see friends shaking hands saying how do you do But they are really saying I love you. I hear babies cry, I watch them grow. They'll learn much more than I'll ever know And I think to myself what a wonderful world." That just about says it for me!

*Louis Armstrong has been gone now for many years, but I do think he had this old world just about right. After all, it is what we make it. So won't you please excuse me while I raise my window shades and let it all in. Amen and Amen*

# DAY 26

Good morning. Have you ever read the book of Job in your Bible? I would highly recommend it if you haven't. It is only forty-two short chapters and a little over fifty pages. You just might find a little bit of yourself hidden there. I would especially suggest that you read Job 38-40:5, the Lord's challenge to Job. Look at these words in Job 40:1-2: "Then the Lord said to Job, 'Do you still want to argue with the Almighty? You are God's critic, but do you have the answers?'" Some of us say, "I don't need this God you speak about. I can do this thing called 'life' all by myself." Can you now? Can you make the dirt upon which you plant your feet? How about the air that you breathe? Can you guarantee that for you, tomorrow will ever come? Can you offer your son to us to die so that we might live? Lord, forgive us for our arrogance and lack of faith in you.

*Perhaps this simple quote by Roy Rolfe can describe a little of how I feel about my faith in this God I cannot see. "Keep your faith in all beautiful things. In the sun when it is hidden. In the spring when it is gone." May your day be filled with His sunshine. Amen and Amen*

# DAY 27

Good morning. It is impossible for everything we say and do to make us feel good. But just in case you have forgotten, Jesus said, "With God all things are possible." (Matthew 19:26.) That thought in itself makes me feel good! It is important to understand what pleases us. Equally important is appreciating it. Here are a few things that work for me. Please recognize that we are not all the same (thank you Lord). You and I may differ and that's perfectly acceptable. I feel refreshed when I take a long, hot shower early in the morning. I've often stated that I don't eat to live, I live to eat. That's not particularly good for me, but it does make me feel good. I always feel delightfully alive when I lie down beside the love of my life in the quiet of the night. I love the feeling I get when I've worked hard and can wipe the perspiration from my brow. Reading and learning new things makes my days more interesting. I have always loved to travel and meeting new friends offers a high that is difficult to explain. I love to write and express myself as my journals readily attest. I have found great joy in the Bible and praying has become increasingly important. There are almost no sports that I don't enjoy. I appreciate anything that brings out God-given talents. I naturally feel good waking to sunshine and nothing is more soothing than walking in a warm summer rain. Snows excite me, though not as much as in my younger days. I love competition, but winning is not nearly as important as it once was for me.

*Most of all, being with my family and my God makes me feel the best. Without these, none of the rest would really matter much. Amen and Amen*

# DAY 28

Good morning. As I awoke in my comfortable bed this early morning, I heard the melodious singing of a single bird. I knew it didn't have to save its song for just this rainy day. What am I saving for a rainy day? Yesterday I spoke with a manager at the restaurant where I was eating breakfast. He was lamenting—or let me clarify, grumbling, about taking inventory. Later, at our local Walmart, another person was unhappy about taking their year-end inventory. When was the last time I took an inventory? I shudder to think about it as I look around our modest abode. Am I an entrepreneur, investor, collector—or hoarder? We have eight closets nearly filled to the brim, not to mention an attic and a storage space for things that never get used. (Does this sound familiar to you?) I have in my closet a tuxedo, bow tie, cummerbund and a frilly white shirt I haven't worn since I was in a friend's wedding. His oldest son is in high school now. My closet floor is strewn with shoes, some older than my friends. I have slacks that are size thirty-two, which I am not. A trunk holds a doll house kit for my oldest daughter, now forty-nine. Count the books, the number is legendary, including a college text from 1965. Every closet, cabinet and drawer is filled with something I'm saving for a rainy day. What would happen if I chose to rid myself of just one item every day? Why, I could finish in a hundred years or so. Still I go shopping for things I'll need some rainy day.

*But I am finally understanding how that little bird can offer me a beautiful welcoming tune on a rainy day. God gave him everything he needs and enough to share, without keeping anything to have to inventory. Amen and Amen*

Selichah

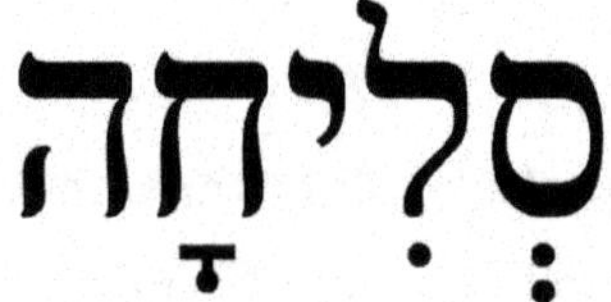


Forgiveness

# DAY 29

Good morning. Let's take a stroll down memory lane when every kid in the neighborhood had a bag of marbles and a favorite "shooter." It was truly a neighborhood school as virtually every child walked there. Minimum wage was $1.25 and a movie cost 25 cents. Aspiring young entrepreneurs became newspaper delivery boys and girls or baled hay in the summer, some weeks making ten dollars. Neighborhood kids played hide'n'seek until way after dark, at least until "I Love Lucy." TV's were black and white, we could only get two stations and sign-off was at midnight, when "The Star Spangled Banner" was broadcast. Hopalong Cassidy and Captain Video were heroes; Howdy Doody and Buffalo Bob preceded them. We had "The Mickey Mouse Club." Most everyone watched Ed Sullivan, Arthur Godfrey, Milton Berle, Jackie Gleason, Jack Benny, Red Skelton, Ruth Lyons, and Groucho Marx. Cherished 45 RPM collections featured Crosby, Como, and Sinatra, at least until Elvis and the Beetles came along. Fats Domino was doing the Twist and every teen knew the words to "A Quarter To Three" or "Peanut Butter." Goose Tatum, Meadowlark Lemon and Marcus Haynes, The Harlem Globetrotters, astounded the world. Pay phones were everywhere and each neighborhood had a corner grocery. A ride in the country or watching passenger planes land was entertainment. The only gym shoes were US Keds and "clodhoppers" were commonplace. Fast food and pizza were new words.

*Looking back, we have to ask, "How did we ever get along?" We got along—with each other. Amen and Amen*

# DAY 30

Good morning. Have you ever cried out, "Pay attention to me!" or "Listen to what I'm saying!" Funny how I always scream louder when somebody else is around. Do you know what it feels like to be the last one picked or maybe not at all? I still remember what it was like when my teacher asked a question I didn't know the answer to. How far could I slide down in my seat? But when I knew the answer, it was pick me! as I practically stood on my chair. Did you ever have a crush on a boy or girl but they didn't know you existed? What about the job you didn't get or the time you stood on the sideline, waiting to hear your name called? waited patiently for calls from a son or daughter far away. Have you ever walked down a busy street or a long hallway hoping that someone, anyone, would notice you? I once attended a new church and I thought maybe I was invisible. Have you been sick or in the hospital for an extended stay? Do you ever tire of offering your ideas and nobody seems to be listening? The pharaoh didn't listen to Moses and Aaron. Job didn't think God was listening when he cried out for an audience. Even Jesus would exclaim "Why have you forsaken me?" But He really knew! It was for you.

*If you need some place to be heard, get down on your knees and pray. God always listens, even when we doubt His presence. And He pleads for us to pay attention to the lonely, the homeless, the sick, the destitute, the widow, the hungry, the smallest child, even the stray dog or cat and the robin with a broken wing. Are you listening? He is speaking to us right now, can you hear? Amen and Amen*

# DAY 31

Good morning. Some of you may be asking, "What's so good about it?" That's a great place to start. First and foremost the Lord saw fit to give you yet another day. He has given you three hundred and sixty-five of these potentially glorious days every year of your life and if you happen to be eighty years old, he has even thrown in an extra twenty, just because he loves you so. For me that's approximately 26,800 days. Now I have to tell you that most of them have been good and a few have even been great! How's that for starters? He's offered you your daily bread, hasn't He? Approximately 1,095 meals, give or take, in the past year. Can you remember a few of the really good ones? Did you thank the one who prepared them? Did you give thanks to him? Has He given you freedom, protection, liberty, a chance to love and to be loved? Did He give you eyes to see, ears to hear, a mouth to speak and a mind to think? Did He offer you sunshine, rainbows, flowers and oh, those mountains high? Don't forget the little things; meat loaf and escalloped potatoes, great art, crayons, basketball and football, largemouth bass, lace, pineapple upside down cake, warm pajamas and a good night's sleep.

*And the most precious of all, He gave his very own Son. So yes, we can, without hesitation, say Good Morning! and know that it's true. Amen and Amen*

# DAY 32

Good morning. The days, how rapidly they seem to pass. Why, it was just Monday. It was just January. It was just 1961, 1965, 1995. It was just 2000, a brand new century! I surely can't be in my seventies. My former students can't be grandparents. My children's children can't be nearly grown. The most important part of time is not the past, nor even the future. For you and me it is today, this day, right now. What will you do with it? There is no time to waste. Live fully every hour, every minute, every second. Every day I still thirst to know more so I am currently reading five books. Because I have nothing better to do? Not at all. Because it is part of living my life fully. I'll share my current book titles with you. A friend has asked if I might read his book, Becoming Silas, Volume 1, 2nd Ed, the story of his life living with ADD. I have just begun The Life Changing Magic of Tidying Up by Marie Konde. Our Wednesday evening small group is studying Growing Slowly Wise by David Roper, exploring the book of James. I will be teaching our Sunday School class using John, the Gospel of Light and Life by Adam Hamilton. Lastly, every morning finds me reading The One Year Chronological Bible. Some are saddened by the sand clock's sifting, constantly emptying the hour glass of life itself. As for me, there is no remorse, for I have been offered more than the clock can hold—a piece of eternity from the Creator of the Heavens and Earth!

*So look at what's in your daily sand clock, trickling from the top of the hour glass to the bottom, and look at what God offers when the sand runs out! Amen and Amen*

# DAY 33

Good morning. I was being held hostage by my wife until we arrived here in sunny Florida. Just joshing with you, but now I have something more important to talk about. Have you ever heard the phrase "the time of your life?" What do you think that is? It is actually the time period between two dates separated by a dash. What you choose to do with it is entirely left up to you. Will it be memorable, tragic, fun filled, spirit filled, exciting, tepid, disgusting, caring and bathed in love? Let's explore a few of the possibilities and options. Have you tried counting the stars? Have you sailed the seven seas? Did you taste everything there is to taste? Have you ever seated yourself in the first seat of a roller coaster? Did you sneak into a drive-in movie? Have you read every book? Have you kissed a new born baby or danced with your daughter at her wedding? Have you ridden on an elephant or maybe a camel? Can you say the Greek alphabet forward or backwards? Have you stood at the top of a mountain? Have you shared with someone just how much you love them? Have you spoken seriously with Jesus? Have you asked the Lord to forgive you?

*Choices, there are millions more, why not try them all? But start and end with Jesus. Amen and Amen*

# DAY 34

Good morning. Two plus two equals five. Is there something wrong with that statement? Only if you know how to count. When man fights man or nation wars against nation, is there something wrong? Only if you truly know God and the Son that He sent to save our wretched souls. There are some things that just don't add up in life. So often we are concerned about the present when we ought to be seeking His presence. In Philippians 4:6-8 are these words: "Don't worry about anything, instead pray about everything. Tell God what you need and thank him for all He has done. Then you will experience God's peace, which exceeds anything we can understand. His peace will guard your hearts and minds as you live in Christ Jesus. And now brothers and sisters, one final thing. Fix your thoughts on what is true, and honorable, and right, and pure, and lovely, and admirable. Think about things that are excellent and worthy of praise."

*Are you counting on the things of this world to add up? I'm counting on the Lord and His word, because I know He will always be right! Amen and Amen*

# DAY 35

Good morning. Is there any other way? Surely you've asked yourself this a time or two. Most of our lives we repeat the same things over and over, for we are creatures of habit. At this morning's men's breakfast I could predict what each of the men at our table would be ordering. Clairvoyant? No. First of all, the men tend to congregate at the same table week after week and to order the same breakfasts. I usually begin my days by brushing my teeth, grabbing a Kleenex and taking my meds in the exact same order. It's right sock, left sock, tie right shoe, tie left shoe, button my shirt always from top to bottom. I test my sugar, read my Bible, drink my coffee and write in my journal. It all seems so comfortable. Is there another way? We travel to and fro, to work and back, we even tend to sit in the very same pew in church. They say changing things up stimulates the mind and enhances our creativity. God offered the Israelites a different way and still they resisted. The Pharisees wanted it no other way. Many of our own colonists wanted it just as it had always been. Thank God for the likes of Moses, for Jesus and all the rest who were willing to see there was another way. I can name more: the frontier pioneers, John Wesley, Martin Luther, Abraham Lincoln, Thomas Edison, Wilbur and Orville, Mother Teresa, MLK, Neil Armstrong, Michael Collins, Buzz Aldrin. . . .

*Finding another way does not mean you're out of step. When you are being told you can't get there from here, don't believe it for even a moment. When experts tell you that's just the way it is, don't be afraid to say "Is there any other way?" Amen and Amen*

Amets

Courage

# DAY 36

Good morning. Have you ever been faced with a dilemma and you felt you needed to ask for help? If you haven't, you are indeed a "rare bird." Often times we look for someone close to us to talk to; mother, father, grandmother or perhaps a longtime trusted friend. In many situations you may just need someone to listen to you while you sort through your thoughts. In marriage we say it like this: "To have and to hold, from this day forward, for better, for worse, for richer, for poorer, in sickness and in health, until death do us part." That certainly is comforting, isn't it? The last words you would ever want to hear are "it all depends." We all want to know that there is someone there for us. When there seems to be no one there to help you, know that the Lord will always be there. How long? For a thousand generations. That's twenty thousand years or so. Is that enough? His promise in Deuteronomy 7:9 says, "Understand therefore, that the Lord your God is indeed God who keeps His covenant for a thousand generations and lavishes His unfailing love on those who love him and obey His commands."

*Never be afraid to ask him for help as He will never forsake you. His love will never fail. Amen and Amen*

# DAY 37

Good morning. Aren't our journey and the trails we choose to take amazing? Notice that I did not qualify this journey in terms of good or bad. I have seen at least five different doctors since becoming a Tennessee resident. There was a time in my life when I must have felt invincible. The only time I saw a doctor was when I was very ill or really hurting. The less I saw one, the happier I was. Now, most of my visits are to keep from being sick or hurting. I have just returned from a visit with an eye doctor. The good news is that my eyes show no diabetic damage. I am thankful for the quality care we receive here in Tennessee. I am thankful to be blessed, able to do so much. It is imperative that we all seek wellness. But allow me to make this clear, wellness is three-fold and no aspect of it should be taken for granted. Physical wellness is key for all of us; good health habits are essential (sleeping, eating, exercise) but don't overlook mental wellness. Keep your mind active. Don't fall into the trap of the dumbing down of America. Reading and learning help keep us alert. Try new things, be creative, keep old friends and develop new relationships. Our third category is perhaps the one we pay the least attention to and yet it will carry us long after everything else has disappeared. It will open the gates to eternity itself. Spiritual wellness provides the very Light of our existence. It offers hope, faith and love. Can you think of a better elixir? How could we possibly live without these three? There is nothing in our physical, mental and spiritual wellness that supersedes a relationship with the Three Fold God.

*Stay well my friends, stay well! Amen and Amen*

# DAY 38

Good morning. There is something very spiritual about walking along the ocean or the Gulf. Yesterday we traversed the water's edge at the beach for nearly two miles. I would recommend shoeless if you really seek the full effect. There is certainly a rush when you take a dip in the open water, feeling the power of the waves pushing all around you, but to walk beside this great creation of God's is all one needs to feel his Presence. What a sense of being fully alive I experienced ambling back and forth between water and shore (of course being careful not to fall prey to the waves pounding the sand) while getting soaked up to my belt line. Isn't that what sunshine was designed to take care of? It seems to charge my adrenaline, almost decreeing that I joyfully run (note that I said almost). There is absolutely nothing on this earth quite like it! If you are not enchanted by all this activity, then let the constant rolling of the waves in the evening calm your senses. Lots of folks love to extol the peaceful effect that it has on them.

*Sunrise or sunset, excited or peaceful, here on these shifting sands I began to understand why the Lord proclaimed: "Let the water teem with living creatures, and let birds fly above the earth across the expanse of the sky. So God created the great creatures of the sea and every living and moving thing with which the water teems, according to their kinds, and every living bird according to its kind. And God saw that it was good." (Genesis 1:20-21) Amen and Amen*

# DAY 39

Good morning. I wonder! Have you ever driven down a busy street or highway and said to yourself, I wonder where everybody is going? Did you ever say, I wonder what I will be when I grow up? I wonder who I will marry? Will we have children? Where will we live? Will I be successful? Did you ever ask in wonderment what's over that wide ocean or beyond the mountains? How about beyond the stars in the heavens above? Did you wonder about growing old or what is to follow? Have you ever wondered why God made you or how much He really loves you? Here are a few scriptures you may have wondered about: Lamentations 3:22 "His steadfast love endures all the day; Psalm 52:8 "I trust in the steadfast love of God forever and ever." Romans 8:39 “Nor height nor depth, nor anything else in all creation, will be able to separate us from the love of God." And John 4:9 "In this the love of God was made manifest among us, in that God sent his only Son into the world, so that we might live through him."

*Once you've found him, know him, and love him, there is no need to wonder about His love for you anymore. That is what I call a wonderful love letter! Amen and Amen*

# DAY 40

Good morning. Have you paid your light bill? Everyone pays for their lights and electricity lest they find themselves in darkness. "Light" it is one of my favorite words. We find ourselves using it in so many bold and beautiful ways. The song, "Light of My Life" tells us, "Wandering like a leaf upon the wind I have been searching for someone, Holding out for a love to shake my soul. Heaven or nothing, then you walked into my life in a blaze of light. I've never wanted someone more. You are the one I've waited for. Light of my life." We see the light when we see the sunlight, when we observe the morning's dawn. There are the shining lights of the stars on a clear winter's night. What mariner doesn't look with appreciation at the lighthouse beacon shining through the darkness and fog? Psalm 119:105 puts it this way: "Your Word is a lamp to guide my feet and a light for my path." And the light of love can best be found in the Bible when we read John 8:12. "When Jesus spoke again to the people, He said, 'I am the Light of the world. Whoever follows me will never walk in darkness, but will have the light of life.'" He came to be the light shining in the darkness. What darkness? The darkness of fear, terror, sin, disbelief, death, losing our way. That darkness. But He offers us another way; forgiveness, love, grace, mercy, compassion, kindness.

*So again I ask, is your light bill paid? Jesus, the Light, has paid my bill so I will never have to be in darkness. Now, that's a Light worthy of following! Amen and Amen*

# DAY 41

Good morning. “I'd rather do it my way.” Does that sound at all familiar to you? Oftentimes we get full of ourselves, believing that our thoughts and our decisions are the only ones. Sometimes, maybe even often, we want to go our own way rather than follow the ways of God. That is exactly what happened to Saul, the first king of Israel, and it ended in ruin for him and his kingdom. King David would follow with a different mindset, found in Proverbs 3:5-6. "Trust in the Lord with all of your heart and lean not on your own understanding. In all your ways submit to him, and he will make all your paths straight." The Bible offers continued testimony to the same instruction in Jeremiah 17:7-8, putting it graphically this way: "But blessed is the one who trusts in the Lord, whose confidence is in him. He will be like a tree planted by the water that sends out its roots by the stream. It does not fear when heat comes; its leaves are always green. It has no worries in a year of drought and never fails to bear fruit." In Psalms 143:8 David himself writes, "Let the morning bring me word of your unfailing love, for I have put my trust in you. Show me the way I should go, for it is to you I entrust my life." And this promise appears in Isaiah 43:2, a scripture that I personally have found a great solace. "When you pass through the waters, I will be with you, and when you pass through the rivers they will not sweep over you. When you walk through the fire, you will not be burned; the flames will not set you ablaze." Do it my way? No way!

*For thine is the Kingdom, the Power and the Glory forever! Amen and Amen*

# DAY 42

Good morning. Life has its ups and downs. We find them at every turn. There are lyrics about them like "up on the mountain tops," and "down in the valley." Think of all the places we find these words: grow up, get up or lay down, sit up, shut up, let down, put down, step up or step down. There is uppity, why not "downity"? There is up, upper, down, downer, why not "uppest" or "downest?" Its sun up or sundown, we split up and shake down. Some rack up while others track down. Some are just plain low down; others need a hand up and instead we offer a hand me down. Lift up your spirits so you won't feel down or be let down. We've got upright and downright, upscale and downsize, download and upstart. We go uptown and downtown. There's upheaval everywhere and folks just being up or down and never giving up. The Bible is replete with ups and downs, too. In Isaiah 60 I see "Rise up and shine, for your light has come." The Bible speaks twenty-three times about not giving up. Colossians 2:7 says, "Rooted up and built up in him..." Thessalonians 4:17 tells us, "We who are still alive, who are left, will be caught up together with them in the clouds to meet the Lord..." In Matthew 10:39 Jesus tells us, "If you cling to your life, you will lose it; but if you give up your life for me, you will find it."

*Knowing all this, I'm sure glad I "woke up" and "got up" this morning! Amen and Amen*

El Shaddai

# אֵל שַׁדַּי

God Almighty

# DAY 43

Good morning. When you awoke this morning what was your reaction? Was it, “Why don't you go on without me?” But maybe this will be the day that a miracle is coming your way! Wouldn’t that be enough to get up for? Don't be afraid to ask for miracles. You do believe in them, don't you? After all, Jesus promised the impossible more than once. Here's the best part: He always delivered! If you want to live every day miraculously, here’s how. Every morning when you rise up, plead the blood of Jesus over the day. The Kenneth Copeland Ministries explains it this way: "When the accuser says we are guilty, our plea before God, the Righteous Judge, Is the blood of Jesus. It changed everything. The blood of Jesus began a new and better covenant between us and our Lord. The blood has become our defense. It has declared that we are not guilty, but free from all penalty of sin. The blood also gives us the authority and dominion to resist Satan and put him out of the affairs of our lives. Because of Jesus' sacrifice on the cross, the devil has no legal right to interfere in our lives any longer. He says we are guilty; we plead the blood! It has given us the right to walk in victory through the precious blood of the Lamb."

*We have the right and the authority every day to declare what the blood of Jesus has done for us. Do not give the enemy even one small inch in you heart and mind and soul. Satan is defeated and you have become the victor! With Jesus, all things are possible, especially miracles! Amen and Amen*

# DAY 44

Good morning. Guilty! Have you ever taken a lukewarm shower, or taken a sip of your favorite ice cold drink only to find it tepid? Or how about a hot cup of coffee that wasn't? Maybe the heater in your car never gets past lukewarm. So what if someone suggested that my faith was just lukewarm? Nonsense, I'd say! I go to church nearly every Sunday, except maybe when we are vacationing or if we have a picnic planned. I read the Bible almost every day, at least five or six pages. No, I don't take notes, or challenge thoughts or ask questions. But I volunteer for several different organizations though I don't overdo it. There's only so much time. I admit that I do some things so others will recognize what all I do, but I never purposely sin against another or doubt God. I pray that my family and friends will be safe, do well and prosper and when others are sick I call on the Lord for healing. What do you mean, when did I ask God for forgiveness? Do I confide in God? Do I deny myself worldly things for the opportunity to do God's work? Do I give as much time to spiritual growth as I do entertainment? Do I view tithing as mandatory? What do I sacrifice to be a disciple of Jesus Christ? Am I honest with others, with myself, with God? Does everyone know the "real" me? Who's asking all these questions?!

*Jesus said he would spew me out of his mouth if I am a lukewarm follower. Just 2.4 hours a day with the Lord is only 10% of my time; He's available 24 hours, that's 100% of His time. Yes, Lord, I've got a lot of work to do before I'm more than lukewarm. Amen and Amen*

# DAY 45

Good morning. Picture winter rapidly waning. Signs of the coming spring begin to appear, although when you look beyond the gray skies and barren trees the grass has yet to don its emerald suit of clothing. Still, there can be no doubt God and nature have begun a transformation. The days do become steadily longer. Crocus and tulips begin to pop up from the bare ground. You may even see a yellow flower here and there or the budding of a maple tree. Songbirds begin to reappear and soon will be nesting to produce another generation of singers. For those of us who can hardly wait for this miraculous transformation each year, plans are being laid for spring house cleaning, oiling and sharpening tools, and making lawn mowers ready. And don't overlook the golf clubs and fishing gear! It is a time of preparation in anticipation of the annual rebirth of God's creation. Summer, fall, winter or spring I can't help but think that Jesus awaits our rebirth. He seeks to heal our discontent and discouragement, to lift us up and renew us. In any season, as I look forward or recall the early flowers, the new green leaves, the golf tees, the fishing lures and all the rest, my true focus is on awaiting the entrance on Earth once more of the King of Kings.

*Have you readied yourself for His return? He's coming. Have you begun your preparations? Are you ready for His eternal renewal of us and all the Earth? Amen and Amen*

# DAY 46

Good Morning. The days of giants are gone forever and the days of heroes are waning. There was a time when every kid could find a hero: Babe Ruth, John Kennedy, Ted Williams, Helen Keller, Jimmy Stewart, Thomas Jefferson, Jackie Robinson, Anne Frank, Rosa Parks, Oskar Schindler, Mother Theresa, Maya Angelou and so many others. There is something to be said about following, striving, achieving to be like our heroes, maybe to be even better, stronger, wiser. We need to be able to look up to our politicians, our faith leaders, our favorite sports figures, but in today's world we often find them tarnished. I remember growing up watching one of my heroes, Jim Andrews, number twenty-one, star halfback for the Fairmont Dragons. He was five or six years older than me and the "best halfback" in the whole wide world. I may never have been quite as good, but I wore his number and played his position on a Fairmont team that only lost two games in three years. Thanks Jim! Another one of my heroes was Jim Valvano, the North Carolina basketball coach for national champion North Carolina State, who died of cancer. His legacy was not so much about coaching as it was courage. He said, "If you laugh, you think, and you cry, that's a full day. That's a heck of a day! You do that seven days a week, you're going to have something special" and his best of all "Don't give up, don't ever give up."

*I've had other heroes, and bet you have, too. So who is your hero? Maybe it was a soldier, a teacher or professor, a minister, a friend—not to mention the greatest hero in the universe, Jesus Christ. Amen and Amen*

# DAY 47

Good morning. I have a question for you. Have you ever been on trial? No, I am not referring to trial in a court of law. That is about dealing with consequences of your behaviors and your actions. If you are speeding down the road at eighty-five miles an hour or if you shoot your neighbor's cat, or your neighbor, you will surely go on trial as a consequence. I'm talking about life trials, the kind that Job experienced. If you are going to tell me that you have never been on trial, you are probably only fooling yourself, and if you truly haven't, get ready. God will surely test His sons and daughters. In Job 23:10 the Bible says, "He knows the way that I take; when He has tested me, I will come forth as gold." In Romans 8:18-20 Paul stated, "I consider that our sufferings are not worth comparing with the glory that will be revealed to us. The creation waits in eager expectation for the sons of God to be revealed. For the creation was subjected to frustration not by its own choice, but by the will of the one who subjected it, in hope that the creation itself will be liberated from its bondage to decay and brought into the glorious freedom of the children of God." In Hebrews 12:5-6 it is written, "My son, do not make light of the Lord's discipline, and do not lose heart when He rebukes you because the Lord disciplines those He loves, and He punishes everyone he accepts as a son."

*Trial is a part of life and our loving God will always be there to see us through even the hardest times. If today is your day of trial, rest assured that the Lord has your back, now and forever more. Amen and Amen*

# DAY 48

Good morning. This morning I was made painfully aware of the fact that I am not the man I used to be. There was a time in my life when I felt that I was invincible. But now I think of the old Camel cigarette commercial, "I'd walk a mile for a Camel." Today it's more like I'd have to ride a camel to make it a mile. Just kidding of course, I can still walk several miles at a time. However, running and jumping, those are challenges that I dare not attempt. It is apparent that my weaknesses have become more and more evident. It is disconcerting that I cannot do all the things that I used to be able to do, both physically and mentally. This old quote rings true: "There are three things I can't remember; faces, names and I can't remember the third." Frustrating and sometimes even embarrassing, I must admit, but then I read 2nd Corinthians 12:9-10, "My grace is all you need. My power works best in weakness. So now I am glad to boast about my weaknesses, so that the power of Christ can work through me. That's why I take pleasure in my weaknesses and in the insults, hardships, persecutions and troubles that I suffer for Christ. For when I am weak, then I am strong."

*So on this day as I travel to Nashville to see an eye surgeon, I am bolstered by the knowledge that God is traveling right along beside me, every step of the way. Amen and Amen*

# DAY 49

Good morning. How important is it for you to feel important? From our very beginning we cry out, "Pay attention to me!" As little children we sought to have our own way. I wanted to be the first one chosen for Red Rover; in fact, I wanted to be the chooser. "I have more marbles than you" grew into "my yard is larger than yours" then as I grew into an adult my car, my house, my job, my church, my team, my city, my nation... they were bigger, better, more important. So now what is it that is more important to us? To be richer, stronger, more powerful, more intelligent? Soon enough we find that our legs will no longer carry us faster, the size of our house or the breadth of our job changes. Kings, presidents and generals are replaced. Fathers give way to sons. What's important then? Is it finding peace, contentment, happiness? Being loved? Loving someone, anyone, everyone? Is it to love God? Is it to know He loves you?

*Nothing could possibly be more important. Seek him first in your life and you will be more and have more than you could have ever imagined. He will show you the way to pure joy! Amen and Amen*

# Mattanah

Gifts

# DAY 50

In biblical history the Hebrew word “zekar” means “a memory.” It becomes a “pointer,” something prominent to assist helping us to remember. In the English word of today we might refer to this as a mnemonic device, or a reminder. The Bible is replete with reminders of the past. In Deuteronomy 16:3 the Lord tells his people to set aside Passover to remember the exodus from Egypt. Psalm 77:12-13 tells us: “I will consider all your works and meditate on all your mighty deeds.” Jesus made it clear when He shared with his disciples and with us; “Do this in remembrance of me.” If that isn’t enough for you, allow me to share one more in Psalm 78:4: “We will not hide them from their descendants; we will tell the next generation the praiseworthy deeds of the Lord, his power, and the wonders he has done...”

*My friends, it is imperative that we become the “memory” and the “reminder” of our God and our Savior, Jesus Christ. Without that there is no Hope! Amen and Amen.*

# DAY 51

Good morning. Can you hear Him? He is speaking very softly, but be assured He is speaking directly to you and me. He says that He has offered us the greatest gift of all, the gift of love. Now that you have received such a precious gift, I charge you with the responsibility of not wasting one ounce of that love. Have you ever kissed a new born baby? They may never know your face or your name, but they will never forget the feel of your loving touch. I think that today He has charged us with a simple but very important task. Smile. Smile at everyone you see. Someone may need that smile more than you will ever know. Smiles can often become the seeds of lasting relationships. I believe that a smile from you is one way God spreads the love He has given you. Have you ever noticed when your glass feels only half full and someone smiles at you, your glass suddenly seems fuller? Imagine what giving a hug or a kind word might do!

*I think that you will find that tonight when you take off your shoes or sandals and begin to count the blessings of the day, smiles (yours to others and the ones extended to you) will find their way to the top of the list, right where God intended. Amen and Amen*

# DAY 52

Good morning. Is there something you'd like to say on this bright and sun filled morning? I repeat the prayer God's Son offered long go. Forgive me for my sins is forever appropriate. To my wife, though I've spoken these words a million times ,I say I love you with all my heart and soul. To my parents, who have joined ranks with those in Heaven, I say thank you a thousand times over. Why do I write nearly every morning? I feel compelled to put my thoughts into words. Years ago the Lord spoke to me saying, "Let's talk." Some days it's mostly me and some days I'm sure that it's him. I often wonder how many of my thoughts have been lost into the vast universe for never having been spoken or written. If you have something that needs to be said, then by all means say it. Write it. Don't be afraid! You say, what if I do it wrong? How will it sound? You won't know unless you capture your thoughts. Say or read them out loud. That is what your ears are for. In time you begin to hear the words that aren't even spoken. It is in the quietest times that I hear the Lord speaking most clearly to me.

*So when you hear words like, "talk is cheap," "put your money where your mouth is" or "actions speak louder than words," don't be afraid. God Is always listening and He is waiting to hear from you. Amen and Amen*

# DAY 53

Good morning. Why don't we take a chance once in a while? "You mean gamble?" you ask, shocked. No, gambling is something else entirely. Gamblers pay no heed to the probability of failure and throw caution to the wind. Risk takers recognize the possibility of failure, accept the challenges and take action. We aren't talking about money here. Have we missed making friends because we were afraid to at least take a chance on them? This age old quote from an unknown source is still applicable: "It's impossible, said Pride. It's risky, said Experience. It's pointless, said Reason. Give it a try, said the Heart." Why not go for that job that seems out of reach; take that vacation you always thought was too far away; bind those wounds that have been holding you hostage. Take a chance on love, on life, on God; you'll find they are all well worth it!

*When your days are done, wouldn't it be wonderful if you could say, "I took a chance on life with God and I won the lottery!" Amen and Amen*

# DAY 54

Good morning. What time is it? How many times have I asked, “Where has this week gone?" Many of us have exclaimed how time flies or the years have absolutely flown by. We say, “There never seems to be enough time,” that is unless you’re sitting in a history class on the hottest day in May or at your work desk at two o'clock on a sunlit Friday afternoon. I would be among the first to attest to the supersonic speed of time. The only time we see it move slowly is when we watch it. Take your temperature or your pulse, the slowest minute ever. How about waiting for the bus to come or the arrival of your daughter or son coming home? There is nothing slower than the final two minutes of a football or basketball game, unless you are losing. My wife proclaims that a nine inning baseball game takes forever and a day. None the less, time is a sacred commodity, not to be wasted. It's been 27,645 days since the doctor at St. Anne's hospital spanked my little pink rear end. It is amazing how fast it has all gone. How much of that time have I offered to and for the Lord? Not nearly enough, I'm sure, and to think He has offered me eternity with him! No more clocks, no watches, no more hurry, scurry and worry.

*And while we are talking about it, remember, there is no time like the present. Have a great day. Be sure you share it with him! Amen and Amen*

# DAY 55

Good morning. I wonder, have you ever wondered how a pelican can fly? How does a spider weave its web? What makes the colors of the rainbow? How fast can a dolphin swim? Do bears really sleep in trees? Why are diamonds and gold more precious than cabbages and carrots or wheat and barley? Why is ninety-eight point six considered to be a normal adult temperature? What is normal, anyway? How did mountains get so high? What lies beyond the stars? How long does a turtle or a butterfly live? What's so important about the past? What does the future hold? Who made me just as I am? Am I actually made mostly of water? Who designed our DNA? There's so much to know in this wonderful world, and beyond, that God created for you and me. It's because of these and trillions and trillions more to wonder about that I believe God is real. What is it that you wish to know, perhaps about the oceans, mountains, the seas or the air we breathe? Maybe you'd like to know about the birds and fishes or the butterflies and bees. I look to the heavens and wonder how far we can go. Jesus, who holds the world together and knows all the answers, said "Seek and you shall find."

*So what do you say, let's get busy, there's so much to know and so little time to learn it. Who knows, maybe we'll even find a little wisdom along the way. That leaves me with only this left to say, "Thank you Lord for sharing each and every day." Amen and Amen*

# DAY 56

Good morning. I wish I could do or say something that would make this life better for you. But I am not a medicine man or miraculous healer. I am not the richest or most powerful man on the face of the earth. I am definitely not the smartest or wisest man in the world. I'm not even 100 percent consistent. Sometimes I question and challenge my beliefs. That leaves my pockets pretty empty, but not my heart, because I can offer thanks to the Lord who created us all in His own image. And He placed you squarely in my life, so I can pray and truly care for your well-being, physically, mentally and spiritually. My world would not exist without the Lord God and it would not be the same without you. My life has been blessed because of each and every soul that I have met and experienced, even those of you who have only offered a smile or a handshake. Hopefully, because of my prayers and actions, Someone will bring new life to you. His name is Jesus. He said in Matthew 25:40, "I say to you, inasmuch as you have done it unto one of the least of these my brethren, you have done it unto me." How awesome that is. I bless you and that blesses him!

*As one of the least of us myself, I thank the Lord that He has allowed me the honor of caring and praying for you. Amen and Amen*

Emunah

Faith

# DAY 57

Good morning. Mark Twain tells of his friend, Brian Cavanaugh, who made the mistake of telling Twain that he had planned a trip to Mt. Sinai and that he was going to climb to the mountaintop and read aloud the Ten Commandments, to which Twain responded, "Why don't you stay at home and keep them." That happens to be pretty darn good advice for all of us! My good intentions are not always the success they were meant to be and guess what, sometimes my intentions aren't that good. We don't need a walk to the mountaintop, we need a daily walk with the Lord. He is never very far away. He doesn't need you to repeat the commandments aloud. He hears you when you whisper them in your actions. The fact is there are a great many holy places throughout the world, but thanks to our Lord and Savior, Jesus Christ, the Holy Spirit indwells each and every one of us who believes in him. C. Austin Miles (1868–1946) wrote "In the Garden" and one of my favorite performers, Merle Haggard, recorded it in 1994. "I come to the garden alone while the dew is still on roses, and the voice I hear falling on my ear the son of God discloses And He walks with me, and He talks with me and He tells me I am his own and the joy we share as we tarry there none other has ever known. He speaks and the sound of his voice is so sweet the birds hush their singing, and the melody that He gave to me within my heart is ringing And He walks with me and He talks with me..."

*You don't have to climb a mountain to impress God or wait until you are in a garden with Jesus. Why not just begin your daily walk where you are with, "Our Father who art in heaven, hallowed be thy name..." Amen and Amen*

# DAY 58

Good morning. I have always been one who was up for a dare. Just what does that mean? The dictionary describes it as having the necessary courage or boldness for doing something. Melville wrote, "What I've dared, I've willed and what I've willed, I'll do!" William Danforth, the founder of Ralston Purina, was also the founder of the American Youth Foundation in 1925 and the author of the well-known book titled I Dare You. It has become one of the top ten self-help books ever written. In it he challenged the youth of America to step out of their comfort zone to become all that they could be. The dominant thought throughout his book was that the four key components in life need to be in balance with one another for a person to be truly healthy. These components are physical, mental, social and spiritual. Though I have never actually read Danforth's classic, his philosophy and mine are compatible. As a teacher, coach and father, I desired most to help shape the whole person. Being a winner was important to me, but being the best you were meant to be was essential. In that way we are all winners! So don't be afraid that you might fail; likewise don't fear that you might win.

*I simply love what it says in Galatians 6:9-10: "So let's not get tired of doing what is good. At just the right time we will reap the harvest of blessing if we don't give up." Be the best you can be, and be ready for the harvest. Amen and Amen*

# DAY 59

Good morning. If someone were to ask me to write them a love song, I could only answer that I am sorry but I cannot. If one were to ask me to paint them a masterpiece I would not be able to respond. If you wished me to give you a million dollars, that would assuredly be an impossibility. However, if you asked me to be your friend, I would certainly agree. If you needed someone to love you and to care for your needs, you need only ask. And I would pray for you without even hearing a request. The talents and gifts that the Lord has bequeathed to me may be limited, but what it takes to make a difference He has offered abundantly. The beauty of it all is that it doesn't require any special talent on my part, only a desire to truly practice these three things: faith, hope and love.

*Billy Graham shared these words: "The greatest legacy one can pass on to one's children and grandchildren is not money or other material things accumulated in one's life, but rather a legacy of character and faith." Martin Luther King offered these thoughts: "Love is the only force capable of transforming an enemy into a friend" and "Faith is taking the first step even when you don't see the whole staircase." Amen and Amen*

# D A Y 60

Good morning. Have you ever experienced "just out of reach?" You know, the very high cupboard, just beyond your tiptoe. Then there was that football pass for the winning touchdown that was just out of reach. Was the score required for admission to college or graduate school a point or two short? I remember the dream house that had a down payment just beyond our budget. How about the daughter who lives too far away, and seldom remembers to call? Did you give up? I remember what my father used to say, "Reach for the stars." Harriet Tubman wrote, "Every great dream begins with a dreamer. Always remember you have within you the strength, the patience and the passion to reach for the stars to change the world." Maya Angelou penned these words, "The desire to reach for the stars is ambitious. The desire to reach hearts is wise."

*There is one who is never out of reach, and His name is Jesus. He is never more than a prayer away. So when your tiptoes aren't quite enough and you can't quite reach the stars, call on him and He's sure to lift you higher. You know what? I feel taller already! Amen and Amen*

# DAY 61

Good morning. Once again I find myself reading 1st Chronicles in the Old Testament. How easy it would be to simply pass right by these genealogical pages that list hundreds of names, most of which I cannot pronounce. Unimportant one might say, but what if it was your name that was omitted from the annals of God's roll call? As I perused each clan, one by one, a name or a town would ring with familiarity. Doesn't that sound strangely connected to what we call family? After all, where would we be without those who came before us? I think that it is sad that so many of us cannot identify anyone in our families beyond our grandparents. Were they doctors, lawyers, fishermen or hunters, pioneers or city folk? Where did they live? Were they strong minded or compromising? Did they cry out to the Lord or ignore him completely? Did they love their children and look after their grandparents? I wonder, do you suppose any looked like me? No matter what our matriarchs' and patriarchs' genealogies might reveal about our ancestors, the New Testament tells us in Hebrews 12:1 that there is a great cloud of heroes surrounding us, faithful witnesses who have lived before our time. Hebrews 11:1 explains, "Now faith is the assurance of things hoped for, the conviction of things not seen. For by it the men (and women) of old gained approval (from God)." They are part of that great cloud, along with the faithful of our own family genealogies.

*It turns out that we have a lot of spiritual ancestors to look up to and a lot to live up to! Amen and Amen*

# DAY 62

Good morning. What is it that you really want? There are few questions we ask ourselves more often than this. As long as we live, this question lies in wait. Yes, I've heard it said, "I want nothing out of life" or "there's nothing I really need." Incredible, if I do say so myself. We all have our own built in Google just waiting to have the search button pushed. For the most part our wants seem pretty simple; I want some black socks or a pair of warm pajamas. I want breakfast, lunch and dinner and of course an evening snack. I want a college degree or a job. I would love to become an artist or plant flower gardens. Life is pretty easy, isn't it? Easy for me to say. What about the children in Niger who have nothing to eat? How about those in Malawi who thirst for even a cup of water? We have difficulty deciding what to wear from overflowing closets. How about those in Somalia who have only the clothes on their backs and no shoes? Far too many have no schools to attend, no churches to pray in and no freedom from their oppressors. There are more orphans in the Ukraine than just about anywhere in the world, with no parents to care for and love them. Some say, "What can I do about all that?" or worse "It's not really my concern." But it is our concern, isn't it? The need is so great we just don't know where to begin.

*What I really want cannot be found on Ebay, Google or Yahoo. It can be found only within my heart. I want to know God better, I want to follow him, I want to make a difference somehow, somewhere. In 1 Corinthians 13, Paul said we should want faith, hope and love, "And the greatest of these is Love." Let's all start right there and see where it leads us. Amen and Amen*

# DAY 63

Good morning. How many of you recall the commercial in the 70's where three brothers are looking at a new cereal for breakfast they don't think they'll like and the older two decide to "Let Mikey try it!" first. Mikey likes it. How about the Alka Seltzer ad touting "try it, you'll like it?" Mom's and dad's everywhere agreed, "Like it or not you're still going to do your homework." What is it you don't like? For example, Karen is not a big fan of Brussels sprouts or butter beans. Two of my children don't like sliced tomatoes and when my brother was small he'd take twenty lashes with a wet noodle rather than eat a spoonful of lima beans. Here's a list of what I don't like. I don't like cottage cheese, very dry wines, liver, and Pon Haus; not much else when speaking of things that one eats. I don't like other things, though, like bullies, arguments, poverty, pain, warfare, ungodliness. I don't like spilling spaghetti sauce on my white shirts or having to go to the men's room when none exists. I am definitely not a fan of warts, dirty finger nails, spiders, ticks, and chiggers. I don't care much for heights or being alone. I definitely don't like it when I know someone doesn't like me because I'd "like" to think that I'm the "Mikey" of people; that is, I try very hard to like everyone I meet. Alright, if I must admit it, I don't like to lose, either. God has been working on me about that!

*You might have noticed I have not used the word "hate" throughout this entire writing. I just "hate" that word! On the other hand, liking is kind of like smiling. You're bound to feel better when you do. Try it, you'll like it! Amen and Amen*

Emet

Truth

# DAY 64

Good morning. Perhaps one of the most difficult challenges we face is the difficult adjustment called "change." How easy it is to say, "I like it just the way it is," or "it's always been that way." No matter whether it is about yourself, your family, your community, nation or the world, there is and always has been a need for change. One must caution that change is a two sided proposition; it can be for improvement or for decline. If the only thought is "those were the good old days," we would still be chopping wood and hunting wild turkey for our dinner. Now, I know that some might find pure joy in that scenario, but as a people, we need to move beyond that. Believe me when I say that I am no advocate of change for change's sake. If it ain't broke, don't fix it! But be careful that you listen to all views. Don't be so closed minded that you find yourself saying, "It's my way or the highway." There are several components and requirements to making a good change; patience, perseverance, study and research, communication, a pinch of love and I must mention a whole lot of prayer!

*Don't you suppose Martin Luther King prayed as he walked down the streets of Selma, Alabama? Remember what I said at the beginning; change is never easy, but don't make change the automatic enemy. Amen and Amen*

# DAY 65

Good morning. Prayers, large or small, are never wasted, the Lord hears and answers them all. Are you worried or concerned about your son or your daughter? Is there a health issue with you or someone close to you? Are you concerned about the state of our nation, our world? Are you struggling with marriage issues, your job, your faith? You say, “I can't sleep” or “I have unrelenting pain.” Finances, uncertainty, the future, aging, anger or hatred, sinfulness, dying—they all strike fear into someone's heart, perhaps yours, this very moment. You cry, “If only God could fix this!” The good news is He can! Offer others’ needs and your own to him. Pray to him. Believe in him. He already knows your need. He is the answer!

*May the Grace of God touch you this very moment. Amen and Amen*

# DAY 66

Good morning. I once heard an engineer speaking about his doctoral thesis. Even the title was unintelligible to me. My very short study with a mathematics professor in college was much the same. Even mechanics leave me clueless. Scientists and astronomers just make me starry eyed and when it comes to fine cuisine and even plain cooking, I am stuck at the first stage, boiling water. I struggle with books that have no pictures and legal documents are, for the most part, baffling to me. I would find it simply impossible to write a novel or paint a masterpiece. I must admit, however, that I do have an affinity for coloring books. When it comes to gardening, I'm just beginning to understand the differences between dirt and soil. There's so much in life that I don't know! Even though we try to fake it for much of our lives, "You can't know what you don't know." But here is what I know for sure. There is only one God of the Universe and all it contains, and He offered His only Son to save us from our sinfulness, because He loves us that much.

*How can you be certain of this? My answer is simple, as I am but a simple man. Because He told us so. There are those things in life that require no theorems, axioms or scientific proofs; just belief and trust in the Lord's hallowed name. Amen and Amen*

# DAY 67

Good morning. In our lifetime we may do a few great things, but for the most part it's the small things that count most. It is those small things that determine our quality of life; little things like changing the oil in our cars or checking the air pressure in our tires, flossing and brushing our teeth and trimming our nails when needed. Eating our breakfast and physical activity are simple things, but very important for us. So you think that hugs aren't important? Try living without them. We all need to challenge our intellect. We should never give up learning. Reading the Bible may seem small or unimportant, but it connects us to the Spirit that lies within us. If you doubt that prayer works, it probably doesn't, whereas those who place their trust in the Lord have no doubts that it does. Tell someone you care, and don't be afraid to say "I love you." Three small words mean so much. A small kiss can touch a heart. Happiness doesn't depend on amusement parks, theaters and basketball games. It comes from experiencing ordinary kindness, beauty and love and passing it on. God isn't looking for extraordinary people, He is searching for ordinary people willing to do extraordinary things.

*Remember: Three small stones and a sling shot saved a nation, and a wooden cross on a hillside saved you and me! Amen and Amen*

# DAY 68

Good morning. If every moment of our lives is precious, why do we waste so much of it in idle time? Do you have plans? Do you set goals for yourself? What are your worthwhile plans for today? I don't mean for twenty years from now, just for today. Are you like the forest or the trees? Perhaps you are like Bugs Bunny when you arise in the morning with "What's up Doc?" Seriously, I'd like to share a thought from my morning Bible reading (NIV, Life Application Study Bible) speaking about Bathsheba, the wife of King David: "From her life we see that the little day to day choices we make are very important. They prepare us to make the right choices when the big decisions come. The wisdom to make right choices in small and large matters is a gift from God. Understanding this should make us more willing to include God in our decision making. Have you asked for His help in making today's decisions?" Most of our time is actually spent silently within our heads, thoughts unshared with anyone but yourself. You will probably have more than eight million thoughts over the next year. Multiply that by seventy years or more, and wonder how many of them will just be "space fillers."

*Why not allow God to have a piece of the action? The Lord will help you prioritize your thoughts and put them into action, if only you are willing to let him in. You might be very surprised at what you are capable of, if you're willing to seek God first then put your mind to it! Amen and Amen*

# DAY 69

Good morning. Have you ever been to a doctor's office where the nurse gave you a page or two and asked you for your history? Wow, one or two pages and my life is an open book! While many of us regard I Love Lucy, The Honey Mooners or Howdy Doody as part of our history, there are others who would designate the Blitzkrieg, Viet Nam or Baghdad as their history. Still others suggest that history has little if any relevance in today's world. Here's the truth as I see it: history is the summation of all that ever was and the building blocks for all that will ever be! It begins with His Story, Genesis Chapter 1, "In the beginning." You can paint it any way you wish and you will see we weren't there—but He was! As babies and wee folk we first learned, "Once upon a time." Later on we learned of Genesis, Exodus, Leviticus, Matthew, Mark, and Luke. There are a few of us who sought to know more: Jesus Christ, Paul, the Roman Empire, the Reformation Discovery, the Industrial Revolution, World Wars and even more. Some sought to know grandpa or great, great, great grandfathers. It may be a little disconcerting, but do you realize that you will become the history of your grandchildren and those that will follow them?

*What do you think the history books (or should I say the gigabytes) of tomorrow will say about the part we played in our world? Only God knows the answer to that! Amen and Amen*

# DAY 70

Good morning. Wake up, wake up! No alarms needed for me! How do you most like to awaken in the morning? Do you love to be awakened as your wife or husband snuggles up very close, or perhaps with a gentle kiss? Could it be the sounds of the birds whistling their morning tunes or the warmth and glitter of the sunshine as the morning dawn erupts? How about the smell of coffee wafting through the air or of pancakes on the griddle? Will you finish that final morning dream? Some prefer the fresh morning air from an opened window. Did you feel God's caress as the darkness of night gave way to a brand new day, a brand new beginning? He was watching over us all night, you know. Is it any wonder that I seek first to read a devotional followed by the wisdom of the Word? Then I am ready for that morning cup of coffee! Doesn't it make you want to sing? It does me!

*Here are a few morning songs just for you: (1) Boo Radley's "Wake Up Boo," "Wake up, it's a beautiful morning. Feel the sun shining in your eyes." 2) Bob Marley's "Sun Is Shining," "Sun is shining, weather is sweet. Makes you want to move your dancing feet." 3) U2's "Beautiful Day," "It's a beautiful day, don't let it get away." 4) Primal Scream's "Movin' On Up," "I'm movin' on up now. Gettin' out of the darkness. My light shines on." 5) Cat Stevens' "Morning Has Broken," "Morning has broken, like the first morning. Blackbird has spoken, like the first bird." 6) Carole King's "Beautiful" "You've got to get up every morning with a smile on your face." (7) Take That's "Greatest Day," "Today could be the greatest day of our lives." Amen and Amen*

Sharath

Serve

# DAY 71

Good morning. "You are the wind beneath my wings." Our Monday morning men's group sang this beautiful song, made famous by Lee Greenwood (1982) and Bette Midler (1988). I find the third verse extraordinary. "Did you know that you're my hero, and everything that I'd like to be? I can fly higher than an eagle, 'cause you are the wind beneath my wings." In this fast paced world heroes are becoming extinct. Are there any heroes in your life, someone to look up to, someone to become the wind beneath your wings? Let's be clear about it, heroes aren't perfect, they are not angels. Heroes are men and women, just like you and me. They make going beyond perceived limitations possible. They provide standards that exceed our estimates. They prod us forward when we are tempted to quit; Joshua, David, Peter and Paul, Joan of Arc, George Washington, Lincoln, Kennedy, Mother Teresa, Lou Gehrig, Martin Luther King, heroes all. Have they all disappeared forever? No! Perhaps you can become another's hero, so that they too can fly higher because you are the wind beneath their wings. Who knows, maybe you're a hero to your son or daughter, perhaps to a student, or a neighbor; why, maybe even to a perfect stranger. What does it take? A hero is "Someone who is admired or idealized for his/her courage, outstanding achievements, noble qualities or spiritual strength." Which one is you?

*Remember this. Wind and hot air are definitely not the same! Amen and Amen*

# DAY 72

Good morning. Whenever it comes, the first day of spring is a time for barren trees and golden brown grasses to be nearly done, at least for a year. The invitation goes out. You can almost hear trumpets announcing a new season! As the grass begins transforming from browns to greens, the woods appear like colorful umbrellas opening for the coming rains. Flowers pop up along winding mountain roads and stand proudly upright along the river's valleys. Birds and squirrels begin busily building their nests, creating a place for still another generation soon to come. Songbirds offer welcoming, melodious sonatas. Caterpillars quietly await their emergence and eventual transformation into majestic butterflies. The sun seems brighter and the breeze whispers more gently. The fields lie naked, silently anticipating the plows and plantings and harvests to come. We wait patiently for new rainbows following the thunder that awakens the landscape to display its full array of colors. These are the sights, sounds and smells that only God can create. Rebirth is His unequaled, glorious idea, and the invitation includes us in any season of the year or of our lives.

*How is it, with you and your soul? Will you give rebirth in you a chance? Here's my answer to His invitation. Yes! Hallelujah!!! Amen and Amen*

# DAY 73

Good morning. Have you ever found yourself saying that it's been a bad day? Or a bad night? Or a really bad day? If you have never answered yes to at least one of these, it'll be coming your way in due time. Into every life rain must fall and sometimes it is stormy and some even experience cyclonic events. I know about our Lord blessing us all, but calling such events a blessing seems preposterous! Nevertheless, Paul shared in 1st Thessalonians 5:16-18, "Be joyful always. Never stop praying, be thankful in all circumstances, for this is God's will for you in Christ Jesus." There are no fewer than twenty-one scriptures that are directed at the "difficult times." What about those you and I have experienced? Devastating divorce, depression or serious illnesses, loneliness, watching your child suffering, standing at the graveside of one that you love. I wish that were all! We all know a bad hair day or a bad day at work. Some will experience sleepless nights in pain. Truthfully, when terrible things happen there doesn't appear to be anything to be thankful for. It is alright to hurt, to struggle, even to be angry. We do not live in a pretend world. What God is asking us to do is to acknowledge that He is good. We need to really believe that God has a plan for us; superficial faith will not suffice. He will walk right beside us, He will even carry us when we cannot make it on our own. He can and will bring us peace even in the toughest times.

*We give thanks because we know him, we trust him and yes, we celebrate him. David said give thanks for the Lord is good and His love endures forever. Max Lucado says God's love is wide enough for the whole world. Amen and Amen*

# DAY 74

Good morning. I'll believe it when I see it. Is that you? If it is, that is not belief at all. The Latin root word "cred" means believe. From it come words like credentials or incredible, something that can hardly be believed. Do you believe there is wind? You cannot see it, only feel it or see its results. I am simply astounded by it as I sit here watching the waters of the Gulf being churned into thrusting whitecaps racing toward the shoreline. Last night I awoke to its sound just outside my window, but I could not see it. Then there is the air we breathe. Can you watch as it makes its way into your lungs to offer you the gift of life itself? Until very recently we could only trust that the earth was round or that the universe went on beyond and beyond. Can't you see, without him there is no wind, no air, no sea, no stars in the sky. So let me ask you, when was the last time you saw God? Do you believe in His existence? It is not enough for us to say just that He exists. The Bible says even devils know that. What we are asked to do is acknowledge His Son Jesus as our Savior and trust the Father, God the Creator, with all our heart, our soul and our strength. Is that too much to ask for all He has done for us? Is it too hard to believe? Believe it! It is true. Just ask him.

*By the way, if you listen closely when you pray, you may even hear him speaking to you! Amen and Amen*

# DAY 75

Good morning. I lightly stepped on the weight scale this morning. The epiphany of this unremarkable event was the realization that I weigh exactly one hundred pounds more than the day the love of my life said, "I do." I bet she did not realize how much more she was getting for her money. You could say there is just that much more to love. It didn't happen all at once; on average it represents less than two pounds per year (every year!) We all knew we would grow up, but who said anything about growing out? That includes out of my clothes. How do you suppose that happened? Blame it on metabolism if you wish, but it had more to do with meat, mashed potatoes and gravy, second helpings, large portions, fast food and decreased physical activity. I'm told, "You haven't changed a bit." Tell that to my diabetes doctor, my eye doctor or the lovely lady who cuts my hair! What am I going to do about it? Resolutions are not working. I am not going to become a vegetarian or a vegan and diet pills or surgery are totally out of the question. So here's my plan: less roast beef, quarter pounders, Reeses cups and second helpings. Cut the size of my portions, seek out more exercise and far less TV and Internet. Did I mention the snack attack? Now, that is a difficult one; maybe more tangerines, pears, apples and fewer potato chips and spice drops. I'll see you on the golf course or the walking track. I want to "waist" away, like maybe from a 42 to a 36 or so. I know how to resist other temptations, so I can't "weight" to see how this all turns out!

*By the way, if someone asks you your favorite fruit, don't answer, apple pie ala mode or lemon meringue pie. Just sayin'.*

*Amen and Amen*

# DAY 76

Good morning. Have you prayed the prayer that our Lord taught us, today? Why not? I Just didn't have time.? To tell you the truth, I didn't think about it, either. It's not Sunday. Funny how we can pray for rain or for sunshine, for improved health, for a promotion or a victory, but His prayer all to often passes through our lips without much real thought. Let me ask, is his name really hallowed? Do we believe his Kingdom will come? If we really want our trespasses to be forgiven are we ready to forgive others their trespasses against us? Do we really believe that He is the Kingdom, The Power and the Glory forever and ever? Hear what Israel had to say about our Lord over four thousand years ago in Deuteronomy 6:4-9: "Hear, O Israel; the Lord our God; the Lord is One alone. Love the Lord your God with all your heart, with all your soul and with all your strength. Those commandments that I give you today are to be on your hearts. Impress them on your children. Talk about them when you sit at home and when you walk along the road, when you lie down and when you get up. Tie them as symbols on your hands and bind them on your foreheads. Write them on the door frames of your houses and on your gates."

*So let me ask again, did you pray the prayer the Lord taught us, today? It's not too late! Amen and Amen*

# DAY 77

Good morning. The wind is one of the mighty forces of God, and we have no control over it, whatsoever. The winds, the rains, the snows, the hot sun, the frigid cold are under God's control and occasionally He reminds us. A respected friend penned a devotion message I feel compelled to share with you. "'He causes the clouds to rise over the whole earth. He sends the lightning with the rain and releases the wind from his storehouses,' Psalm 135:7. Have you ever seen huge wind farms appearing on the horizon? From a distance they look like angels doing their morning calisthenics. As you get closer, you can admire the towering pinwheels on the prairie. Up close they are even more majestic. They are taller than the Statue of Liberty with blades bigger than the wings on a jumbo jet...and there are whole fields of them neatly arranged as far as the eye can see. Wind force has been present since creation, but only lately have we attempted to harness these invisible horses and put them to work. It was simply a matter of putting something up to catch the power. Think about all the other forces in our lives just waiting to be tapped...your friends always in the background but available to help...the energies available from positive attitudes like optimism, hope, courage and decisiveness. Arthur Gordon captures my simile: 'Be bold and mighty forces will come to your aid.' Consider the magnetic power of prayer to attract God's infinite help... always at hand, waiting. He is never too busy, and always understands our need."

*It's a no brainer. We should boldly tap the power of prayer available to us 24/7. Amen and Amen*

Come,
follow me, Jesus said

Karen DuBro

and I will make you
fishers of men. Matt 4:19

# DAY 78

Good morning. Has anyone ever asked you, "Where are you going?" You may have answered, "Just down the road." That's pretty open ended, isn't it? There are lots of roads we can choose, in many different directions. I want to share just a few of those choices. Many of us have been like the familiar comic strip character, the Roadrunner, always headed somewhere at break neck speed, "beep, beep." Willie Nelson shared with all his country western fans, “On the Road Again." The Beetles gave "Penny Lane," Elton John offered "Goodbye Yellow Brick Road" and Bob Dylan connected with "Highway 61." Books and movies offered "The Road Less Traveled' by M. Scott Peck, "The Road Not Taken" by Robert Frost, "On the Road" by Jack Kerouac, and "The Road to El Dorado.” Add "Tobacco Road" and Dr. Seuss’ "Oh, the Places We Will Go." As for my travels I chose "The Road to Emmaus." The Bible speaks often and directly about roads countless times. In Isaiah 42:16, "I will lead the blind by ways they have not known, along unfamiliar paths I will guide them...I will turn the...rough roads smooth. These are the things I will do; I will not forsake them." In Jeremiah 29:11, "’For I know the plans I have for you,’ declares the Lord. ‘Plans to prosper you and not to harm you, plans to give you hope and a future,’" and in Matthew 7:13-14, "Enter by the narrow gate, for wide is the gate and broad is the way that leads to destruction and there are many who go in by it. Because narrow is the gate and difficult is the way which leads to life, and there are few who find it."

*The next time someone asks you where you are going, which road will it be? Amen and Amen*

# DAY 79

Good morning. When I was very young (a long time ago) my mother used to tell me what I should wear. Oftentimes I would disagree, but I'm sure you could guess who usually won out. My father had a penchant for wearing outfits of robust colors and felt no remorse at mixing stripes and plaids. Oh, how my mother cringed at the thought! As I grew older I learned what should be worn with what. White socks to church just wasn't cool and black socks and Bermuda shorts wasn't a good match. Mind you, I could never start a haberdashery, but over the years that followed there were things I learned about what everyone should wear. For example, Tony Bennett, Janet Leigh, and Dick Van Dyke taught me to "Put On a Happy Face." "Pick out a pleasant outlook, stick out that noble chin, wipe off that full-of-doubt look, slap on a happy grin! And spread sunshine all over the place, just put on a happy face." Then there was "When You're Smiling," taught to me by Louis Armstrong. "When you're smiling keep on smiling, the whole world smiles with you and when you're laughing, oh, when you're laughing the sun comes shining through." And one more that I like very much comes from Ephesians 6:11-18. "Put on the full armor of God that you may be able to stand against the strategies of the devil... Above all, taking the shield of faith ever with you, you shall be able to guard all the fiery darts of the wicked..."

*Open up your Bible. It really offers quite an outfit for all of us to wear. And Keep smiling! Amen and Amen*

# DAY 80

Good morning. On a gloomy, stormy day, have you ever really stopped to count your blessings? I think we need a starting point. 1 Thessalonians 5:18 sounds like a good place to begin. "Be joyful always, pray continually, give thanks in all circumstances, for this is God's will for you in Christ Jesus." Now I am willing to wager that most of us have never heard of the name Johnson Oatman Jr, born 1856 in Lumberton, New Jersey. As it happens his father possessed the finest singing voice in all of Lumberton. It was natural that Johnson would have a desire for music himself. Not having the talents of his father, he turned to writing song lyrics (mostly Gospel). So every year more than two hundred songs would flow through his pen. He found a way to preach the Gospel through music. He would eventually write over 5000 songs, among them "No, Not One" and "Higher Ground." But the one that stands out above them all is "Count Your Blessings" written in 1897 and still one that "men sing, boys whistle (can you still whistle?) and women rock their babies to sleep to." How easy it has become to take our blessings for granted. Here is the chorus that he composed. "Count your blessings, name them one by one. Count your blessings, see what God has done." In the lyrics he advises, "When you are discouraged thinking all is lost...Count your many blessings...every doubt will fly And you will be singing as the days go by."

*See if this helps make your day go better. Try writing a blessing down every morning when you rise. You could even sing it! Amen and Amen*

# DAY 81

Good morning. Have you ever found yourself in a situation similar to these two? The gas light just came on or a bathroom can't come soon enough. How far is it to the next exit? Time for a little prayer, perhaps. "Please Lord, just get me there!" I distinctly remember once several years ago in the mountains of Eastern Kentucky, near Hazard, when the miles between exits seemed considerably longer than I expected. "Come on Betsy, just get me there and I'll never try this again!" Can you remember when your kids were small, every bathroom along the way had a built in magnet. But the highways don't provide our only exits. How many habits have you vowed to break that you never quite got rid of? This will be my last cigarette or drink. Did you ever anxiously anticipate graduating or changing jobs? What about thoughts of retirement or relocation? "Perhaps someday I will be out from under this debt." Have you ever noticed that nearly every exit has an entrance nearby? That exit, what a relief it is, but how about the exhilaration of the entrance with a full tank or an empty bladder? Next time pay closer attention to the physical and spiritual gauges in your life and the exits won't be nearly so scary.

*By the way, how full is your spiritual tank? Amen and Amen*

# DAY 82

Good morning. There is an old adage that says there are only two things that are certain in life and they are death and taxes. I certainly hope and pray that is not how you see it. There is a great deal more to life than that! It has been said that an apple a day keeps the doctor away. An apple may not do it, but healthy eating and physical exercise can certainly increase your chances. I've heard that April showers are sure to bring May flowers. April's coming, just wait and see. How do I know? It's been said that for every drop of rain that falls, a flower grows. That'll do it for me. The world and everything in it is always changing and that is for certain. James Baldwin saw it this way: "If you are treated a certain way you become a certain kind of person. If certain things are described to you as being real they're real for you whether they're real or not." That may attest to why some of the things we see around us today are as they are. But Amy Grant sees it this way: "I can look at the future with anticipation and it's comforting to know that someday as Christians, we'll be able to look back and have a little more clarity on why certain things in life happened."

*There is one thing of which I am absolutely certain, and that is that Jesus loves me! And how do I know this? Because the Bible tells me so! That's the old adage I choose to believe. Amen and Amen*

# DAY 83

Good morning. I've heard it said, "Never say never." The word "never" itself has some very interesting dynamics. We use it in so many ways. "Never do that again," "Never a dull moment," "Never is a very long time." There's "Never, Never Land" as James Barrie's Peter Pan would put it. Dr. Seuss uses it often. "You're never too old, too wacky, too wild, to pick up a book and read to a child. If you never did you should. These things are fun, and fun is good." Consider "Sometimes you will never know the value of a moment until it becomes a memory," or "Never take no for an answer" and "Never give up!" There's more. "Never back down, never let me go, never been kissed," and of course "never mind and never too late." Karen and I sweetened our romance over fifty years ago with Johnny Mathis and "The Twelfth of Never." If you don't remember or are too young to remember, the lyrics follow. "You ask how much I need you, must I explain? I need you, oh, my darling, like roses need rain. You ask how long I'll love you, I'll tell you true. Until the twelfth of never, I'll still be loving you. Hold me close, never let me go. Hold me close, melt my heart like April snow. I'll love you till the bluebells forget to bloom. I'll love you till the clover has lost its perfume. I'll love you till the poets run out of rhyme, until the twelfth of never and that's a long, long time..."

*Just remember what the Lord tells us: "It is the Lord who goes before you. He will be with you, He will never leave you or forsake you." We should never forget to celebrate the never ending story of Jesus our Lord and Savior. Amen and Amen*

# DAY 84

Good morning. A change of plans. "The best laid plans of mice and men often go awry." An often quoted statement, but from whence did it come? It's actually an old quote of the Scots in a poem by Robert Burns, circa 1785. It refers to turning up the mouse's nest by the plough. It would become the title of John Steinbeck's 1939 novel Of Mice and Men. It is used to signify the futility of making detailed plans when the ability to execute them is uncertain. All of us have been there, haven't we? How about these plan spoilers: health, weather, finances, and disposition. Many a soldier has heard these words, "You're in the army now, not behind the plow." I can share with you that my journal entries seldom end up where I originally thought our conversation was headed. I am absolutely positive that the love of my life, whom I have been blessed to spend fifty-four marvelous years with at this writing, never would have guessed in her wildest dreams that we would be joined in holy matrimony, never to be put asunder. In college, my first major was pre-dentistry. Not my path. Our first child was going to be a boy. Nope. Our second wasn't even in the plan book. What a wonderful change of plans! I claimed I would never become a Lay Director on an Emmaus Walk, but I did. I never thought I was capable enough to pray in public (or privately for that matter) but I do. Tennessee was never in our plans for retirement, but here we are.

Perhaps the big*gest change that occurred in my plans was when I recognized I'm not the one in control of them. Only the Lord knows the plans of both mice and men. Amen and Amen*

Ahavah

Love

# DAY 85

Good morning. Lord, will you care for me and love me, today and forever? I pray to you every morning—well, almost every morning. Some mornings I get up too late or have important matters to accomplish. Lord, I try to read your Word every day. I believe I spend at least fifteen to twenty minutes, sometimes more. Don't ask me to repeat what I've read. Many times I just don't get the message. Lord, I do my best to love my neighbor as I love myself but I just wish she'd take better care of the yard next to us. I must admit that I don't even know most of my neighbors. I love everyone, except maybe the Muslims, the Russians, the politicians, the "druggies," and Michigan football fans. Lord, what more do you want from me? You suggest I start by reading Psalm 8? Okay. "Oh Lord, our Lord, your majestic name fills the earth! Your glory is higher than the heavens. You have taught children and infants to tell of your strength, silencing your enemies and all who oppose you. When I look at the night sky and see the work of your fingers, the moon and the stars you set in place, what are mere mortals that you should think about them? Yet you made them only a little lower than the angels and crowned them with glory and honor. You gave them charge of everything you made, putting all things under their authority, the flocks and the herds and all the wild animals, the birds in the sky, the fish in the sea and everything that swims the ocean currents. Oh Lord, our Lord, your majestic name fills the earth!'"

*Dear Lord, I am so ashamed. Please forgive me for my nonchalance; it does not honor you. Amen and Amen*

# DAY 86

Good morning. When Solomon was to become the king of Israel he prayed to the Lord, not for power and wealth, but only for wisdom that he might rule his nation justly, to improve the lives of his people. God was pleased and in return granted him much more. Have you prayed recently for wisdom? Have you found it within your heart to pray for your nation? Your world? Your leaders? Your neighbors? Your families? Your enemies? For the sick, the lame and the destitute? For the lonely, the homeless and those who hunger? The addicted and the dying? The powerful and the powerless? We can go on and on, you know. Prayer is like a poem that has no end, it should never be abandoned. As you pray, be mindful that you are not the healer, only the intercessor before the Lord. He listens and acts. When someone asks for your prayers, don't ignore them or put them aside. If you say "I will keep you in my prayers," do just that! No prayer is too large or too small. God hears them all and will respond to each and every one. In case you have overlooked it, or need a gentle reminder, have you prayed for the servicemen and service women, the police and firemen as well as those in emergency services who have placed their lives on the line so that you might be free and safe as you pray? God knows them, every last one! If you let intercessory prayer be the intersecting point between you and the Lord He will fill your heart with compassion and His love will bless you, too. Be thankful.

*Remember, 1 Thessalonians 5:18 tells us to always, "in everything, give thanks." Psalm 69:30 says to "Glorify him with thanksgiving." Amen and Amen*

# DAY 87

Good morning. This has been a blessed week and it has gone by so rapidly. But life isn't perfect. What do you say we talk candidly and personally a minute? So, how are you feeling? Really feeling? You miss that special someone in your life? You're fighting that thing called aging and it is an uphill battle? You love the changes in the weather each season, but dread the new requirements of some of them? You can't wait for a spring break in the late winter, while others are sorry that the snow melted so quickly? As for me, I am deeply saddened that our eldest daughter just can't seem to find permanent (or at least prolonged) healing. When I speak to my Lord, I find myself saying enough is enough. He asks, "Where is that eternal optimism that you so often exude?" Actually, I know it is right here, just waiting for me to ask for it, so I will. Lord. We know the struggles of life. We really don't expect every moment would be free of struggle, anxiety, loss or failure. I hear your answer that the elixir for our pains and sorrows is our faith and trust in you, Lord. You wait for us so much more patiently than we do for you. You say "Ask and I will respond." I know you hear my prayers for my daughter. I know the answer may not be what I want. But I am asking for your healing touch for her. Others can ask about their loved ones, their fear of change and the challenges of aging. I know you will hear and answer each of them, too.

*The bottom line is that you, Lord, are my rainbow in the midst of every storm, my sunshine overriding the darkness. So Lord, as always, I give praise to you for my blessings. I give thanks for the sunshine that I am sure will follow the rain. He will be your sunshine, too, if only you let him. Amen and Amen*

# DAY 88

Good morning. If someone were to ask you what you are good at, how would you answer? The easy way out would be to say "I'm not good at anything." The truth is, I find that hard to believe. Now it is possible that you may not realize what you are saying. It may be true that you don't excel at baseball, dancing or fishing and you are likely not equipped for the NFL. You may struggle with mathematics or mechanics and writing. Perhaps your talents lie in cooking, sewing or building. What's that? You're happy just to be able to boil water? You see that these talents and more take time, effort and hard work; but God has offered us things we can all do well. You ask what these things might be? I direct you to Galatians 5:22-23, "But the Holy Spirit produces this kind of fruit in our lives, love, joy, peace, patience, kindness, goodness, faithfulness, gentleness and self-control. There is no law against these things." And it goes on to say in Galatians 6:10, "Therefore, whenever we have the opportunity, we should do good to everyone."

*So, my friends, doing good to everyone you can do good to may be the best thing of all to be good at doing. That's good enough for me! How about you? Amen and Amen*

# DAY 89

Good morning. My New Living Translation One Year Chronological Bible is beginning to show some serious wear. There was a time in my life when I didn't have a Bible or if I did it sat in a not so prominent place, hidden away from my sight. There was also that time when I treated my Bible as though it was so fragile that extreme care should be taken not to desecrate its pages. My Bible became much like an egg. Be careful not to crack the shell! There was a problem here. What I needed remained hidden away within that protective shell. When I finally became brave enough to risk seeing what was inside, it took a long time for me to carefully work my way through the "white" of its contents. As I became more assured, I attempted to scramble it all together (the white and the yolk). And it was just that, scrambled—scrambled and confusing. Often, I found myself missing the message altogether. Then one day, I can't tell you exactly when, I came across the "yolk" of it all. God wasn't offering me a sixteen hundred and ninety-two page book to be a decoration or bed time reading. He was offering me his very Self in the Living Word, the Bible from Alpha to Omega, from "In the beginning God created the heavens and the earth" to "Amen! Come Lord Jesus."

*The tattered cover, torn and turned up pages, and the scribblings of my thoughts and questions in the margins, have become part of my conversations with my Lord and Savior. He invites you to meet with him in His Word. Amen and Amen*

# DAY 90

Good Morning. Whose turn is it, anyway? Everything and everybody has a turn at one time or another. It is so because it is a part of God's plan. How carefully he has scripted it all. He has offered us the night and the day that's sure to follow. How beautifully He has introduced them with the dawning of the morning sunlight and the robust, majestic sunset of eventide. There is nothing accidental about the seasons as we experience the rebirth of springtime, where all creation once again renews itself. The buds on the trees transform to blossoms and leaves of every shade of green with floral displays in designs and colors only God could create. The summer grasses come alive, the birds and bees and butterflies receive their invitation to His wonderful dance. (OK, Ok, flies and mosquitoes, I guess He welcomed you, too.) It will soon be time for planting in preparation for fall feasting that surely follows. Autumn's crazy quilt will color the trees then blanket the ground until cold weather brings frost and snow that become the décor of gardens, yards, fields and woods. Then it happens all over again. First the daffodils, some even willing to peek through the last of the fallen snows, then trilliums, tulips, rosebuds, and water lilies along the nearby shore. All in God's time.

*Don't forget that you, too, are a part of this magical merry-go-round. Give thanks to the Creator and as the seasons follow one another, celebrate Jesus' promise to return. For as sure as summer follows spring and winter follows fall, His turn will come all in God's time. Amen and Amen*

# DAY 91

Good morning. So how have you been thriving lately? Thriving is the gerund or present participle of the verb thrive. To be perfectly honest, that means nearly nothing to me. What I do understand are the synonyms: flourish, prosper, blossom, do well, succeed, mushroom (not Morels). Do any of these fit you? Just what do you consider success to be? Is it prosperity, good health, happiness, power, faithfulness? Yesterday evening we were blessed to attend a music performance (really a testimonial to what worship can be). God was in attendance, I am sure! One piece among many that affected my senses deeply was a song by Casting Crowns, entitled "Thrive." Perhaps you have heard it: "Here in this worn and weary land Where many a dream has died Like a tree planted by the water We never will run dry. So living water flowing through God we thirst for more of you. Fill our hearts and flood our souls With one desire. Just to know You and To make You known. We lift your name on high. Shine like the sun make darkness run and hide. We know we were made for so much more Than ordinary lives. It's time for us to more than just survive. We know we were made to thrive. Into Your word we're digging deep To know our Father's heart. Into the *world we're reaching out To show them who* You are. So living water flowing through God we thirst for more of You. Fill our hearts and flood our souls With one desire Just to know You and To make You known."

*"Joy unspeakable, faith unsinkable, love unstoppable, anything is possible We were made to thrive!" I believe it completely, don't you? Amen and Amen*

# Hallel

# הלל

Praise

# DAY 92

Good morning. In the Christian world we celebrate Maundy Thursday during Easter Week. So just what does that mean? Sadly, very little to a great many Christians and others alike. There are some who would say those who attend Maundy Thursday and Good Friday services are a bit over the top in their beliefs. I must plead guilty, then. I know of no other place that the word "Maundy" is used in everyday language. It is a shortened form of "mandatum" (Latin), which means "command." It refers to the day Jesus celebrated Passover with his disciples. John 13:4-5 says, to their dismay and embarrassment, "He got up from the table, took off his robe, wrapped a towel around his waist, and poured water into a basin. Then he began to wash the disciple's feet, drying them with the towel He had around him." Jesus told them, "You don't understand what I am doing, but someday you will. You call me Teacher and Lord, and you are right, because that is what I am. And since I, your Lord and Teacher, have washed your feet, you ought to wash each other's feet. I have given you an example to follow. Do as I have done to you." What did He mean? He explained, "A new commandment I give to you, that you love one another: just as I have loved you, you also are to love one another." John 13:34

*His example was washing the dusty, road weary feet of His friends. His command was to love as He loves. How does He love? Humbly, kindly, thoughtfully, unconditionally. If we want to obey His command, we need to take a really good look at how we love. Amen and Amen.*

# DAY 93

Good morning. How long has it been since you received a report card? Some refer to it as a progress report. Do you think it's time for you to receive an update on your current standing? Mind you, I'm not much on grading on the curve. Comparing ourselves with everyone else doesn't say much about our progress or our ability. In life, are you where you hoped to be, where you want to be? Do you care about others or about yourself? Matthew 22:39 and Mark 12:31 instruct that "Thou shalt love thy neighbor as thyself." How's that going for you? And don't ignore the one before that, "Thou shalt love the Lord thy God with all thy heart." It goes on, "with all thy soul, and with all thy mind." Careful, that mind thing can get you. Here are a few more instructions for a good progress report: Leviticus 19:18, "Do not seek revenge or bear a grudge against anyone among your people, but love your neighbor as yourself." Here's another one, 1 Corinthians 10:24, "No one should seek their own good, but the good of others." Then there is Galatians 6:2, "Carry each other's burdens, and in this way you will fulfill the law of Christ," and Philippians 2:3, "Do nothing out of selfish ambition or vain conceit. Rather, in humility value others above yourselves." There are lots more and I know just where to find them. Look further in the Bible.

*The bad news is that our report card doesn't end at the twelfth grade or even graduate school. The test is how we are living our lives right now. The good news is that we can get a better "grade" if we pay attention to God's word and do it. Amen and Amen*

# DAY 94

Good morning. Here is one of the insights the Lord has given me. He has shown me that we have all received gifts and talents. They are different, don't you know. Our talents are attributes that we are proficient in. Art or athletics for instance. He challenges us to make good use of them, whereas our special gifts are freely offered to each of us to edify one another as the Body of Christ. Let me explain. I often find myself relating to songs that I have known over many years. Some remain in my memory bank. I cannot sing worth a plug nickel, but I love to sing and I love to hear the words that honor the Father, Son and Holy Spirit. Someone was gifted with the words from the Spirit. Someone used their God-given talent to create the tune. Someone recorded it for the rest of us to hear. Songs have become standards that I choose to live by. Some are a joyful noise unto the Lord. Some are prayers. I've shared a few already and here is yet another that makes me happy. If you know it, I invite you to sing along out loud with me. "Author of the world, walk with me Ruler of the earth, walk with me Calmer of the storm, walk with me Healer of my heart, walk with me How I need you How I need you Oh, Jesus, walk with me Light for every step, walk with me Giver of each breath, walk with me How I need you How I need you Oh, Jesus walk with me In your presence there is peace, there is rest In your presence Lord there is life that never ends In your presence Lord there is joy, there is joy In your presence there is life that never ends."

*So there you have It; don't you feel better? I sure do! Amen and Amen*

# DAY 95

Good morning. Just what is it that the world needs now? Hal David had an answer back in 1965 when he wrote the lyrics to "What the World Needs Now is Love." He collaborated with Burt Bacharach who supplied the musical score recorded by Jackie DeShannon, creating this masterful selection. David stated that these were the most difficult lyrics he had ever chosen to write. The first two lines came easily, "What the world needs now is love, sweet love. It's the only thing there's just too little of." What could be compared to that? No answer, until his conversation with God led him to write the antithesis, what we didn't need! "What the world needs now is love, sweet love. It's the only thing that there's just too little of. What the world needs now is love sweet love. No not just for some but for everyone. Lord, we don't need another mountain. There are mountains and hillsides enough to climb. There are oceans and rivers enough to cross, enough to last until the end of time. What the world needs now is love, sweet love. It's the only thing that there's just too little of. What the world needs now is love, sweet love. No not for some but for everyone. Lord we don't need another meadow. There are cornfields and wheat fields enough to grow. There are sun beams and moon beams enough to shine. Oh, listen Lord, if you really want to know. What the world needs now is love, sweet love. It's the only thing that there's just too little of."

*What the world needs now is love, sweet love...and you must know, God is Love! 1 John 4:8 says, "Whoever does not love does not know God, because God is Love. Amen and Amen*

# DAY 96

Good morning. I think about the paradox of life as we see it today. I have often heard it said, "How I long for the simple life, like it was before." Before what? Was that when you were a child and spoke like a child with no real responsibilities? Perhaps you were referring to those days when we flung the windows wide open to cool our sweltering homes or hung the sheets out to dry on the clothes line all day. Maybe it was the days of mix masters, sewing machines, pressure cookers or push lawn mowers and planting our own gardens. Could it have been the times of iron lungs, whooping cough and scarlet fever with doctors who carried little black bags? There are some who might call for the return of protractors, slide rules, multiplication tables and cursive writing. If that's not enough consider hunting and fishing for your next meal, walking ten miles to the nearest town or general store, riding your horse or mule to church and using barrels of salt to preserve your food. Yes, those were the "good old days," weren't they?

*Now, if you are talking about abiding by the Lord's Commandments, helping your neighbor, taking care of your elders, appreciating our nation's flag, schools that didn't just teach subjects but taught children, Bibles that didn't just sit on the bookshelf, believing that Jesus and one's faith were not a danger to others, and loving thy neighbor as thyself, well, bring it on my brothers and sisters! I can handle all the rest. Amen and Amen*

# DAY 97

Good morning. How does it make you feel when you finish something? Are you saddened, are you elated, or is it something in between? I love it when I finish that old crinkled up tube of toothpaste or when I've used the very last drop of cologne. When that last blade of grass has succumbed and sweat rolls down my brow, I feel a special tinge of joy. I could have tears run down my cheeks at the end of a sad movie, though I am pleased that I possess the capacity to care. I'm not always pleased at the end of the eighteenth hole or the tenth frame and there have been times at the end of the final bell I've been disappointed, but almost always I'm glad that I attempted to do my best. It is important to remember that for every ending, there is a new beginning. Even when it's the darkest night the dawning of a new day is not very far away. There will always be a tomorrow. I would be remiss if I did not share with you the most awesome finish of all time. John 19: 28-30 records it. "Jesus knew that his mission was now finished, and to fulfill Scripture He said, 'I am thirsty.' A jar of sour wine was sitting there, so they soaked a sponge in it, put it on a hyssop branch, and held it up to his lips. When Jesus had tasted it, He said, 'It is finished!' Then He bowed his head and released his spirit." It was Friday—but Sunday was coming.

*When someone tells you there are no tomorrows, don't believe them for even a moment. Jesus rose from the dead that Sunday. He lives! And He has made all our tomorrows possible, now and forever. You can believe it! Amen and Amen*

# DAY 98

Good morning. Who can you trust? We live in an upside down world overflowing with terror, anger and fear. We expound that the government can't be trusted and that the police and others chosen to protect us are no better. We lament Wall Street and the big financial institutions exist only for themselves and schools and universities could care less about those they are charged to teach. Brother against brother, father against son, where can one turn for help? Solomon understood our dilemma over three thousand years ago. In Proverbs 3:5-6 he wrote, "Trust in the Lord with all your heart; do not depend on your own understanding. Seek his will in all you do, and He will show you which path to take." You may be asking, "How can I possibly do that?" First, don't depend on yourself. Trust God. This isn't always easy. Spend more time in God's presence. Put God first in your life. Stay close to the Word—God uses it to guide us in the right direction. Third, listen and receive the Holy Spirit. John 14:26 explains, "The Counselor, the Holy Spirit, whom the Father will send in my name, will teach you all things and remind you of everything I have said to you."

*It's never easy, though. Matthew 16:24 reminds us that trusting God takes a whole-hearted commitment from dawn to dusk. But we're never alone, and this is His assurance: "And surely, I am with you always to the very end of the age." Matthew 28:20. So, where will you put your trust? I know where I put mine. Amen and Amen*

La'Netzach

Forever

# DAY 99

Good morning. God created the heavens and the earth. God created man and woman. God gave man and woman free will—oops!—the will to choose whatever we will be. What an awesome responsibility. He offered us his entire domain, his prized creation. So how well have you done with it? Better yet, what will you do with it? You know you still have time. He offered rainbows. Do you chase after them or do you cherish their beauty? He offered you mountains. Do you climb them or do they become your barriers? What will you do with the fields and the streams, the rivers and the valleys? You say, "But I cannot hear, I cannot see, I cannot speak." Tell that to Helen Keller. You say, "I am lame and cannot walk." Tell that to Franklin Delano Roosevelt. You say, "I am poor." Tell that to Mahatma Gandhi. You say, "I'm just a woman." Tell that to Mother Teresa. You say, "I am the son of a slave." Tell that to Martin Luther King. You say, "I don't have the time." That is all we do have!

*So what time is it for you? What will you choose to do with the choices that have been offered to you? By the way, free will has a cost: full responsibility for the choices you make. You can choose to accept God's sovereignty and forgiveness; or you can reject him. Are you willing to pay the price? Jesus paid the price for me. And for you. Accept him. Amen and Amen*

# DAY 100

Good morning. My how the years fly. As I sit here this morning I can't help but remember and reflect on those many days that have passed so swiftly. There were cereals like Rice Krispies, Corn Flakes and of course “the breakfast of champions,” Wheaties. Windows stood wide open in the summer and no one ever locked their doors. There were free peanut butter sandwiches distributed at lunchtime in the school cafeteria. Baseball cards were pinned to our bicycle wheels with clothespins and sheets could be seen blowing in the wind on clotheslines in every yard. We took turns washing and drying dishes after every meal. There were bow ties and Easter bonnets and there really were blue suede shoes. I couldn't wait to lick the bowl after mother made fudge, no worry about salmonella. We used bus tokens and transfers that took us "downtown.” We listened to the radio at bedtime and were entertained by Fibber McGee and Molly, The Inner Sanctum and Amos and Andy. George Burns repeatedly told Gracie Allen, "Say goodnight, Gracie." Elvis Presley shook the world as well as his hips and Dezi Arnaz was not the only one to love Lucy.

*Many things have changed, but one thing will never change—just like the song I learned so long ago—“Jesus loves me, this I know.” Amen and Amen*

# DAY 101

Good morning. In Luke 3:4-6 of the Gospels, Luke wrote about the words John the Baptist recited from the prophecy proclaimed by Isaiah many generations earlier. "A voice of one calling in the desert, prepare the way for the Lord, make straight the paths for him. Every valley shall be filled in, every mountain and hill made low. The crooked roads shall become straight, the rough ways smooth. And all mankind will see God's salvation." The people asked, "What shall we do?" John immediately answered, "The man with two tunics should share with him who has none, and the one who has food should do the same." This remains a very strong message for us today. Luke 4:13 tells us that after Jesus spent forty days in the desert the devil stopped tempting him and left until an "opportune time." What temptations are lurking in your shadowy places? We must be willing to identify the temptations for us and our nation. For starters, there's neglecting God, impurity and lust, hatred, anger, discord, jealousy, greed, selfish ambition, dissension, arrogance, envy, idolatry, drunkenness, lying, cheating, and thievery.

*Jesus came to offer freedom from all of these and more. Don't give the devil the chance to find the "opportune time" to tempt you. Instead, ask the Holy Spirit to become your shield and your armor. Amen and Amen*

# D A Y 102

Good morning. When I was young, a long time ago, I used to ask my Dad, "How are you feeling?" to which his often repeated response was "with my fingers." Though not the answer I was seeking, I knew it meant that he was Ok. Many of us are very cautious about allowing anyone to see our "real" feelings. That, of course, is in direct contrast to those we say wear their feelings on their sleeves. Why is it that some, maybe many, go to such great pains to mask what's really going on in that gray matter we call a brain? It is even worse when we hide what's in our heart. The old proverb used by many coaches is "never let'um see ya sweat." The world and a great many households would be much better off if they allowed their true feelings to emerge. Do your kids really know how you feel about them? Many a sad child has said, "I never knew he/she felt that way." For that matter, how about your spouse? When you are really down and out or feeling quite depressed, it can make a big difference if you can share with someone you can trust. Who would want to listen to you? The One who always listens and can provide the right answers. His Book is chock full of great solutions.

*I guarantee He is there just waiting to become your friend, confidant, sounding board, your safe place. The Lord is waiting twenty-four-seven, even on the darkest nights and in the deepest valleys. Try him. He invented feelings! Amen and Amen*

# DAY 103

Good morning. Jesus has sent you an invitation to become His disciple. In case you haven't noticed, it carries with it an RSVP. It is simply not enough to answer "I am a Christian." That is the easy part, but it's not the response that He is searching for from you. He is seeking your commitment to following him NOW, not tomorrow or next week! He wants you to enlist in service to those who need you. They can be found at every turn. Can you see them? There is the lonely one in the corner of the library. Did you notice that desperate soul at McDonalds yesterday? There is a little girl across the street that could use your smile and a comforting word. The old man you see on his porch when you take your daily jog, did you know that he is dying of cancer? Or that sad looking woman who lost her husband not so long ago who works the cash register at your grocers? Don't ignore the guy with the tattoos and all that metal, he is the one that Jesus wants you to greet first. For some who cry out, tomorrow may be too late. You might be their only hope.

*As I looked across the room earlier this morning, I noticed what was written on my wife's t-shirt: "Work for Jesus. There are lots of openings." So tell me, are you ready to return your RSVP? Amen and Amen*

Yeshuah

יֵשׁוּעַ

Jesus

# DAY 104

Good morning. I have prayed this morning, have you? You have nothing you need to pray about? Why not pray about that! Pray for the blessing of having a God you can pray to, One who will listen to every word. Pray in thanks for the blessing of His Son offered for you. Pray for yet another day. Pray for your family, your friends, your country, your world. Pray for peace, justice, redemption, and by all means pray for Salvation, yours and that of others. This morning as I read Deuteronomy 32:15 I substituted America for Israel. "But Israel (America) soon became fat and unruly; the people grew heavy, plump, and stuffed! They abandoned the God who had made them; they made light of the Rock of their Salvation." This occurred in about 1400 BC. Are we there once more? Moses wrote Psalm 90 as if it was written today: "Lord, through all the generations you have been our home: Before the mountains were born, before you gave birth to the earth and the world, from beginning to end, you are God. . . You spread out our sins before you—our secret sins—and you see them all. . .Let us, your servants, see you work again, let our children see your glory. And may the Lord our God show us his approval and make our efforts successful. Yes, make our efforts successful!"

*And that is the exact reason that I pray every day! Amen and Amen*

# DAY 105

Good morning. It has been said that Solomon, King of Israel, was the wisest man who has ever lived. I don't know about that, but I can't help being impressed by his words. I know that we could truly benefit if we were to experience an ample portion of wisdom in ourselves, our nation and our world today. The fact that Solomon's kingdom lived in peace and prosperity for many years tells us something, does it not! Oh, where is our peace and prosperity? We could find much worthy of our learning if we were taught the principles exhibited in the Proverbs. It is no wonder that kings and nations sent legions to learn and understand his wise words. Proverbs 1:1-7 speaks volumes; why not give a listen. "These are the proverbs of Solomon, David's son, King of Israel. Their purpose is to teach people wisdom and discipline, to help them to understand the insights of the wise. The purpose is to teach people to live disciplined and successful lives, to help them do what is right, just and fair. These Proverbs will give insight to the simple, knowledge and discernment to the young. Let the wise listen to the proverbs and become even wiser. Let those with understanding receive guidance by exploring the words of the wise and their riddles. Fear of the Lord is the foundation of true knowledge but fools despise wisdom and discipline."

*There are thirty-one groups (chapters) of Proverbs handed down to us. Why not spend a little time there? Who knows, if we glean the fields of the wise, perhaps we too will reap the harvest. Amen and Amen*

# DAY 106

Good morning. I rose up early to greet your morning wonders, Lord. That is, after I partook of one strong cup of coffee. How easy it is to digest your words when I am sitting where I can feel your glorious creation. The sun is trying its best to find a way through the early morning fog that rests upon the still waters of the bayou in my view. The birds have already begun their morning rendition of nature's sonata and what a beautiful composition it is. As I read your Word this morning there is a feeling of peace that rests upon me and this place. Lord, we begin another new week together. I'm looking forward to it and know you are, too. You've called on me, and all who hear you speaking to them, to become your disciples and I will do my best to follow your ways. We have heard you in Jeremiah 29:11: "For I know the plans I have for you declares the Lord; plans to prosper you and not to harm you, plans to give you hope and a future" and in Jeremiah 29:12-13: "Then you will call upon me and come and pray to me, and I will listen to you. You will seek me and find me when you seek me with all your heart."

*The day begins and ends with you, Lord. You are my way, my truth, and my life. Amen and Amen*

# DAY 107

Good morning. Tell me about the good old days—part two. Ok, let's step out of our comfort zone for a little while. June 28th, 1914 Franz Ferdinand is assassinated in Bosnia-Herzegovina and WW I is underway. Seventeen million deaths. The US lost 279 men per day. October 29th, 1929 the US stock market crashes beginning the Great Depression, financial disaster in America lasting nearly ten years. 1939 Adolph Hitler invades Belgium and WW II has begun. December 7th, 1941 Japan attacks Pearl Harbor and we are in the war. Hiroshima and Nagasaki 1945 two atomic bombs end the war, but not before an estimated 50-80 million deaths are recorded during the war years. Over 400,000 American soldiers died in this tragic war. The Korean War lasts from 1950 to 1953, more casualties! President Dwight Eisenhower intervenes in the Little Rock school crisis in 1957. November 22nd, 1963 John F. Kennedy is assassinated, followed later by assassinations of Robert Kennedy and civil rights leader, Martin Luther King. 1965-1968 Vietnam and more US war deaths. 2019 the pattern hasn't stopped.

*In 33 AD Jesus died on the cross so we can be forgiven. So there you have a different glimpse of the "good" old days. Deaths and destruction then and now. Wars and rumors of wars. The only solution is the victorious Kingdom of God. Come, Lord Jesus, Thy Kingdom come. Amen and Amen*

# DAY 108

Good morning. Is there someone you wish to pray for this morning? Pray to God, the only true God, the God of the Universe. How do we know that our God is God? Because He says so. He tells us, I AM. He is Always Listening. He will listen to you! He is Always Wise. He listens to our prayers for our nation! He is Always Caring. I will pray for those who are traveling this morning, knowing he cares about them. He is Always Present. He is Alpha and Omega. We are all somewhere on the way to our finish line. He was present at our beginning. Is there anything in this lifetime more important than finishing that life well? He is present at its ending. He is Always Patient. He waits on us to ask, so I pray that my children and grandchildren will know you, Father God, and be blessed by you. I pray you have heard His Word to you and respond to him. Bathe us all in the blood of Jesus, so Satan will be powerless against us, as he possesses no authority over Jesus Christ, the Lord of all creation.

*We must keep this scripture in mind constantly: "Let your light so shine before men, that they may see your good works, and glorify your Father which is in heaven." (Matthew 5:16) Just how can we do that? By being an example for others in word, in conversation, in relationship, in charity, in spirit, in purity, in courage and in faith. Can it be done? Yes, if we pray, pray, and pray and when we have done that, pray some more. Amen and Amen*

# DAY 109

Good morning. It is time for everyone to stand up and be counted! Have you ever wondered why there are only a few who ever say or do something profound? You may think you will never do anything that anyone will remember. “I'm just an average person,” you say. Do you suppose Abraham Lincoln or Thomas Edison thought that way? What do you suppose made them different? Was their intellect superior? Did they possess power or wealth? Was God on their side? I got it! They were just lucky. Yep, it's just the "lottery" of life. Some will win, some will lose and some are rained out. Do you believe that to be true? I sincerely hope not! They and others were focused. Oh, they failed as so many of us have, but they always got back up. Quitting, giving up was not an option. They possessed a quality that we all have available; it's called faith. They were focused, determined, persevering and believed they could. When the road ahead of you seems narrow, get your shovel and make a new road. When the water is too deep to cross, build a boat. When you have no answers, pray to the Lord and He will show you the way.

*My friends, I am sure that Peter never dreamed he'd be a fisher of men until he met Jesus. Find something to believe in, have faith and never give up. The whole world awaits you! Amen and Amen*

# DAY 110

Good morning. Which of your walls have fallen into disrepair? What are you doing about it? Are you planning to rebuild? One of my Facebook friends, Laura, wrote this to me: "'End' is not 'the end.' In fact, END is 'Effort Never Dies' and if you get NO for an answer, then remember NO is 'Next Opportunity.'" Always be positive! My Bible readings this week have taken me to the Old Testament books of Ezra and Nehemiah. They would participate in the rebuilding of the broken and the battered. Ezra would return from exile to rebuild the faith of the Jews in Jerusalem and Nehemiah would follow to lead in the rebuilding of the walls of the once great city. Amazingly, he would get it done in just fifty-two days. (With God's help of course.) The entirety of the New Testament is all about rebuilding and repair. God promised He would send his Son so our brokenness would be forgiven and we could become whole again. Randy, another friend, wrote this: "Blessed are those that spread the Gospel to the ends of the earth—which means everywhere past the end of your nose."

*So is it time to fix that broken relationship? Just as our bodies sometimes need rehab, so do our minds and our hearts. Is your faith in need of restoration? Read the Bible; let its instructions become the building blocks for whatever needs to be repaired in your life. And it wouldn't hurt to bend a knee in daily prayer. Amen and Amen*

Teshuvah

Repentance

# DAY 111

Good morning. I awoke this morning to the sounds of thunder. As I prepared for this new day I asked the Lord, “Where is the sunshine and the warmth that I have become so accustomed to? Will the wind and the rain ever cease?” As I was leaving to share in breakfast thoughts with my valued Emmaus brothers, I asked the most precious woman in my life, "Will you get the lumber and I'll get the nails?" In a state of confusion, she asked, "What are you talking about?" To which I responded sullenly, “For the Ark, of course.” All I could see was depressing clouds. Where was the beauty, the promised sunshine? I wondered. Do you ever feel like that? So with that thought in mind, I'll share a devotion that speaks volumes to me. "More Than Beauty,” by J. Stephen King from Alive Now, 1982. “O God of loveliness, we are a people who praise you readily for the lavender sunsets, the rhythm of the tides, the birds that bring in the morning, the rainbows and all the painted things of life. Yet how we box you in! Ah, you are more than a God of dorm room posters. You are a God of blood and thorns, dust and sweat, and yes, a God of tears, a God of wounds. We close our eyes and look away, embarrassed, or disturbed, or so perplexed, not thinking that the dear God of butterflies and lilies came down to live with lepers, beggars, rogues, walking the dusty roads, walking a road to wounds that end in death, a broken heart, a broken soul. You are the God of loveliness, for on this wounded world you place your loving hand. All ugliness is in our eyes, for through the eyes of love you see not ugliness, but burning need. Lord, will you forgive me my insolence?”

*Let the thunder roll! Let it rain, let it rain! Amen and Amen*

# DAY 112

Good morning. "I gave at the office." Just what did you give? Did it make you feel better? What about the man in the tattered clothes? You know, the one that smells as though a shower has eluded him for a long time? Did you see him struggle with barely enough to purchase a kid's meal at McDonald's? How about the little boy whose shoes have no soles? Did you walk away, saying "I gave at the office?" Did you offer to pray with the old woman sitting on the park bench with tears streaming down her cheeks? Did you offer to help the blind man cross the street? I'm sure you must have welcomed the lady who came to church in less than what would be called appropriate church clothing? Was the Bread of Life shelter too far away to offer your help or were you just too busy? Have you offered to share your love of Jesus with anyone lately? How about your kids, grandkids or your neighbor? Jesus said in Matthew 25:43-45, "For I was hungry and you gave me no food; I was thirsty and you gave me no drink. I was a stranger and you did not welcome me, naked and you did not clothe me, sick and in prison and you did not visit me. Then they also will answer saying, Lord, when did we see you hungry or thirsty or a stranger, or naked or sick or in prison, and did not minister to you? Then He will answer them saying, Truly I say to you as you did not do it to one of the least of those, you did not do it to me."

*How's giving at the office working for you? Amen and Amen*

# D A Y 113

Good morning. What are your plans for the future? The end of the school year or possibly graduation? Maybe you are readying yourself for that long anticipated vacation. You may not know it, but God has chosen you to be a part of His plan. What plan could He possibly need me or you for? We have been called to make His love known. Why is it that we so often treat God as though He exists to satisfy our needs, as temporary as they might be? We seek pleasure and prosperity above him. Turn to him, and find him and you will find purpose and joy, not temporarily, but forever. How does that sound? You know He loves you. He has always loved you. You can know him, serve him, love him. He is our hope and we are His hope for a world filled with love and beauty, just as he planned. You do remember the mustard seed, don't you? In Matthew 17:20-21 He said, "Because you have so little faith I tell you the truth, if you have faith as small as a mustard seed, you can say to this mountain, 'Move from here to there,' and it will move. Nothing will be impossible for you."

*So let's get busy, there is so much to do to restore the Earth and Its people to their full beauty as was and still is His plan. Amen and Amen*

# DAY 114

Good morning. When you turn to the Bible, what are you looking for? Finding answers has a lot to do with knowing where to look. If someone asked me, “Where should I begin?” I would probably respond, "Why not start where it all begins, in Genesis." If you want to know The Lord Jesus, then read the first four books of the New Testament and the book of John (the Gospels). There are many other great places to visit, and here are a few of my favorites: Romans, Galatians, Esther, Isaiah, Psalms, Proverbs, and of course Genesis and the Gospels. You have most likely heard said, "The Lord knows," or some variation of it. It's true! Why not ask him when you want to know about something. Bible reading and prayer conversation is a great way to approach him for answers to your thoughts, hopes and fears. Here are suggestions from Psalms: To Find Comfort- Psalm 23; To Meet God Intimately-Psalm 103; To Learn a Prayer- Psalm 136; To Learn a New Song- Psalm 92; To Learn More About God- Psalm 24; To Understand Yourself-Psalm 8; To Find God Daily- Psalm 5; To Find Forgiveness for One's Sins-Psalm 51; To Feel Worthwhile-Psalm 139; To Find Clarity-Psalm 119 (be prepared to spend some ample time here as it is the longest Psalm in the Book); To Praise the Lord-Psalm 145; To Know That God Is In Control-Psalm 146; To Give Thanks-Psalm 136; to please the Lord-Psalm 15; To Understand Why You Should Worship the Lord-Psalm 104."

*I pray that these scriptures will provide some of the answers you are seeking. Amen and Amen*

# DAY 115

Good morning. Decisions, decisions, decisions! What should I do? That's life as we know it, isn't it? What time should I get up? What should I wear? Breakfast or not? Do I have time for the Word or prayer this morning? What time is that meeting or class? Should I plant the garden or mow the lawn? What checks do I need to write today? Groceries, what do I want, what do I need? The car needs maintenance. House cleaning is on the list, I need to fix the toilet and wash the dirty dishes! What doctors' appointments? Not another meeting! My Sunday school lesson hasn't been read. I nearly forgot soccer practice or dance lessons, which is it today? Got to go to the bank. Did I forget a birthday? Who's coming to visit? When are we going to visit? Did I promise to help? What's for dinner? Did you buy the tickets? Is she still in the hospital? What, when, where, who, why? Can I just go back to bed?!

*Alright, back to the beginning. Did you settle into the Word first of all? Did you ask the Lord what to do? You don't have to do it all alone. Remember this, God is a twenty-four-seven God. He is with you always, If you choose to follow him. By the way, He is the best decision I have ever made. Amen and Amen*

# DAY 116

Good morning. What time is it? Well, that depends. For me, it is just past 6:30 AM and it is my time with the Lord. For others it may be time to get up, and for some there is still time for a dream or two. Time. It is one of the many gifts that God has offered to us, his children. As Solomon observed a long time ago, "There is a time for everything, and a season for every activity under heaven." In Ecclesiastes 3:2-8 King Solomon notes that there is "A time to be born, and a time to die, a time to plant, and a time to harvest, a time to kill, and a time to heal, a time tear down, and a time to build, a time to weep, and a time to laugh, a time to mourn, and a time to dance, a time to scatter stones, and a time to gather them, a time to embrace, and a time to refrain from embracing, a time to search, and a time to give up, a time to keep, and a time to throw away, a time tear, and a time to mend, a time to be silent, and a time to speak, a time to love and a time to hate, a time for war, and a time for peace." He also writes that God made everything beautiful in its time. Besides time, God gives us the gift of choice. What time is it for you? What will you do with the gift of time offered to you? The choice is yours.

*Now, just a personal recommendation on my part—make the most of the time you have because we move through it so very rapidly. So my prayerful wish for all of you is, "Have a good time!" Amen and Amen*

# DAY 117

Good morning. Who would have ever guessed that Rob became a seismologist or that Lory is known as one of the best geriatric doctors in the land? Skip and Richard are managers of cities. Nonsense. Donnie, that little boy deep in the heart of Eastern Kentucky, surely never imagined becoming a jet pilot! Was precocious Karen fashioned to become a teacher of children in distress? As for little Jimmy, he's a teacher. Are you kidding? So who would have ever guessed? You see, things thought to be impossible, or not thought of at all, do become true. I am sure Bill Clinton never thought that he would become the President of the United States; and Neil Armstrong never imagined that he would walk on the moon. Mother Teresa never dreamed that sainthood would be the exclamation point to her life's work. Our journeys take us down many roads, some wide and easy, others narrow and difficult. We experience crossroads and dead ends, but every road leads somewhere. Where have you been? More importantly, where are you going? Is anybody walking along that unfamiliar pathway with you? Hebrews 11:1 explains, "Now faith is the assurance of things hoped for, the conviction of things not seen." In 2nd Corinthians 5:7 it says "For we walk by faith, not by sight." Matthew 28:20 reads " And behold, I am with you always, to the end of the age." Never, I say never, overlook this quote from Matthew 19:26, "With God all things are possible."

*So when somebody asks, "Where are you going?" you can tell them, "Your guess might be as good as mine, because I don't know where I'm going exactly, but I do know who's going with me, and I know that He knows!" Amen and Amen*

Lis'moakh

To rejoice

# DAY 118

Good morning. Have you ever heard someone say, "Whatever happened to..." or "I have never thought about that?" It seems to me that we have given up thinking to artificial intelligence. Children sit at the dinner table with their hand-held games, mothers and fathers text and e-mail. Whatever happened to conversation? Television, computers and smart phones have been traded for reading, exercise and relationships. Internet, twitter, face time and innocuous entertainment have replaced creativity, poetry, cursive writing, multiplication tables and good old fashioned sweat equity. Do you know what your children and grandchildren are thinking? Have you taken the time to share with them what you know? Have you walked and talked the extra mile with your neighbor, your friends, your brothers and sisters? Years ago, I used to ask my students "critical questions," expecting real reasoning and thinking. Does that still exist? When someone asks, “What do you think?” will your answer be, "I have never thought about it?”

*Perhaps it's time to turn off the hand-helds, the computers and the televisions and sit around the dinner table talking to each other. Who knows, maybe the Lord will join us. You know He's standing by, just waiting for the opportunity! Amen and Amen*

# DAY 119

Good morning. There are a great many who would proclaim that only the strong survive. Herbert Squirer coined the phrase, “Survival of the Fittest” as a result of the Charles Darwin theory about the biological mechanism of natural selection and social dominance. Great generals, emperors and warriors have always displayed their skills as leaders through warfare, by conquering other nations and subjecting them. Among them are the likes of King David, Julius Caesar, Cyrus the Great, Alexander the Great, and Napoleon, just to name a few. Today’s world seems always ready to race for dominance as well, both the old fashioned way in battles, and in more modern competitions for preeminence. The business world and the sport’s world both weed out the weak and empower the strong. Jesus shared a different way to survive with his disciples in Matthew 5:5. “Blessed are the meek for they shall inherit the earth. Blessed are the poor in spirit for theirs is the kingdom of heaven. Blessed are those who mourn for they will be comforted. Blessed are those who hunger and thirst for righteousness for they will be filled. Blessed are the merciful for they will be shown mercy. Blessed are the pure of heart for they will see God. Blessed are the peacemakers for they will be called children of God. Blessed are those who are persecuted because of righteousness for theirs is the kingdom of heaven.”

*Move over, Squirer and Darwin. I’ve decided I’m going to cast my lot with God. His survival plan is much better. Amen and Amen*

# DAY 120

Good morning. Do you believe the best things in life are free? Did you ever walk on a mountain trail with the warmth of the sun shining down on your back? How about sitting by a rushing brook with your bare feet dangling in the cold, sparkling water? Have you ever planted seeds in your garden soil and watched as little plants popped through the surface and unfurled their leaves? Have you stood on the ocean's shore and watched as the sun slowly flattened on the sea? Have you ever watched an eagle soaring high above the trees? Have you kissed someone and instantly known that this is the one that God has chosen for you? Have you ever seen a baby born and heard her very first cry? Have you offered a stranger a helping hand only to recognize that you were the one being blessed? Have you ever thrown a pebble into a quiet pond to see the ripples grow?

*Have you prayed to God, knowing that He is listening to your every word? It's true, the best things in life are free. By the way, God has scheduled another sunrise tomorrow morning. Don't miss it! Amen and Amen*

# DAY 121

Good morning. I have a friend, a writer who wrote these words in one of his books: "I almost wish people didn't know the Bible so well. Most of us have just enough familiarity with it to keep us from hearing what it really says... We tend to get to a certain place, a certain point in our relationship with God and then we simply...stop." Is that where you are? Have you stopped short of your intended objective? You may not want to hear this, but we may be only one generation away from extinction of the Living Word, the watch tower of our faith. We are called and must be the stewards of our Christian faith for those who come after us. How else do you think the next generation is going to receive what we know to be truth, His Truth? It is not an accident or a coincidence that the chain has remained unbroken for more than two hundred generations. The Truth has met countless challenges, but through prophets, disciples and believers it has survived and even thrived. You cannot just hear the Word, you are called upon to be the Word. Those who will follow us don't need just a good story; they need real meaning. Do you remember what it felt like when you found Jesus as your personal Savior? You wanted to shout it for the whole world to hear! What has happened to that zeal? Was it lost, is it hiding in the closet? When our descendants repeat "God is Dead," and add "Jesus died, period," or maybe don't speak of him at all, do you want to be one of those who had kept silent? Will the Bible become just another storybook?

*It is time for all of us to drink deeply from the well, so we can dispense the living water for a thirsty population before it is too late. Amen and Amen*

# DAY 122

Good morning. "Always," that's a mighty big, powerful word. Careful when you use it as it is a very important Promise. I like the word "always" much better than "swear," even though they share the same meanings, like to vow, to pledge, to guarantee, to give one's word. Sometimes we use this solemn word lightly, as in I always tie my shoes or I always go this way. Careful now, I always treat people nicely and respectfully; I always listen to the words and thoughts of others; you can always depend on me. Then there are the super important ones as in I will always love you, I will always trust in the Lord. Remember Peter the night before Jesus was crucified? Though the Constitution of the United States doesn't actually use the word "Always," its synonym, "Promise," becomes the cornerstone of the entire document. The same is true of our wedding vows and our statements of faith. There are eleven Bible verses about always praising Jesus. Isaiah 41:10 says do not fear for I am with you always. Philippians 4:4 uses it this way: "Rejoice in the Lord always. I will say it again, Rejoice." Thessalonians 5:16-18 repeats the idea, "Rejoice always, pray continually, give thanks in all circumstances; for this is God's will for you in Christ Jesus." And of course Jesus' great promise to one and all for all time, Matthew 28:20: ". . .And surely I am with you always to the very end of the age."

*Other than "love," could there be a word any more comforting? Amen and Amen*

# DAY 123

Good morning. I awoke this morning to the sound of the wind blowing through our trees. I wondered for a moment just what this phenomenon of sound is. So...I looked it up in my trusty dictionary. Sound is "vibrations that travel through air or other mediums that can be heard, or sound produced by continuous and regular vibrations, as opposed to noise." But wait a minute, my source says it's also a verb, "to convey a specified impression when heard." Huh? Oh, I get it. "You sound worried," or "that's a sound idea." That got me to thinking what are the sounds in my life? I love the sound of the wind, but intensified it can become frightening. The sound of a crackly fire makes me happy, but that of a raging forest fire can be more than scary. The sound of music is exhilarating. The harp and the lyre played hallelujahs to accompany God's angels. When Moses approached the burning bush, I wonder if he heard God's vibrations. Was it Jesus's vibration that tore the curtain in the tabernacle? Did the Spirit's vibration set the flames flickering over the heads of those gathered in the upper room?

*The wind is mentioned fifty-six times in the Bible, but the time I like best is John 3:8 "The wind blows where it pleases. You hear its sound, but you cannot tell where it comes from or where it is going. So it is with everyone born of the Spirit." Amen and Amen*

# DAY 124

Good morning. There are simply no words to explain it. Have you ever tried to tell someone what something tastes like? For example, an apple or a pear. Usually we refer to another object to compare them. How does coconut cream pie taste, not like, but simply taste? How does a rose, lilac or dogwood tree smell; a blade of grass or a dandelion? Often, we resort to saying, "It's beyond compare." When you tell someone that you love them, they can't possibly know just the way you feel, unless they, too, have felt the exact same feeling. When I say that I love you, do you really know what I mean? I tell you that knowing the Lord gives me great joy. Do you understand? To know him is to feel that same joy. Do you know him? He waits so patiently to meet you, to greet you, to bring you joy. By the way, He already loves you. He loved you before you were even born. You know He created the universe, the sun and the stars, the earth, the mountains and the streams; why not you? The only way to know how craw fish or pineapple upside down cake tastes is to experience them. The only way to know how the ocean wind feels on your skin is to experience it. The only way to feel the height and depth of love is to experience it. The only way to feel the joy of the Lord is to experience it.

*Come on, friends, we've got a lot of experiencing to do! Amen and Amen*

Ruach

Wind, Spirit, Breath

# DAY 125

Good morning. My daily Bible readings have taken me through the Psalms and the struggles that David expressed in many of them. Our Sunday School class is studying the book of Hebrews in the New Testament, reading about the tribulations of the Jewish Christians of the first century and the encouragement they received to stay the course. In addition, I have picked up an old edition of Uncle Tom's Cabin to ponder. The struggles and challenges of God's children never seem to cease, do they? It's the same for those of us living in this world now, hearing cries for peace as it experiences some of its greatest challenges: terror, poverty, despair, hunger. Who could overlook the loss of faith and trust in this fallen world that is our home. There is only one answer, my friends, and that is to turn to Jesus Christ, the one and only true Son of God. He can dispel all our fears, even the fear of death. He modeled for us the way to overcome each fear as well as our daily mistakes and missteps. No magic potions or sacrifices required, simply give it all to Jesus and listen to His directions. Do you trust him with your life? There is nothing else that can impede you as you seek to find first joy and ultimately eternal life through Jesus Christ.

*Some may say, "But I'm not perfect." That's exactly why God came to us in human form—as Jesus—to help us get what we can't have by our own doing. He offers peace and eternal life with him. Just say "Yes" when He calls you to him. Amen and Amen.*

# DAY 126

Good morning. You've all heard the well-worn statement and sometime warning, "Be careful what you ask for..." In the Good Book it tells us time and again to ask. As I see it, this is one of the fundamental blessings of belief and of prayer. Note that I say one. There are more. First, we must bless the Lord our God for without him we would not exist, nor would anything in the vast universe. Secondly, we pray for the needs of others, both friend and foe. Now we can pray that our prayers will be answered. In Matthew 7:7-8 it is said, "Ask and it shall be given you, seek and you shall find, knock and it shall be open unto you; for everyone that asks receives and he that seeks finds and to him that knocks it shall be opened." A parallel verse comes to us in Luke 11:9. If that doesn't "seal the deal" try Matthew 21:22, "If you believe, you will receive whatever you ask for in prayer." It is here that I offer you caution; this is not three wishes from the bottle of a genie. John 14:14 states, "You may ask me for anything in my name and I will do it." Do you need more clarity? Here's more for your search: John 6:38; 1 John 9:14, Matthew 6:33, Romans 12:1-2, John 16:24. Guess what! There are even more, some going way back, like Psalm 37:4, "Delight yourself in the Lord and he will give you the desires of your heart." You see, we really find that we receive everything that we need in him.

*Remember this. All things are measured in His time not ours. My friends, if you allow him, He will fill you to overflowing. Isn't that quite enough? Amen and Amen*

# DAY 127

Good morning. Have you ever had a Yahoo! moment, when suddenly ordinary things became extraordinary to you? I have found the experience depicted in the Bible on a number of occasions. It's those times that celebrate the good times. Do you recall the lyrics of the song, "Celebration," by Kool and the Gang? A portion of the song went like this: "It's time to come together. It's up to you, what's your pleasure? Everyone around the world, come on! Yahoo! It's a celebration, Yahoo!" The tradition in the biblical days was to celebrate the good times with feasting and frolic, sometimes for days on end. Whatever happened to tradition, celebration, and of course the feast? When was the last time you put out your finest tablecloth, best dishes and silverware and celebrated? When did you wear your best Sunday clothes, just because? Would your husband faint if he came home to a candlelight dinner and you were dressed to the nines? Would your wife go into cardiac arrest if you arose early and greeted her with the finest breakfast and fresh cut flowers? It doesn't have to be a fiftieth anniversary or a wedding feast. What if you celebrated being married for eighteen years and 11 days or just because you were in love or both?

*You ask why? Why not? Every day is God's day, and isn't He worth a good party once in a while? Even every day? Amen and Amen*

# DAY 128

Good morning. Have you prayed yet today? Have you fallen to your knees to thank the Lord for the blessings of yesterday and the day that has yet to unfold? Would you be willing to prostrate yourself for him who has sculpted you into who you are and what you will become? Do you need to ask that He forgive you for your trespasses? You are fully aware that we possess imperfections, aren't you? He says to you, "That's alright, that is why I sent you my only Son." Is there someone who needs your prayers? Is there someone that would benefit by hearing your prayers? Did you pray for those that you cherish and love? Have you prayed for those that are your enemies? Not so easy, is it? Do you know God? He knows you! If we only prayed when we needed him—guess what, we would pray constantly! Do you believe that prayer can heal? That our prayers are answered? That the impossible can become possible with the Lord? I do!

*Give him a try. Any place, any time, any praise, any plea. He will listen to you and touch your heart and mind in response. He will never give up waiting to hear from you. Amen and Amen*

# DAY 129

Good morning. I have a friend who was a math teacher. I have a friend who is a cop. I have a friend who was a jet pilot. I have a friend who is a garbage collector. (Excuse me, politically incorrect, a Sanitation Engineer.) I probably shouldn't admit it but I have a friend who is a lawyer, and there is that politician, too. I have a friend who is black and a yellow one and a red one. Then there are my Baptist and Catholic friends. (Shhh, must I apologize for my new Muslim friend?) I have a number of female friends and a few friends who are under thirty-five, not to mention a host of over the hill guys like me. I have democratic friends and one who voted for Donald Trump. I have two friends under five feet tall and a man who is six- eleven, I'm sure. I have some skinny friends and several overweight, just like me. Why, I even have a friend who spent some time in jail. You see, I don't qualify my friends by the vocation they pursue, the color of their skin, their political or religious persuasion, or the fit of their suit.

*I select my friends by the size of their heart and the love they wish to share. Could it be that's why I have such a friend in Jesus? Won't you be my friend, too? Amen and Amen*

# DAY 130

Good morning. I've got some reading for you today. I hope you're ready. I was caught up again in my reading in the Bible this morning by a particular word: "promise." It's been with human kind from the very beginning. God offered it as a covenant with Adam and Eve, as a commitment and bond between him and them. Sadly, we humans broke that promise; it was our original sin. Think about it for a moment and sin takes on a new meaning. It wasn't murder or larceny, burglary or lying, greed, cheating or sexual promiscuity—it was a broken promise. Yet we break our promises to him, to one another, to ourselves. Thankfully, God has never given up on us. He loves us so much that He has continued to give us a second, third, fourth chance. In Genesis 15:18-2, the Lord promised Abraham a new beginning, then confirmed the promise to his son Isaac in Genesis 26:3 and again to Isaac's son Jacob in Genesis 28:13. The Bible contains 262 references pertaining to "promise." Here are several that might benefit you: Exodus 6:8, Genesis 12:7, Genesis 13:15, Deuteronomy 9:1, Genesis 17:8, Genesis 50:24, Leviticus 20:24, Numbers 14:8, Deuteronomy 6:10, 31:20, Joshua 5:6, Judges 2:1, Hebrews 11:9-10. And that's not all. The Gospels show him offering his only Son as a brand new Covenant to save our souls. Take some time to seriously read His Word, His Promise, His continued Covenant to us! It's vitally important.

*John reveals His final promise in Revelation 22:5, "There will be no more night. They will not need the light of a lamp or the light of the sun, for the Lord God will give them light and they will reign forever and ever..." Amen and Amen*

# DAY 131

Good morning. Mark Twain was known to quip, "Life is short, break the rules, forgive quickly, kiss slowly, love truly, laugh uncontrollably and never regret anything that makes you smile." He was also known to say, "The two most important days of your life are the day you were born and the day you found out why." I wish I could have known him. William Penn penned this: "I expect to pass through life but once. If therefore there be any kindness that I can show, or any good thing, let me do it now, and not defer or neglect it as I shall not pass this way again." Abraham Lincoln pondered, "In the end, it's not the years in your life, but the life in your years." Actress Mae West famously said, "You only live once, but if you do it right, once is enough." Maybe you'd like to try journalist Hunter S. Thompson's advice: "Life should not be a journey to the grave with the intention of arriving safely in a pretty and well preserved body, but rather to skid in broadside in a cloud of smoke, thoroughly used up and totally worn out and loudly proclaiming, 'Wow, what a ride!'" All interesting quotes, but here are the only ones that really count: "I am the Way, the Truth and the Life;" "For what shall it profit a man, if he gain the whole world and suffer the loss of his soul," and "I have come to give life and give it abundantly."

*Now that's what I'm talkin' about! Here's my two cents: Be all that you can be and how about living every day of your life knowing that you'll live forever with him! Amen and Amen*

Chayim

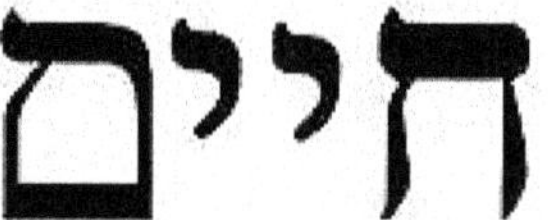


Life

# DAY 132

Good morning. Greetings and salutations. They are actually one and the same. Greeting is derived from the Latin "salutare," meaning "to greet." This morning as I was sitting up in bed, I gazed across the bedroom at the mirror above the dresser and what did I see but a sleepy soul looking back at me. I waved and he returned the favor. There are mornings when I whimsically make a funny face and you guessed it, he always responds in like manner. God has offered some very auspicious ways to greet us. There is nothing more welcoming than the sun bursting forth above the horizon or the sweet sound of songbirds at first light. Who would turn away from the sound of wind gently whistling through trees, or waves breaking onto shore, or a gurgling mountain brook? Don't you love the smell of a spring rain and the sound of thunder rumbling through mountain valleys? I can feel nothing but love for the Lord Almighty when I see the rainbow after a storm, proof of his ancient covenant. Our greetings fall short when compared to his wondrous salutations, but they are important none the less. My greeting of choice is the age old hug. I'd offer up a hundred or more every day if I could. Then there is the smile, a wink, a nod or a warm handshake. There are excited greetings when a son or daughter comes home from college or war. Did your dog ever kiss you when you returned home after a long day? There's that, too!

*They all beat the daylights out of the greeting "to Whom it may concern" or "to Occupant," but by far and way beyond any of the others, the best ones are surely greetings from God! Amen and Amen*

# DAY 133

Good morning. Where have all the great poets gone? Poets who used verse to offer thought and message to an accepting audience. Are they lost forever? Just how does one describe poetry? I especially appreciate this explanation: “Poetry is lofty thought or impassioned feeling expressed in imaginative words." We can trace these kinds of words as far back as the Old Testament and the New Testament of the Bible. We see poetry as early as the Song of Moses in Exodus 15:1-21. Actually, nearly one-third of the Old Testament is portrayed through poetry: Job, Psalms, Proverbs, the Song of Solomon, Lamentations, as well as large portions of Isaiah, Jeremiah and the Minor Prophets. As for the New Testament, who would deny the poetic words of Paul in 2 Corinthians 4:8-9: "We are hard pressed on every side, yet not crushed; we are perplexed, but not in despair, persecuted but not forsaken; struck down, but not destroyed."

*Poetry has captured the emotion of mankind’s story throughout time. Writers like Robert Frost, Edgar Allan Poe, William Shakespeare, Emily Dickinson, Tennyson, Whitman, Kipling, Longfellow and Maya Angelou should never be forgotten or overlooked. They tell our story, the story of life itself—through poetry. Amen and Amen*

# DAY 134

Good morning. I often search for words that say just what I mean. It is kind of like the statement, "A picture is worth a thousand words." An artist searches for just the right colors and shades in all the right places and the musician looks for all the right notes and the perfect voices and instruments. Aren't we all searching for something? This morning while reading several of the Psalms written by David, two words popped into my head: “congruently” and “perpetuity.” These are definitely not words that I would ordinarily use. Let me explain. While writing, David said many things that seem to fit congruently with our thinking today (at least mine). That is to say that they are congruent, fitting concurrently, at the same time, yesterday and today and tomorrow. That being said, his thoughts could well be my thoughts. Let me share just three from today's Bible reading: "Oh, the joys of those who are kind to the poor! The Lord rescues them when they are in trouble..." and "Only fools say in their hearts, there is no God" and finally "Give your burdens to the Lord, and He will take care of you. He will not permit the godly to slip and fall."

*As for the word perpetuity, meaning the quality to last forever, the whole Bible is surely just that! Lord, You are the Word, and You are forever. Amen and Amen*

# DAY 135

Good morning. Danger! Warning! Thinking in Process. What does that mean? It's simple, our thoughts are constantly with us, fourteen hundred and forty minutes a day. This occurs even when we sleep. There is never a time when our minds are not working. Now, that is not to say that some of it may be wasted effort, or "stinkin' thinkin'." Being multi-taskers, you and I are not limited to just thinking. So how do we use our time? Perhaps an inventory of our usefulness is in order. Most of us sleep or at least rest between 25 and 30 percent of the time. You say you walk at least three days a week for thirty to forty minutes. That is about eight hours a month (96 hours a year). Translated, that comes to about 1.8% of your allotted time, and you wonder why you are not losing any weight! I am proud to say that I spend at least 30 minutes a day reading the Bible, about 15 hours a month or 180 hours a year (7-1/2 days or a little less than 3% of available time). Now let's compare internet time, approximately 50 hours per month and television 80 hours a month. Stinkin' thinkin', you say. How much time do I spend in prayer? Too small to calculate; I should be ashamed. My calculations tell me that I spend nearly three times the amount eating as I do with the Word. I use about 5 days (100 hours) of my year playing golf and about six hours a year brushing my teeth. There is one place I really save, that is brushing and combing my hair (I'm bald). Needless to say, it seems that I need to make some adjustments to how I spend my time.

*Is my time something I should tithe? Lord, forgive me for spending so little time with and for you! I promise I will do better. Amen and Amen*

# DAY 136

Good morning. Hebrews tells it this way: "So we must listen very carefully to the truth we have heard, or we may drift away from it." Just how far have we drifted? The writer of Hebrews extoled the second generation of Jewish-Christians to maintain their faith and trust and it had only been thirty years or so. What about those of us who live today? When the hard times come where do so many of us turn? There's 9-11-2001, Viet Nam 1955-1975, 1963 John Kennedy Assassination, World War II 1939-1945, World War I 1914-1918, The Civil War 1860's , (What was that war about?), Revolutionary War 1776, (what revolution?) Fall of Rome 476 AD (Why? Who cares anyway?), Jesus and the cross! (Something we used to believe and trust), David and Goliath (Something about giants), Moses and The Red Sea(Is that near the Great Lakes?), Genesis In the Beginning: God. (What do you mean?) Jesus came to save us from our sins." (What sins?) How far we have drifted away!

*Lord, help us listen very carefully to the Truth we have heard, so we can share it with those who haven't been taught, so this generation does not drift farther away from it. Amen and Amen*

# DAY 137

Good morning. There are many who say the New Testament is the only relevant portion of the Bible and nothing prior really matters to our salvation. Really? Then why did Jesus pay such close attention? Do you think Genesis, Exodus, Leviticus, Numbers and Deuteronomy have no relevance? We are a product of all that came before us, for better or for worse. Consider 2 Kings 17:34-40 printed here: "To this day they persist in their former practices. They neither worship the Lord nor adhere to the decrees and ordinances, the laws and commands, that the Lord gave the descendants of Jacob, whom He named Israel. When the Lord made a covenant with the Israelites, He commanded them: 'Do not worship any other gods or bow down to them, serve them or sacrifice to them. But the Lord who brought you out of Egypt with mighty power and outstretched arm, is the one you must worship. To him you shall bow down and to him offer sacrifices. You must always be careful to keep the decrees and ordinances, the laws and the commands He wrote for you. Do not worship other gods. Do not forget the covenant I have made with you, and do not worship other gods. Rather worship the Lord your God; it is He who will deliver you from the hand of all your enemies." They would not listen, however, but persisted in their former practices. Even while these people were worshiping the Lord, they were serving their idols. To this day their children and grandchildren continue to do as their fathers did."

*Are we continuing to serve our idols? Have we forgotten His covenant? "Our Father who art in Heaven, hallowed be thy Name...Thy kingdom come, thy will be done..." Amen and Amen*

# DAY 138

Good afternoon. How is your vision? Very few of us possess perfect sight. There are those who are near sighted and others who are far sighted. Some have cataracts while still others have macular degeneration. But I know a blind man who sees things far better than most of us. He is spiritually awake and aware. He “sees" clearly. We need to pray the hymn Open My Eyes for his kind of sight. “Open my eyes that I may see Glimpses of truth Thou hast for me; Place in my hands the wonderful key That shall unclasp and set me free.” Barbara Streisand made the lyrics of On a Clear Day famous in 1970. “On a clear day, rise and look around you, and you’ll see who you are. On a clear day, how it will astound you, that the glow of your being outshines every star.” Now we have the opportunity to actually put the song into motion in our daily lives. I don't need a clear day, an eye chart or even glasses to “see.”

*“Silently now I wait for Thee, Ready, my God, Thy will to see; Open my eyes, illumine me, Spirit Divine!” Amen and Amen*

Berith

# בְּרִית

Covenant

# DAY 139

Good Morning. Just remember this—you are one of a kind, not one of a thousand, a million or even more; you're truly one of a kind. Why? Because God said it would be so! There will never be another quite like you. Have you ever wondered why you are just as you are? If everything under the sun and all that's beyond exists without coincidence, then you are no exception. Why are my eyes so... blue? Why was I born to be here and now, at this time somewhere between the Alpha and Omega? Why were my parents just who they were chosen to be; in my case a Jewish city boy and a country Methodist girl. Why did you offer to me such a love that one like me could never deserve? Of all the variations of those you have created, you chose that I would become a father and a teacher. Why? I know it's like asking what makes the sun and the stars shine and the sky so blue. You made me! How blessed could a man be?

*This I surely know, you've chosen where I've been, what I would become, who would share my life and where I'll spend eternity, with you, my Lord. This is your promise to each unique being who responds to your love. I'm counting on it! Amen and Amen*

# DAY 140

Good morning. When was the last time you wrote a letter to someone? I don't mean an invitation, thank you note or a birthday card. I am talking about a real live communicating document, one that starts like “dear mom and dad” and ends with “sincerely” or “love.” I can still remember the first letter that I wrote over sixty years ago. It was to my grandmother. I was about eight or nine years old. How proud I was. I didn't really say much that was very profound. Wait a minute, there was one thing; I finished the letter with “I love you and I miss you.” You know, when my grandmother passed away a few years ago that letter was still with the items she cherished and saved. I remember how important those letters were that I received while I was in college. Yes, they did contain spending money and once in a while they came with a package full of cookies but that was secondary to the love I felt. Then there were those love letters that we exchanged, Karen and I, in our formative years. They would become part of the foundation of our relationship. I never threw them away. As the years went by letters became postcards and postcards became phone calls or emails. And here we are, Twitter, Facebook or nothing at all. How do you think it would make someone feel if you sent them a real hand written letter? After all, Paul wrote a letter to the Galatians in 49 A.D. and we are still reading it today.

*I wish I could write a letter to each of you readers in my own handwriting. And I'd like to write a love letter to you, Lord. Love, Jim. Amen and Amen*

# DAY 141

Good morning. It is said that if you have God in your life you will never be alone. How does that make you feel? There are some of us who might think that we are not worthy. Even if you don't believe in him, He believes in you. What about those times when you have said, "I just want to be left alone." Does that include him? You know, I love the thought that He is with me always, and that includes the good times and the bad. He has seen me when I was at my best, but He has also seen me when I have been angry and when I have been at my very worst. There are times when I wish I could say, “I'll be back in a while." Guess what, He is still right there. He would have never sent His Son if He had not known me at my worst. Has He forgiven me? He offered His Son so that I might live. Holy God, how great thou art!

*Remember this: it's not just WWJD, but what will you and I do? God will be with you every second of your life. Invite him into your home, not just the sitting room, but the bedroom, the attic and the closets. Make your home His home. He will love you all the more. And by all means pray that your children, your family and your friends will come to know him, too. Amen and Amen*

# DAY 142

Good morning. My thoughts today are focused on an individual's journey. A friend shared a small slice of his story with our Sunday school class recently. His journey carried him through five hundred miles and sixty hours on a Greyhound bus. Who would do that? Perhaps a man seeking to know himself, to clarify his story, hoping to meet the Lord head on. He told us the first person he met on that bus was Jesus! That was a pivotal point on his journey, a remarkable meeting but it is only a part of his ongoing story. So what about the rest of us? Where will our journeys lead us? Could my journal writing be telling my story? Yes! Over seventy years and my journey is not done yet. God is leading me and walking with me. What does He say about my journey? James 1:22-25 tells me "But don't just listen to God's word. You must do what it says. Otherwise, you are only fooling yourselves. For if you listen to the word and don't obey, it is like glancing at your face in the mirror. You see yourself, walk away, and forget what you look like. But if you look carefully into the perfect law that sets you free, and if you do what it says and don't forget what you heard, then God will bless you for doing it."

*I have to listen, obey and remember on my personal journey. And so my story continues...Amen and Amen*

# DAY 143

Good morning. "And forgive us our trespasses..." I'm sure we all recognize this statement's origin. Have you ever seriously thought what that means? The dictionary puts it this way, "Trespass: a violation of moral or social ethics, transgression, especially sin." First of all, we should attempt to grasp what trespass or sin really means. The Hebrew words that identified sin were "chet" which basically means "missed the mark'; "avon meaning "desire;" and "pasha" which means "rebellion." Knowing that, I can be sure I for one have missed the mark, been rebellious, and most assuredly indulged in fulfilling my own desires. I've trespassed repeatedly. An acclaimed religious teacher once wrote, "As long as we deny where we stand today, we will find that we are still there tomorrow."

*And so, Lord, it is fitting that I should ask forgiveness. I know that you truly understand when I pray, "Forgive me for my trespasses." Amen and Amen*

# DAY 144

Good morning. Is there any better way than to start the day with a heartfelt "good morning?" It can provide the setting for what is sure to follow. With that as your outlook, it becomes nearly impossible to grumble or be forlorn. Practice your smile, you might be surprised to notice that it actually works at such an early hour, and you don't even need a cup of coffee to jump start it. God says, "Rest in me." That applies to rising as well as seeking a nights rest. What are you in such a hurry about? Don't make your days become a race. Even runners settle themselves before they begin the competition. No need for a false start. Try focusing on the things that bring you joy and what you are thankful for. Why not invite the Lord to join you; He loves the mornings. Why else would He offer such awesome sunrises, or entice the birds to begin their songs? He allows the rooster to be your wake-up call. It seems more than appropriate that I offer up a hearty "Thank You!" I am sure it makes him smile; it surely does me. Are you smiling yet?

*Now I can begin my day. Where is that cup of coffee? Now I'm ready to go, and go, and go. God, would you come along with me and help me do your will? Amen and Amen*

# DAY 145

Good morning. Who would have imagined? For many, our wildest dreams would not have taken us to where we are. My family, my friends, my students, my associates—we have virtually traveled the world. Our footprints can be found in Maryland, Kentucky, Tennessee, Florida, Texas, Colorado, Kansas, North Carolina and South America just to name a few. We have traveled to the four corners of the earth, from Alaska to Australia to Viet Nam, Japan and back. We've become teachers, preachers, doctors, lawyers, bricklayers, chaplains and soldiers, too. We've danced and sung, we've worked and slaved. We've lost our way and we have found a way, we've met the Lord who's here to stay. I've become a teacher, husband, father, businessman and most important of all, a disciple of Jesus. Who could possibly have guessed all this? I've been to the mountains big and tall, and to the lowest of places and crossed broad seas that at times seemed impossible. As Dr. Seuss said in Oh, The Places You'll Go: "You have brains in your head. You have feet in your shoes. You can steer yourself, any direction you choose. You're on your own. And you know what you know. And you are the one who will decide where to go. So be sure when you step, step with care and great tact. And remember that life's a Great Balancing Act. And will you succeed? Yes! You will indeed! (98 and 3/4 per cent guaranteed...) Kid, you'll move mountains!"

*I leave you with this thought: "You're off to Great Places! Today is your day! Your mountain is waiting. So...get on your way!" Amen and Amen*

Shama

Hear, Obey

# DAY 146

Good morning. When is your favorite day? That is a very open-ended question. It all depends on your perspective, doesn't it? Many might answer, TGIF—"Thank Goodness It's Friday." There may be a few who say, "I can't wait until Monday comes around." Some may answer, "Saturday" or "Sunday, the Lord's Day." Then there are those who answer "I love Christmas," or "Easter" or "Halloween." A number may respond a birthday or anniversary (if it can be remembered). Then there are those who choose "the day we got married" or "the birth of our first child." There could be someone who enthuses "the day the Reds won the World Series" or "Graduation Day." Lots of choices, wouldn't you say? A few tell us "It's the day that Christ was born" while others suggest it's the day the telephone or the internet was first invented. How about these next three choices: yesterday, today or tomorrow? Do you remember the lyrics to the song, "Tomorrow" from the play (and movie) Annie? It goes like this: "The sun'll come out tomorrow Bet your bottom dollar that tomorrow there'll be sun Just thinkin' about tomorrow, clears away the cobwebs and the sorrow till' there's none When I'm stuck in the day that's grey and lonely I just stick up my chin and grin and say Oh, the sun'll come out tomorrow So you got to hang on till' tomorrow, come what may! Tomorrow, tomorrow, I love you tomorrow, you're only a day away."

*As for me, I love my memories of yesterday and there is no question that today was made for me. The truth is that every day is my favorite. I just love God's gift of being alive. Yes Lord, because of you every day is Special. Have a great day. I'm going to! Amen and Amen*

# D A Y 147

Good morning. The times they are a changin'—or are they? As I continue to study the words of the Bible, from Genesis to Revelation and everything in between, I cannot help but recognize that man's greatest struggle lies within himself. Throughout history Assyria, Egypt, Persia, Greece, Rome and today, man's greatest enemy has been man. We have encountered and overcome earthquakes, floods, volcanos and hurricanes, but we continue to fall prey to violence, dissension and wars. From Cain and Abel to the present day, it has been brother against brother. Yet there is so much to be said for "love thy neighbor." Let me share an example. Father Flanagan, a young Catholic priest, began the Noyes Home for Children in 1917, opening it for six troubled, neglected boys. It grew into what we know as Boy's Town which has served and saved thousands of troubled youth. In 1943 Boy's Town adopted a logo with the picture of a boy carrying a younger boy on his shoulders, with the words, "He ain't heavy, Father... he's my brother." As The Hollies recorded it, it goes like this: "The road is long with many a winding turn that leads us to who knows where. Who knows where, but I am strong, strong enough to carry him. He's not heavy, he's my brother. So on we go, his welfare is my concern. No burden is he to bear. We'll get there, for I know he would not encumber me. He ain't heavy, he's my brother."

*Mark 12:31 quotes Jesus saying, "Love your neighbor as yourself." So the questions are who in the world is your neighbor? Who will be your brother? Amen and Amen*

# DAY 148

Good morning. Bobby McFerrin wrote a dilly of a song a number of years ago entitled "Don't Worry, Be Happy." Though written tongue in cheek, it still makes very good sense. Given a chance between happiness and sadness, I believe we would unanimously choose happiness. The big question is how do you do that? We complain that we can't be happy all the time, but sometimes we just don't have the choice to make. But as is often said, we can make lemonade out of lemons. It is amazing what a prayer can do or how much better a smile can make you feel. Laughter has been an elixir since the beginning of time itself. A warm heart and a helping hand can do wonders for the one who needs uplifting, and it serves well the one offering. Fear, sadness, anger are of little value as we travel through a lifetime. I believe that is why God offered us a song as well as the harp and the cymbal. His greatest gift, love, makes happiness much more achievable. Do you need to ask me why I am happy almost all the time? It doesn't take a pill or a drink to make us feel good, because a prayer and a happy face can do wonders.

*By the way, there is a lot of truth in that small book by Charles Schulz titled Happiness is a Warm Puppy. You might want to read it. Amen and Amen*

# DAY 149

Good morning. Let today become a breath of the mountains' fresh air, as free as the sparkling streams that find their pathway down into the magnificent valleys below. The early morning mist and fog makes everything seem surreal, but the glorious sun soon breaks out, clearing the air and lighting the Lord's wondrous creation. How blessed to be free to call upon The Creator, to claim him as Abba, Father! Do you know the feeling of taking a deep breath, inhaling all that you possibly can, knowing that it is more precious than gold or silver? Michael W. Smith expressed it this way: "This is the air I breathe, your holy presence living in me. This is my daily bread. Your very word spoken to me. And I'm desperate for you. And I'm lost without you....

*Lord God, what could I ever do to possibly deserve all of this? Never enough, yet you continue to show me such love! Dear Lord, giving thanks could never be enough, but thank you! Bless your Holy Name with Praise and Glory and Honor. Amen and Amen*

# DAY 150

Good morning. Could this day possibly become your "one moment in time"? Will it by chance see the best of you? Whitney Houston sang a song by the very same name, One Moment in Time, written by John Bettis and Albert Hammond. “I want one moment in time when I'm more than I thought I could be, when all of my dreams are a heartbeat away, the answers are all up to me. Give me one moment in time when I'm racing with destiny. Then in that one moment of time I will find eternity..." Are you ready for such a time as this? You see, the Lord expects nothing more from you, except the very best you have to give. For those who say it's too late, it's never too late! You can be more than you ever thought you could be, a real winner. The answer, you see, is that with the help of the Lord you can be much, much more, for a lifetime, beginning right now, this one moment in time!

*When you give your whole self to him, He gives himself to you! You are filled with His light. Let it shine, let it shine! Let it shine! Amen and Amen*

# DAY 151

Good morning. Sh h-h-h. Be still. Listen. I heard him speaking to me, not in words, but in the sounds of his creation. He told me it was all created for me, but not just for me, but for all who believe. He affirmed and confirmed that I am a Christian, and He spoke with boldness that could not be mistaken. "But first you are my disciple." We sometimes think we know everything and smugly ask, "What need have I of God?" His response: "Seek the Lord while He may be found; call on him while He is near. Let the wicked forsake his ways and the evil man his thoughts. Let him turn to the Lord, and He will have mercy on him, and our God, for He will freely pardon. 'For my thoughts are not your thoughts, neither are your ways my ways', declares the Lord. As the heavens are higher than earth, so are my ways higher than your ways and my thoughts than your thoughts. As the rain and snow come down from the heaven, and do not return to it without watering the earth and making it bud and flourish so that it yields seed for the sower and bread for the eater, so is my Word that goes out from my mouth: It will not return to me empty, but will accomplish what I desire and achieve the purpose for which I sent it. You will go out in joy and be led forth in peace, the mountains and hills will burst into song before you, and all the trees of the field will clap their hands. Instead of the thorn bush will grow the pine tree, and instead of briers the myrtle will grow. This will be for the Lord renown for an everlasting sign, which will not be destroyed."

*It is through His Spirit He has called us to be His hands and feet, so we might become sowers so that others may eat the Bread. Isaiah 55:6-13. Amen and Amen*

# DAY 152

Good morning. “On a clear day you can see forever....” That may be true with regard to our own personal reflections on our lives. Life is all about making decisions, large and small, every hour, every minute, even every second of each and every day. What an awesome responsibility that is! It is just what our Lord has granted to us, his children, on this earth, his creation. We make big decisions: marriage, family, vocation. We make small ones: brand of coffee or toothpaste. We make good ones and sometimes not so good ones! That's where the clear days become most important; those days when we can reflect on direction as well as decision, the real "whys" of our living. This gift that God has granted us can be a blessing or a curse. He knew that and yet He still made it our reality. In your decisions have you consulted (prayed) with him? He is our Guiding Light. We need to follow him.

*In the words of the chorus of “Lord of the Dance” by Sydney Carter : "Dance, then, wherever you may be, I am the Lord of the Dance said He, and I'll lead you all, wherever you may be, and I'll lead you all in the Dance said He." And He says it all in the final verse: "They cut me down and I leapt up high, I am the life that'll never, never die. I'll live in you if you'll live in me. I am the Lord of the Dance, said He.” Amen and Amen*

Tiqvah

Hope

# DAY 153

Good morning. For those who question, who have doubts—I tell you this: God has a plan. "In the beginning God created the heavens and the earth... And God said, Let there be light... And God said, Let the water under the sky be gathered in one place and let dry ground appear...Then God said, Let the land produce vegetation...And God said, Let the land produce living creatures...Then God said, Let us make man in our own image... God blessed them! Then God said, I give you every seed bearing plant...every tree that has fruit...and all the beasts of the earth... God saw all that He made and it was very good." Genesis Chapter One! So now can you see His plan? If not purposely created with a plan for every detail, not one thing would exist. There is a miraculous and unique symbiosis between you, the earth and sun, the grasses and the creatures of the earth, the sea and the sky. God has a plan.

*The hymn "This Is My Father's World" tells us "He shines in all that's fair; in the rustling grass I hear him pass....All nature sings and round me rings the music of the spheres." So when you smell the clear mountain air and view the trees and the tall grasses, know that it was all His plan. He made it for you. He made you. God has a plan—for you! Amen and Amen*

# DAY 154

Good morning. Have you ever said it's a bad hair day, it's been a bad day, or a bad night, or a really bad day? If you never have, you will in due time. Into every life some rain must fall, and sometimes it even becomes a real storm. I am well aware of the fact that our Lord has blessed us all, but receiving a blessing in such negative events, preposterous! However, I can't ignore what Paul wrote in 1 Thessalonians 5:16-18: "Be joyful always. Never stop praying, be thankful in all circumstances, for this is God's will for you in Christ Jesus." There are no fewer than twenty-one scriptures that are directed at difficult times, like those many of us have experienced: devastating divorce, depression, serious illnesses, loneliness, sleepless nights in pain, watching your child suffer, losing someone you love and I wish that were all! Truthfully, when terrible things happen there doesn't seem to be anything to be thankful for. It is alright to hurt, to struggle, even to be angry, but superficial faith will not suffice. What God is asking us to do is acknowledge He is good on good days and bad days. We must believe that God has a plan for us, that He will walk right beside us, that He will even carry us when we cannot make it on our own. He can and will bring us peace even in the toughest times.

*We give thanks because we know him, we trust him and yes, we celebrate him. David said we give thanks for the Lord is good and his love endures forever. Max Lucado says God's love is wide enough for the whole world. It's certainly wide enough for you and me. Amen and Amen*

# DAY 155

Good morning. "I'd walk a mile for a Camel." That was a well-known advertisement for Camel Cigarettes that first appeared back in 1949. The ads for Camels, Philip Morris and Pall Malls are long gone, but walking still remains fashionable and healthy, to say the least. So who among you is walking today, or every day? Walking is fine, especially with a golf club in hand. My doctor declares that it is as good as push ups, especially away from the dinner table. My wife puts me to shame with her 8000 to 12000 steps every day. Consider this, your walk may well keep you fit enough to be able to walk in somebody else's shoes, and I'm not referring to their Skechers. "Never criticize a man until you've walked a mile in his moccasins." This proverb can be traced back to the Cherokee Tribe of Native Americans. So before judging someone, you must understand their challenges, experiences and thoughts. Walk their walk.

*It may just be that someone is out there waiting to hear your footsteps beside them. It's the way Jesus walks with us. Amen and Amen*

# DAY 156

Good morning. Rain happens. It has been something that a great many vocalists have sung about over the years: James Taylor's "Fire and Rain, and who could forget Gene Kelly's "Singing in the Rain?" Guns and Roses offered "November Rain" and the Temptations gave us "I Wish It Would Rain. There were the Cascades doing "Rhythm of the Rain." The Eurhythmics' second biggest hit was "Here Comes the Rain." Milli Vanilli sang "Blame it on the Rain" and Prince made "Purple Rain" popular. There are many, many more rain songs so it's pretty evident that rain has been talked and sung about forever. Now here's one I bet most of you aren't that familiar with, Psalm 65 by King David, one of the songs in the Bible. Here is a part it (Psalm 65:9-13). "You take the earth and water it, making it rich and fertile. The river of God has plenty of water: it provides a bountiful harvest of grain, for You have ordered it so.  You drench the plowed ground with rain, melting the clouds and leveling the ridges. You soften the earth with showers and bless the abundant crops.  You crown the year with a bountiful harvest, even the hard pathways overflow with abundance. The grasslands of the wilderness become a lush pasture and the hillsides blossom with hoy.  The meadows are clothed with flocks of sheep and the valleys are carpeted with grain.  They all shout and sing for joy!"

*Here is my humble thought: Let it rain, let it rain! Let it rain! Amen and Amen*

# DAY 157

Good morning. Have you ever thought I'll do it when I have some spare time? What is that anyway? Everybody says wait till we retire. That's a laugh. There are seven days a week but I'm working on creating "Addaday" to add an extra day of the week, just for good measure. I create lists in an attempt to stay on track. Yet another laughable matter. I've tried sleeping a little less, but that doesn't work either. Those of you who are still working or still have children at home and think that someday.... I've got news for you, no porch swings or idle hours await you. Am I sounding like I am complaining? Not on your life! I feel blessed to be right where I am. Minutes, hours, days, weeks, months and years are too precious to be wasted. I just wonder why it took me so long to figure that out. Take time for your family, your friends, your God and by all means, yourself.

*So here's my thought to share with you today: There's no time to spare, just time to find joy in each day that is offered to you. Amen and Amen*

# DAY 158

Good morning. Have you ever played follow the leader as a child? Probably we all have participated at one time or another. Were you the follower or the leader? It seems that we all follow as we grow up. We learn by following the examples of others. Sometimes it's to our own undoing. My parents would often warn, "Careful who you choose to follow." In school I learned to follow instructions, though at times with more than a little difficulty. My listening skills and my action skills were often at odds with each other, especially when it came to homework. As for being a leader, that facet of my life took a while. Being the youngest in my family, I was reticent to take the lead with anything. As I grew a little older my competitive spirit and my desire to win would have a hand in changing all that. It worked for me as an athlete but not so much in other matters, although time would provide leadership opportunities as I became a teacher, coach and father. The story in Matthew 9:9-13 speaks to me now. Jesus and His disciples were dinner guests at Matthew's home along with many tax collectors and others considered by Jewish society to be disreputable sinners. When the Pharisees saw this they asked His disciples, "Why does your teacher eat with such scum?" When Jesus heard this, he said, "Healthy people don't need a doctor–sick people do...I have come to call not those who think they are righteous, but those who know they are sinners."

*So now and forever I am ready to follow the leader again. I ant to follow Jesus. Amen and Amen*

# DAY 159

Good morning. I spoke with a lady yesterday evening who is training to become a foster grandparent. How cool is that? It got me to wondering who all is out there needing someone special in their life. Could you become that "special" one? Could you make a difference? No one is expecting you to be another Mother Teresa or Mahatma Gandhi. But you could be! How many un-adopted children do you think there are? How many children and adults are in hospitals awaiting treatment who need someone to care about them? Teens living in the alleys and streets of our cities? Could you make a difference in the life of a teenager who is struggling with drug addiction or is contemplating suicide? The elderly with no surviving relatives in need of food delivery, a ride to the doctor, a friend? Are there neighbors grieving the loss of a lifelong mate? How about the brand new resident to your town, community or country feeling confused or lonely? Can you offer spiritual guidance to your family? Will you at least offer a prayer or a friendly smile to someone, anyone?

*Here is the really good news. I know that you can be the one!*
*Amen and Amen*

He replied, "You of little faith,
why are you so afraid?"

Karen DuBro

Then He got up and rebuked
the winds and the waves,
and it was completely calm.
Matt 8:26

# DAY 160

Good morning. Have you ever exclaimed, Lord, I am afraid? Take heart in all that you do, and know that He will be with you, even to the end of time. That's a long way! Don't allow fear to stop you. Do you seek him first? Then the rest will surely follow. Rivers will be crossed, mountains climbed. Will you allow the rapids to stop you or the cliffs to impede your way? Is the water too deep or the sky too high? Are the walls too thick? They say you can't do it, that you shouldn't even try. No way, it can't be done, there is no cure, it's impossible, you're going to fail. Do you believe them, the ones that have never even tried, when the Lord himself offers assurance? Trust him. "But Jesus looked at them and said, with man this is impossible, but with God all things are possible." (Matthew 19:26.) "For truly I say to you, if you have faith like a grain of mustard seed, you will say to this mountain, move from here to there, and it will move and nothing will be impossible for you." (Matthew 17:20. 6) "Aha, Lord God! Behold, you have made the heaven and the earth by thy great power and stretched out arm, there is nothing too hard for you." (Jeremiah 32:17. 12) "If God is for us, who can be against us?" (Romans 8:31: 13) "In all your ways acknowledge him, and he will make straight your paths." (Proverbs 3:6. 14)

*"Behold, I am the Lord, the God of all flesh. Is there anything too hard for me?" (Jeremiah 32:27) Need I say more, for He has said it all. Now go for it! Amen and Amen*

# DAY 161

Good morning. There is no doubt about it! So what doubts are troubling you today? Do you doubt that you are good enough? That you are loved? That you can go on? That the sun will ever shine again? That we will ever see peace again? That there is a God? Is that all that is bothering you? Well, put aside your doubts for I am here this very moment to assure you that above all else, there is a God. The only God. He is the God of all mankind, all races and all nations! He is the One that makes "all things possible." You can offer him all your doubts and troubles. You are good enough because He created you so He could love you. He will offer you the light, because it is his to offer. He will bring you peace. All He asks is that you give yourself, all of you, to him. How can you trust him? He is the author of the universe. He wrote the Book and He knows the beginning and the end. In 1 Kings 19:4-5 the prophet Elijah cried out to the Lord in the worst of times. "I have had enough Lord...then he lay down and slept under the broom tree. But as he was sleeping an angel touched him and told him, 'Get up and eat!'"

*So to you who are feeling troubled God is saying "Get up and eat! I love you! And if you are mine, the Son will surely shine in your life now and ever more. Amen and Amen*

# DAY 162

Good morning. He's a friendly sort of guy. What do you suppose that means? First let me say that I see "friendly" as someone who has the opportunity of becoming a friend, on the way you might say. You've no doubt heard all the euphemisms; friends forever, never met a person I didn't like, friends through thick and thin, my best friend... For those who say they have no "real" friends, I forgive you. For those who say I'm very selective who my friends will be, my condolences! Just what does being a friend entail? Here is my take. You can never have too many friends. I've always had difficulty with "best" friends. The woman I love and married comes closest to "best." There have been many close friends over the years, but I have chosen not to measure my friends against one another. It should be noted, though, that one definitely stands out above all the rest: Jesus! "What a friend we have in Jesus...."

*Someone once told me "you're not very choosy about your friends," to which I say just the opposite. I choose you, and you, and you, no restrictions! Amen and Amen*

# DAY 163

Good morning. What words belong in your vocabulary? As I am once again spending some time with Proverbs in my Bible it has become apparent that there are those words that we should willingly accept and repeat as well as those that we ought to avoid. So what are the good words? Let's begin with "love." And I don't mean as in I love my Sugar Pops or I absolutely love to play golf. I mean the kind that's defined as strong affection for another arising out of kinship or personal ties. Have you used it lately? How about telling your wife or husband, your children, Mom, Dad, your cherished friends, and yes, the homeless guy on the street corner? Who knows, he may have put his life on the line for you in Viet Nam, Iraq or Afghanistan. The Lord is unrelenting in his love for you, the strong affection for another arising out of kinship or personal ties kind. Is that the kind of love you have for him? There are lots of other good words like thanks, please, trust, bless, faith, joy, sorry, and forgive. There are people who are just waiting, hoping, praying for someone, anyone, to just say "hello." Note the precious nine words mentioned in the Fruits of the Spirit: love, joy, peace, patience, kindness, goodness, faithfulness, gentleness and self-control. So when you are seeking just the right words don't worry about the number of letters in them; think about the positive power they possess.

*Just think of it this way, your words may spell the difference in someone's day or even life. May your own days be overflowing with good words. God bless you, one and all! Amen and Amen*

# DAY 164

Good morning. Have we become wimps and sojourners? Is it ours to be never happy, never satisfied and always ready to convict? What has become of this land is your land, this land is my land? Where is one nation under God? Who still abides by until death do us part and in sickness and health? Do we even know what democracy means in today's world? We don't like our schools. We definitely don't like our elected senators and representatives. We detest the journalists and we say the White House is in a shambles. We question our heritage and our beliefs. We scoff at anyone who says put your trust in the Lord. We seek first to be entertained rather than to be involved or responsible. We lament, after all, what can I do? Maybe Isaiah, Jeremiah, Hosea, Ezekiel, John, Peter and Paul were onto something. Think about this from Galatians 5:1: "It is for freedom that Christ has set us free." And Galatians 5:13-16: "You my brothers were called to be free. But do not use your freedom to indulge the sinful nature; rather serve one another in love."

*"The entire law is summed up in a single command; love your neighbor as yourself. If you keep on biting and devouring each other, watch out or you will be destroyed by each other." That just about sums it up folks! Amen and Amen*

# DAY 165

Good morning. I'm so glad that I got up this morning! You ask why? Because I have the chance to learn something new. All our lives, we are constantly learning something, or at least we have the opportunity. Some of us can recite history all day long, or quote the Bible, name sports teams, pronounce horticultural plant names, explain numismatics, study astronomy and countless other wonderful things. There are those who even relish their knowledge of the trivial. In fact, we've even made a game out of it. When we share our learning we call it teaching. Those who learn an abundance are called "learned" or “intelligent.” It is only when we learn how to use or understand what we have learned that we call it “wisdom.” They say that comes with age. I'm still waiting! Recently I've learned what A1C means. I've learned how to "deadhead” flowers. I've learned that Pennsylvania originally opposed the signing of the Declaration of Independence. I've learned that Daniel prophesied that the statue in Nebuchadnezzar’s dream represented the four kingdoms that would dominate the world (Babylonian, Persian, Greek, Roman) and that all of these would be crushed by the Rock and ended by the Kingdom of God that shall reign forever. Wow, I can't wait for tomorrow so I can learn something else new!

*As for wisdom, I guess I am just too young, although I’ll share two things I learned before I was even twenty-one: Happiness is a warm puppy and God is good, all the time! Amen and Amen*

# DAY 166

Good morning. In the season of planting and tending our gardens, we anticipate the coming harvest. For a while we are all a little bit like "Mary, Mary quite contrary" asking "how does your garden grow?" Today let's explore a different garden, independent of the seasons, a garden not of tomatoes and turnips, corn and cabbage, but of seeds planted in our spirit. Is caring sprouting and spreading? Have compassion and understanding put down deep roots? Is faith resilient even after dark and stormy nights? Are the fruits of the spirit ripening? Can you see any weeds between the rows of love, joy, peace, patience, kindness, goodness, faithfulness, gentleness, and self-control? What does forgiveness look like? Is it wilted? Water it well. Look over everything, and be sure to feed whatever is true, honorable, right, pure, lovely, of good repute, any excellence and anything worthy of praise. In tending your garden, be sure to ask advice from the Master Gardener, who started it all with His very own garden in Eden. That way, you will have a harvest that pleases him and blesses others.

How does your garden grow? If you tend it well, the harvest will be abundant and the blessings plentiful. Amen and Amen

Baruch

בָּרוּךְ

Blessed

# DAY 167

Good morning. Do you know which side your bread is buttered on? In other words, do you understand what is good for you, what is to your advantage? Are you on the right side of things; the winning side? Which friends will be there for you? Do you know who you can you depend on to be there when you need them, when times are tough? Luke tells us we can absolutely depend on the Lord when we need help. All we have to do is intentionally and sometimes persistently "ask and it will be given to you; seek and you will find; knock and the door will be opened to you. For everyone who asks receives, he who seeks finds; and to those who knock, the door will be opened," Luke 11:9-10.

*So take the bread and pass the butter! You now know which side of the bread it goes on. Amen and Amen*

# DAY 168

Good morning. Have you done your homework? When was the last time you studied something, really studied? Was it that high school or college exam you stayed up all night to cram everything you could into you head in a few short hours? Maybe it was for a driver's license or real estate certification. Could it have been planning for construction of a submarine or the building of the Twin Towers? You may have listened to tapes to learn Spanish or Japanese so you could take that long awaited trip of a lifetime. But how many times have you sailed through life “by the seat of your pants?” It is difficult to become a teacher if you have nothing to teach. Whether you realize it or not, life is all about homework. If we spent as much time understanding the Bible as we do becoming a fisherman or an engineer, what would our lives be like? I have decided to study the Psalms more diligently than ever before, doing my homework in the Bible. I am beginning with the first Psalm: "Blessed is the man who does not walk in the counsel of the wicked or stand in the way of sinners or sit in the seat of mockers. But his delight is in the law of the Lord, and on his law he meditates day and night.” Did you hear that? “He is like a tree planted by streams of water, which yields its fruit in season and whose leaf does not wither. Whatever he does prospers."

*God's Homework, the Bible, has been written so it can be studied and understood. Then we can apply it to our own lives. Amen and Amen*

# D A Y 169

Good morning. I have spent much of my life challenging my abilities. Sometimes it resulted in great success and on other occasions not so much. It seemed that when I was competing or when I met challenges I was at my best. When I participated as an athlete I was driven to compete and sought to be the best. It took me quite a long while to recognize the difference between being the "best" and doing my best. If there was one flaw in who I would become, it was in my ability to focus. As a young student I was often more interested in the butterfly on the window sill than the pages of a text or the voices of my teachers. What was so important about nouns, verbs and adjectives or multiplication and division and who really cares about Beowulf? I did, however, have a voracious thirst for reading, especially about others and the past. Who could possibly have known that this would define my destiny and offer me a focus that I didn't know I was seeking? Many years have passed since those formidable early times. I find myself in the fourth quarter of my life now. My days of competing are gone but need I remind you that many a touchdown has been scored in the fourth quarter and many a game won. Now it is my time to offer a synthesis of all that I have been and what I have become. There is much in life yet to do and I intend to use my talents, gifts and skills to fulfill the purposes God has created me for.

*I know all about winning and losing, and I choose winning! Amen and Amen*

# DAY 170

Good morning. Has anyone ever challenged you? Of course they have, in one way or another. Much of life is built upon that premise. Nations rise and fall as a result. Records are broken because of it. Do you remember the childhood game Red Rover? It challenged us to break the lineup against us. Challenges allow us to do things we wouldn't ordinarily do. If I challenged you to jump off a cliff, would you do it? (Just kidding, of course.) It was a mainstay of my teaching and my coaching to challenge my students and athletes to be better (not better than, just better). There is never a day that we don't meet new or old challenges, from following our diets, working harder, listening more intently to our children and our mates, becoming a better foul shooter or pass catcher, reading God's Word, trying a new cuisine, overcoming using the word "very," all the time, and running our best race yet. The list goes on and on.

*Who is the biggest challenger? He's closer than you think. Here's my challenge today: make this the best day that it can possibly be. And don't forget to thank him! Amen and Amen*

# DAY 171

Good morning. I am especially taken by two simple sentences written by the prophet Isaiah over 2700 years ago. Isaiah 22:11 says: "But you never ask for help from the One who did all this. You never considered the One who planned this long ago." That was about 136 generations ago. Would you call the human race slow learners? We can record the outer limits of our solar system but we cannot find what is hidden within our hearts. From generation to generation we've tried and we've failed. Look at the last eight generations: 1883-1903 The Lost Generation, no answers. 1904-1924 The Greatest Generation, thought power and strength was the answer. 1929-1945 The Silent Generation, hoped for answers but searched in the wrong places. 1944-1964 The Baby Boomers, still no answers. 1965-1985 Generation X, ditto. 1985-2005 The Millennials, Generation Z and what some call the Always On Generation, all still groping for the answer. How did we miss it? It's right there in the Word. Psalm 121 directed us straight to the only answer for help in a fallen world. "My help comes from the Lord who made Heaven and Earth! He will not let you stumble, the One who watches over you will not stumble...The Lord himself watches over you! The Lord stands beside you as your protective shade. The sun will not harm you by day, nor the moon at night. The Lord keeps you from all harm and watches over your life. The Lord keeps watch over you as you come and go, both now and forever."

*Come on now, don't you think 136 generations has been long enough to accept His answer? Amen and Amen*

# DAY 172

Good morning. I got up early today so I could travel down the road to pick up a load of food provided by Feed America First. It would have been so easy to complain it's too early, it's too wet, it's too far but a cup of coffee, a few verses of Jeremiah and a loving kiss bye from my wife were all I needed to convince me that it was the right thing to do. It rained all the way down off the Plateau, but I didn't care. I could feel the sun shining in my heart. I arrived plenty early, which provided opportunity to talk with several others who felt the very same way. One of those who inspired me was a man who regularly rose much earlier than I so he could water ski up and down the lake near where he lives. You might think that's no big deal—but he's over eighty years old! Then there was the man who was "simply passing forward the blessings" given to his family. There was a veteran of twenty plus years who just "found another way to serve," and the minister who rose early to drive the big diesel truck for those in need in his church and community. How about that thirteen year old and the grandmother who helped load the waiting vehicles? What about the church that opened its doors before the light of day to be central to the distribution process? What a wonderful day!

*You know, it never did stop raining, but I am certain that somewhere God had a rainbow to share! Amen and Amen*

# DAY 173

Good morning. Early this morning I read and prayed over the words of Psalms 120 - 126. The message was largely the same. Their message could have been written about our times. Psalm 120 speaks my very own thoughts and feelings. "I am tired of living among people who hate peace. I search for peace, they want war!" Psalm 125 becomes our hope in desperate times like ours. "O Lord, do good to those who are good, whose hearts are in tune with you. May Israel have peace!" How about peace for our whole world, dear Lord? Psalm 126 promises the answer to our prayers. "Those who plant in tears will harvest with shouts of joy. They weep as they go to plant their seed, but they sing as they return with the harvest."

*Lord, let our prayers and our tears wipe away the blood of wars that stain our world and may we all come to know the peace that only You can truly grant us.  Amen and Amen*

Sharath

שָׁרַת

Serve

# DAY 174

Good morning. Have you kept all your promises? I can assure you that I have fallen short more than I would like to admit. "I'll be there, I'm praying for you, I forgive you, you can count on me." Regrettably that has been me from time to time! Some might say just don't make any promises. What if our Lord had refused to make and keep His promise to Abraham? Promises are a covenant we make. It is important to keep even those that are inconvenient or may seem inconsequential. When you marry you promise "until death do us part." When you bring children into the world you promise to love, protect and care for them. When you accept Jesus as your Lord and Savior your promise yourself to him and He accepts responsibility for you—loving and caring for you forever.

*So here is my prayer for this day. Lord, I'm ashamed of my broken promises; I'll try harder not to break any more. And Lord, you are and will always be the greatest promise I could ever receive! Amen and Amen*

# DAY 175

Good morning. Did you ever say “I can't?” Of course you did, we all have at one time or another. In fact some of us have made a practice of it. Could that possibly be you? When I was coaching a long time ago, I used to tell my young warriors that there is no such word as can't. Can't places us on the precipice of failure. Is that where you want to be? When someone tells you that you can't, accept it as a challenge. The one thing that most often prohibits us from moving forward is ourselves. Oh, it may take great effort and countless attempts. You may even stumble and fall. So get back up! When the whole world seems to be against you, remember, you have a source much greater than the world. Trust in the God who purposely made you special. He will never leave you, even when the entire world abandons you. So when the wall seems too high, the river too wide, just tell yourself, I can do that!

*Proverbs 3:6: "In all your ways acknowledge him, and He will make straight your paths." Amen and Amen*

# DAY 176

Good morning. A great many of you may hold that "seeing is believing." I would suggest to you that often times seeing has nothing to do with believing! So what is it that I believe? I believe the scriptures: I believe God created the heavens and earth and that God gave man the Ten Commandments. I believe in Jesus Christ my Savior and Lord. Furthermore, I believe him completely! I believe the Lord's Prayer, the Beatitudes and the Fruits of the Spirit. I believe the words of John 3:16: "For God so loved the world that he gave his one and only Son, that whoever believes in him shall not perish but have eternal life." Now that I have the truly important things out of the way, there are a number of things that I believe about the world in which I live: I believe that good will always overcome evil. I believe in America. I believe that hard work pays off. I believe in being honest. I believe in the sanctity of marriage between man and woman. I believe we are all called to mission, to caring for those less fortunate and in need.

*OK, I must admit that I believe in the Ohio State Buckeyes and the Clemson Tigers football teams. It's a human frailty in me, I guess. I Just can't help myself. And finally, I believe in you! Amen and Amen*

# DAY 177

Good morning. Get up! Wherever you are, listen to the warbling songs of early birds. See the extraordinary dawning of a new day. If it's summer, smell the lilacs and the roses, the new-mown grass. Their scents sweeten the air. Jump with elation when you feel the warm waves that frame the majestic ocean or whoop when you skip a rock across a quiet lake. If it's winter smell the wood smoke in the air and listen to the winter song birds chirp. Admire the snowy scene when everything is white and pure. And who could ever turn away from the mountain meadows and the sight of glorious peaks in any season? When the night sky is clear gaze at the full moon smiling at you and smile back. Stand in awe of stars shooting across the sky at night or a rainbow arching across a daytime sky—all wonders to behold, created for your pleasure by our Heavenly Father and brought to you by Jesus His Son. Get up! Get out! Don't miss it!

*Stop, take a deep breath and take it all in every chance you get. It is reason enough to declare each today, no matter what else it holds, the best day of your life. Amen and Amen*

# DAY 178

Good morning. How do you begin your days? I don't mean brushing your teeth, shaving and other sundry tasks. Do you begin the day with a question or a statement? I wonder what kind of day it's going to be—or—it's going to be a great day. You are the primary source in determining what the outcome will be. Let me illustrate what I mean. You may glumly mumble "It's raining, I won't play golf today" while I observe "It's raining, I've been looking forward to having some time to read." Someone will gripe "the mortgage is due again"; I announce "we are one month closer to owning our home." Another will cry "it's too late" while I shout "we have just begun!" Sad life, happy life, it's your choice. Each day is our big chance to fully appreciate our God given five senses. Smell the rain! See the blue sky. Hear the wind! Taste the oranges. Feel a kitten's fur. Now I must mention two other "senses" that are just as important as the first five: common sense and the sensing of time. Common sense aids the way you live in the present. Sensing time is the opportunity to glimpse the future you are destined for. You see, I know God has planned that my days will be filled with joy, laughter and love. He told me so. Hope you will join me!

*For I know the plans I have for you," declares the Lord, "plans to prosper you and not to harm you, plans to give you hope and a future. Then you will call on me and come and pray to me, and I will listen to you. You will seek me and find me when you seek me with all your heart." (Jeremiah 29"11-13) Amen and Amen*

# DAY 179

Good morning. Did you go to church this week? Did you do church this week? They are different, you know. You've probably heard the opinion that church is a verb. What does that mean? Go, strike, travel and love are examples of verbs. It is the essential portion of a sentence. I admit that the proper usage of auxiliary verbs escapes me, but I do indeed understand that the church that I seek is a "verb." It is not about attending or even believing, it's the action that makes a difference. Don't attempt to define church by the length of the sermon or the prayers or the importance of the announcements. Sunday school and church cannot be just "story time." It is great to hear the choir and to sing old hymns and new choruses but if they don't capture your heart they are little more than entertainment. “Go” means proceed, make one’s way. “Do” means perform an action, accomplish something. The church we attended this morning truly "does" church, a verb with a capital V! The minister proclaimed, "I want more! More of Jesus Christ!” More Bible study, more prayer, more Holy Spirit, more relationship. More walking into the world with him.

*Going to church plus doing church equals being The Church.*

*Yes, Yes, Yes. Hallelujah! Amen and Amen*

# DAY 180

Good morning. I love to see men and women (children too) do the very best they can at whatever they choose to do. It doesn't matter whether it's sports, flower growing or painting a picture. But hear so many who declare, "I have no great talents or useful gifts." Nonsense. Every living soul has something to offer, so why not make it the best offering that it can be? There is really nothing to be gained from mediocrity. I must admit that I love to watch the likes of Labron James or Stephon Curry putting forth great effort to use their talent and being rewarded for that effort. The same can be said for Shakespeare, Billy Graham or Mother Teresa, as well as one of the wrestlers, football players or students doing their best. When I watched an ex-marine in the Special Olympics running sprints with no legs, his determined effort and faith that he could do it humbled me and brought me to tears. It is not about being the best, it's about you doing your best. Age, size, intellect and even talent have little to do with achievement.

*Try out these words and see how they fit you: belief, trust, effort. It is amazing how far they can take you. Add in your relationship with the Lord and nothing is impossible! Amen and Amen*

Chofesh

Freedom

# DAY 181

Good morning. What's on your plate today? That's a euphemism for what things are in your busy and hectic pathway today? Up early this morning, ready for a round of golf, we were greeted by the unexpected pitter-patter of raindrops. Not having a close relationship with toads and frogs, we decided to forgo our playtime for the day. To quote Little Orphan Annie, "The sun'll come out tomorrow." How's your plate look? Maybe getting supplies for a weekend adventure you've been planning? Maybe just getting out the sweeper, washing clothes and a little arts and crafts? Do I hear you saying, "Who has time for any of that! My kids have to get to and from school, be at practices on time; there are groceries to buy, doctor's appointments to schedule, and oh, I almost forgot about choir practice." Busy, busy, busy! So much to do, so little time to do it. Stop! Take a deep breath! Take a minute! Let's offer the sacrifice of praise and thank the One who gave the day to us. And what a day it can be! Time to shower love on the kids, to show affection for your mate, to enjoy having an automobile or an umbrella! Smile. There really is something to be said for taking time to smell the roses – even in a vase on the table.

*Just remember: Today is the first day of the rest of your life and the Son shines on you every day of it. Amen and Amen*

# DAY 182

Good morning. What have you have been searching for? More and more at my age it's where are my car keys, my wallet, or even worse—what was it I was looking for? Actually, I am writing about things much more important than keys and billfolds. Were you, or much more importantly are you, seeing results from your search? Are you still working long and hard, hopeful that the results could bring you wealth? Perhaps it is contentment that you seek, whatever that feels like to you. My mother and many more, I'm sure, just "want to do the right thing." Now that can create a real conundrum. Maybe it's happiness that drives you forward or a search for true love. Many seek to become educated. (Don't ever confuse that with wisdom, they are not the same.) Throughout time countless have struggled to understand life itself. Here is my confession, at one time or another I have sought them all. But the most important search of all is to know God, to seek His purposes and conform to them. That's where you'll find what you're looking for.

*Lord, I have been searching. Now I am listening intently! Amen and Amen*

# DAY 183

Good morning. Listen. He is calling you! Don't you remember what He said long, long ago? In Isaiah 43:1: "Do not be afraid. I have called you by name, you are mine." You thought He was only calling Jacob. Isaiah 40:29-31 asks, "Have you never heard? Have you never understood? The Lord is the everlasting God, the Creator of all the earth. He never grows weak or weary. No one can measure the depths of His understanding. He gives power to the weak and strength to the powerless. Even youths will become weak and tired and young men will fall in exhaustion. But those who trust in the Lord will find new strength. They will soar high on wings like eagles. They will run and not grow weary. They will walk and not faint." That can be you!

*Now that you can hear more clearly, listen to what He tells us in Ephesians 2:8-10: "God saved you by His grace when you believed. And you can't take credit for this; it is a gift from God. Salvation is not a reward for the good things we have done, so none of us can boast about it. For we are God's masterpiece. He has created us anew in Christ Jesus, so we can do the good things He planned for us long ago." Amen and Amen*

# DAY 184

Good morning. A friend once said, "It's too late, I missed the boat." I've got news for you, it is never too late. Imagine looking up at a star. "I wish I may, I wish I might..." "When You Wish Upon a Star" is a Disney song. "When you wish upon a star Makes no difference who you are Anything your heart desires Will come to you If your heart is in your dream No request is too extreme When you wish upon a star As dreamers do Fate is kind She brings to those who love The fulfillment of their secret longing Like a bolt out of the blue Fate steps in and sees you through When you wish upon a star Your dreams come true." You don't believe that nonsense? I do. It's all about believing. There was Anna Mary Robertson (Grandma Moses). She began painting at age 75 and died at 101. An Indiana farm boy, Harland David Sanders, became the founder of Kentucky Fried Chicken. And I have friends who believed. There is Lory who graduated with a degree then started over again to become a geriatrics doctor. Dave, a teacher, never climbed or skied until he was in his fifties. John became a teacher and wrestling coach long after a career in landscaping. Laurie left a successful career to enter the ministry and Mamie gave up a fortune five hundred job to become a minister. Greg accepted his first church long after his family was grown. Then there is Karen who found delight in painting and photography and Jim who learned to pray through journaling, long after maturity.

*So what is your wish? It's never too late. God sees the desires of your heart without needing fate or a star, and He delights in fulfilling them when they are the best things for you. Amen and Amen*

# DAY 185

Good morning. I've never been a great proponent of English Literature, but Shakespeare penned some of the greatest writing of all time. Many of us are at least familiar with the famous first lines delivered by Hamlet: "To be or not to be, that is the question." So which is it? I'm not referring here to Hamlet, but to you and me. You've probably heard, at some point in your life, "I don't care what you do, just do something," or "Get off the fence," and “Don't give mold the opportunity to form between your ears.” Life should be more about action than inaction. Definitely about being! Here are a dozen "fy" words calling for action, good or bad: Identify, solidify, amplify, justify, ratify, verify, stupefy, horrify, vilify, satisfy and one that absolutely stands out for me, glorify.

*To be or not to be? That's easy for me. I choose life on God's side of the fence. Hope you join me there! Amen and Amen*

# DAY 186

Good morning. Are you a prayer warrior? Prayer is all about urgency. If someone asks you to pray for them, what is your response? Don't wait or it might be too late! You say it's just not my thing. Why not? If someone is suffering would you turn away from them, using the excuse that it's just too hard or you can't find the right words? If you knew that you could save a life with a prayer would you do it? God is not a grammar teacher. Words come from our head, prayers are from the heart. Start with Dear Lord. He will lead you the rest of the way. Pray in Jesus' Name. Pray for your family, pray for your friends, pray for your church, pray for your nation, pray for your world, pray for forgiveness, pray for your enemies, pray for anyone who asks and certainly for those who don't. Pray for healing, pray for miracles, for blessings. Pray for flowers and trees, the mountains and the seas, the moon and the sun, bullfrogs and bumble bees. Pray for today and pray for tomorrow. Pray for the military, missionaries, the persecuted, and peace. There is plenty to pray about. Won't you answer the call to become a prayer warrior? I am sure there is someone right now needing for a prayer from you!

*Give thanks to God who answers prayer and pray Lord Jesus, Come! Amen and Amen*

# DAY 187

Good morning. Who's calling? While I was coaching, a group of my wrestlers and I were traveling to a wrestling meet when one of my guys pretended to answer an imaginary phone. "Ring, Ring. Yes, this is John. Ya don't say! Ya don't say! Ya don't say...." With great anticipation we exclaimed, "What did he say?" With a wry grin, John responded, "He didn't say!" We laughed at ourselves for wondering what a pretend caller on a make believe phone might have to say. Now, if you are being called by the Lord, it isn't a laughing matter. Have you heard im calling in the night? Samuel did (1 Samuel 3:1-10). "The Lord called Samuel a third time, and Samuel got up and went to Eli and said, "Here I am; you called me." Then Eli realized that the Lord was calling the boy. So Eli told Samuel, "Go and lie down, and if he calls you, say, `Speak, Lord, for your servant is listening.'" So Samuel went and lay down in his place. The Lord came and stood there, calling as at the other times, "Samuel! Samuel!" Then Samuel said, "Speak, for your servant is listening."

*We are always calling God. We never get a busy signal. He answers us. Be sure to listen for His call, then listen to him. Amen and Amen*

Kavod

כָּבוֹד

Honor

# DAY 188

Good morning. Do you know what commitment means? We speak of commitment in educational pursuits, vocations, families, marriages; as political leaders, athletes and followers of the Lord. I am not referring to a sterile dictionary meaning, or the take-it-or-leave-it generic definition carelessly preferred by most of the world. I am speaking of the kind that works its way deep within the soul to the center of our very being, the kind God defined for God's chosen children and those adopted into His family thereafter, His covenant for a thousand generations, Deuteronomy 6:5-6 : "And you must love the Lord your God with all your heart, all your soul, all your strength. And you must commit yourselves wholeheartedly to these commands that I am giving you today." Moses explains why in Deuteronomy 8:3: "He did it to teach people to not live by bread alone; rather, we live by every word that comes from the mouth of the Lord." Be careful! Moses warns in Deuteronomy 8:11: "Beware that in your plenty you do not forget the Lord your God, and disobey his commands, regulations and decrees that I am giving you today." God himself seals that commitment for all time in Deuteronomy 11:18-22: "So commit yourselves wholeheartedly to these words of mine. Tie them to your hands and wear them on your forehead as reminders. Teach them to your children. Talk about them when you are at home and when you are on the road, when you are going to bed and when you are getting up. Write them on the door posts of your houses and on your gates, so that as long as the sky remains above the earth, you and your children may flourish..."

*Are you committed? Amen and Amen*

# DAY 189

Good morning. What are you praying for? Maybe the first question should be are you praying at all? We treat God as if He is our personal valet, expecting him to answer on request, or sadly, on demand. Then, when He doesn't, we are disheartened or even angered. "How could He? I prayed!" we say. "He's supposed to hear our prayers, even the smallest ones." News for you, He answers them, too, though perhaps not as you and I expect. Sometimes I pray for my wants and desires: for good weather, success, victory. I pray for quiet, or highways without traffic. I know He answer prayers, but I often ignore that I am supposed to pray for God's will first and in everything give him thanks. "Lord, forgive me for my shameful requests." There, that's the right start; praying for forgiveness. Oops. I forgot something else. I must forgive before I am forgiven, just as Jesus taught His disciples in Matthew 6:9-13, The Lord's Prayer. "Forgive me for my sins as I forgive those who have sinned against me." Now, I will pray for myself to hear what the Lord is saying to me; for safekeeping, strength to fight spiritual battles, then for my family, for my friends and neighbors, for my local church and The Church....giving thanks and asking in the Name of Jesus, who carries my acceptable prayers to Our Father.

*If you don't know how to pray, start with the Lord's Prayer then make your requests and end with "Thank you, Jesus; I trust you, believe you, need you and love you with all my heart and soul. It's in your name I pray." He'll do the rest! Amen and Amen.*

# DAY 190

Good morning. "Is that all there is?" PJ Harvey's lyrics ask. I haven't searched the world or experienced it all, but I have seen some of Tennessee and SW Ohio near Cleveland, where I met the love of my life at KSU. As far as having done everything goes, I confess I've never been a butcher, a baker or a candle stick maker; never seen an ocean from the other side, never climbed the Eiffel Tower or traversed the Great Wall of China, been to Pismo Beach or downtown New Orleans. I've never been in a submarine or caught a swordfish. I've never been to an Opera (the Grand Ole Opry doesn't count) or danced the Hokey-Pokey (maybe once long ago). I've never picked a grapefruit, dug a sweet potato, painted a picture, written a song or made a hole in one (still trying). So there's a lot left for me to do, but if we hadn't come to this place in Tennessee nestled on the Cumberland Plateau, I never would have played golf on Tuesdays and Thursdays. I wouldn't have taken classes to become a Stephen Minister and a Master Gardener, held season tickets to Dollywood or enjoyed exploring Cades Cove and Smokey Mountain trails, even planting flowers on a mountain top. I wouldn't have servant ministries in Tennessee and Louisiana. Who would have guessed that we would make friends from Maryland, Pennsylvania, Illinois, Michigan and Texas, not to mention Tennessee, all right here where we live now?

*The best thing yet, I've seen the God I love everywhere I've been, but more clearly here than ever before. It's so wonderful to be alive in Christ forever, and never have to ask, "Is that all there is?" Amen and Amen*

# DAY 191

Good morning. I know many of you are at least a little familiar with Sonnet 43 by Elizabeth Barrett Browning in 1850. Most of us know only the first sentence or two: "How do I love thee? Let me count the ways. I love thee to the depth and breadth and height my soul can reach, when feeling out of sight for the ends of being and ideal grace." It continues, "I love you to the level of every day's most quiet need, by sun and candlelight. I love thee freely, as men strive for right. I love thee purely, as they turn from praise. I love thee with the passion put to use in my old griefs, and with my childhood's faith. I love thee with a love I seemed to lose with my lost saints. I love thee with the breath, smiles and tears, of all my life; and, if God choose, I shall but love thee better after death." Now that is what I call love! Could you love that completely? We probably would like to believe that is how we love our husbands and wives, but we know many times we have fallen short. Still, I feel my love growing deeper over the years, don't you? Wouldn't it be wonderful if only we could love our Lord Jesus that way? We can! That's how much He loves us. We need only return His love.

*Read and meditate on His words, talk to him day and night, in every day's most quiet need; let him know the depth and breadth and height your soul can reach, freely, passionately, faithfully. Love him with the air you breathe, with the smiles and tears of all your life. Know that you will love him even better after death, when eternity with Hhim begins. Amen and Amen*

# DAY 192

Good morning. I left my heart in San Francisco. Actually that's a bit of a fib on my part. It is really at the Cumberland Medical Center with the rest of my matured body. I am spending the night here undergoing some tests. At my age, when something doesn't seem quite right, the best thing to do is to check it out. Hopefully, God willing, I will be heading home tomorrow. One thing for sure, this provides an opportunity to fully appreciate the many caregivers that so willingly serve those of us who are here, in need of special attention. I had only been here a few hours when I was blessed with special friends who came to pray with me and offer support. Where would we be without friends, not just friends, but those really special ones? Then there is that truly special one, "in sickness and health," the one I love to the moon and back, and that's the short trip. Significantly, they all bless me with God's love, the greatest love of all.

Dear Lord, as I sit here on the edge of my temporary bed, looking out the window at the mountains in the distance and the cloud studded blue sky, I'm quite comfortable because I feel your Presence. Thank you for the hospital's doctors, nurses, technicians, chaplains, and others who serve You here. Thank you for my special friends. I know that all is well. Amen and Amen

# DAY 193

Good morning. Will you sup with sinners? It's easy enough to break bread and enjoy the company of friends and good companions. When the righteous sit down with us we smile and are pleased, but what about the derelict, the dirty and the disenchanted? Jesus did not pick Matthew to have dinner with him (at the tax collectors house, no less) because he was "righteous." He did not chastise him, either, for what he had been. He simply said, "Follow me!" Peter and the rest of the disciples, who had not been choir boys themselves, followed without a word. The Pharisees wouldn't give them the time of day. After all, they considered the tax collector and his friends the very dregs of society, people who spoiled the kingdom God had created for them. How do you see it? Remember what Jesus said to those who wanted to stone a woman caught in adultery as told in John 8:1-11. "Let he who is without sin cast the first stone." I don't know about you but I don't want to throw "stones." I want to bring others to the Lord, not turn them away.

*We cannot plant seeds unless we are willing to get our hands a little dirty. We can't make a difference if we think "what's the difference." You haven't offered your best until you've offered it to the least. Amen and Amen*

# DAY 194

Good morning. We all say we are seldom angry and never hate. But what about that guy who cut in front of me and shared a little sign language? There was the waitress who never offered to refill my cup. How about the neighbor who refused to mow her lawn or the man who spoke harshly about denominations other than his own? There is the wife who unfairly criticizes the way her husband dresses and the husband who refuses to inform his wife why he will be late to dinner. Men swear when a fishing line breaks or they misjudged a chip shot. Don't get involved in a conversation about drug abusers, gays, illegal immigrants, the police, politicians, and others! I remember once losing a game and the words that came out, I'll never repeat. Do I really hate Michigan, Ohio State or Alabama? Kill the mongrel dog who soiled my lawn or the stinkin' skunk that was only protecting her young? OK. You see I don't need dissidents or war mongers to spew hate, there is literally enough to go around in my own back yard! So what will I do about it? Asking the Lord's forgiveness is a good place to begin, and I could leave judgment to the One who has the power to do something about it. Jesus made a really difficult request in Luke 6:27-31 and in Matthew 5:43-48. "Love your enemies, do good to those who hate you, bless those who curse you, pray for those who abuse you. To him who strikes you on the cheek, offer the other also; and to him who takes away your cloak, do not withhold your coat as well. Give to everyone who begs from you; and of him who takes away your goods, do not ask them again. As you wish that others would do to you, do so to them."

*Lord, forgive me, for I am a work in progress. Amen and Amen*

Yahweh Raah

יהוה יראה

The Lord Is My Shepherd

# DAY 195

Good morning. I'll think about it tomorrow. Good advice? What are you waiting for? Amazing how easy it is to put off until tomorrow what we could do today; mow my lawn or rake the leaves. Fix my car, my bad habits, my attitude; visit my doctor, my dentist, my neighbor, my parents; forgive my doctor, my neighbor, my siblings. We should never have to say, "I wish I had." Don't allow yourself to be like Felix the procrastinator in Acts 24:25 where we learn "as he was discussing righteousness, self-control and the judgment to come, Felix became frightened and said, 'Go away for the present and when I find time I will summon you.'" Just a little kindly advice, do it now, sometimes later becomes never. There are several sayings addressing procrastination that can be found in Proverbs. I particularly like the one about an ant in Proverbs 6:6-8. "Take a lesson from the ants, you lazybones. Learn from their ways and become wise! Though they have no prince or governor or ruler to make them work they labor hard all summer, gathering food for the winter."

*How's that for good advice for today? Amen and Amen*

# DAY 196

Good morning. Who are your prophets and truth tellers? It is irony that those who profess to lead us say, “Trust me,” and yet they spew anger and tell lies about each other. It's not just those who lead, but also the many who follow. Are you contributing to the dysfunction and derisiveness that plagues our nation today? Worse yet, do you not care about the direction we are headed? We are a people divided, not just by race, nationality or even faith, but also by our values. This was also true in the days of Jeremiah, Israel, Judah and Babylon. The Lord said to Jeremiah, "Suppose one of the people or one of the prophets or priests asks you, 'What prophecy has the Lord burdened you with now?' You must reply, 'You are the burden! The Lord says he will abandon you!'" Fast forward, has anything changed? “Stop turning upside down what the Lord has told his people.” That is us now! Has the Lord abandoned us already? When we say leave it to the leaders or even leave it to the people, we have forgotten who our real leader is—the One who knows the way, the God in whom we trust. Are we ready to patch our wounds, abstain from anger, and abandon our divisiveness?

*Whether Democrat, Republican, Liberal, Conservative, Black, White, Brown, Christian, Jew, Muslim, Young or Old we must take a creative look at working out our differences and turn our trust back to the Lord where it belongs. The time to do it is now. Amen and Amen*

# DAY 197

Good morning. Whenever we celebrate our nation, there are those who say we should be praying instead of celebrating. We should celebrate and pray. The fact that we are a democratic nation built on Christian principles makes us a desirable place in the world. Millions want to become Americans. We are Africans, Asians, Europeans, South Americans, Native Americans; black, yellow, red and white. If there was blue we would be that too. We are people of many religions and no religion, a nation of many differences, yet we are all Americans. We are far from perfect, but we are a free people in a world that seeks to be freed from injustice, inequality, persecution and poverty. We celebrate and continue to pray scriptural prayers like this one from Revive Our Hearts: Pray For America. "We pray for kings and all those in authority, that we may live peaceful and quiet lives in all godliness. We pray that God's people will demonstrate a spirit of repentance and prayer, which God will raise up through righteous leaders who will model integrity, so Americans will see their spiritual poverty. Then our citizens will awaken to their spiritual needs. We pray that we will see truth, that error will be exposed, and wicked agendas will fail. We pray that Christians will avoid fault finding, but instead will serve as worthy ambassadors for Christ. We pray for truth in media, that we will place our confidence in God rather than politicians, and that we will look to God to overcome the enemies of truth and righteousness."

*This is my challenge. Join me to pray every day that we will be up to the challenge to pray this way every day! Amen and Amen*

# DAY 198

Good morning. Are you a quitter? When I was a young coach a good many years ago I used to preach to my athletes, "Never quit." What I meant was not to give up or give in. As I have experienced more about living over many years now, I've come to realize that there is indeed a time to quit. Karen, my wife and often my mentor, says this about retirement: "We don't retire, we just repurpose." Quitting is not necessarily a bad thing. As a college student I learned that frequently imbibing alcohol was not a good thing. It may have taken many late nights with my head over a bowl, but I figured it out. One of the best decisions I ever made was when I quit smoking at age thirty-three. It has taken me a lifetime to quit wasting time and I'm still struggling sometimes with sinful behavior or thoughts. If something is not right for you, then quit. As my wife puts it, repurpose yourself. You don't have to be seventy years old to figure it out. Albert Einstein figured it out when he offered this advice: "The definition of insanity is doing the same thing over and over again and expecting different results."

*Take these thoughts with you from the Word. Psalm 119:11, "I have stored up your word in my heart, that I might not sin against you," and from James 4:17, "So whoever knows the right thing to do and fails to do it, for him it is sin." The lesson I have learned: I may quit, but I will never give up! Amen and Amen*

# DAY 199

Good morning. I need it! I want it! Why is it that our wants often exceed our needs? Much of the world experiences poverty and yet we have been blessed with so much. According to Federal standards, even those in poverty here have much more than the great number of living souls occupying the rest of the world. Approximately 85 per cent of the world's population live on incomes of less than 20 dollars a day; and more than 15 per cent live on less than 2 dollars per day. That represents more than 1.3 billion people at less than 700 dollars a year. OK, OK, we've all heard, "Eat your Brussels sprouts, they are starving in Africa," or lots of other places. But we shrug and think, "I give a donation here and there, and after all, we all need three tv sets, two cars, closets filled to the brim and enough cash for a rainy day or two or forever. I need it, I want it, I earned it! Just a thought or two about that from Paul in Philippians 4:11-12. "...For I have learned in whatever situation I am to be content. I know how to be brought low and I know how to abound. In any and every circumstance I have learned the secret of facing plenty and hunger, abundance and need..." and in 2 Corinthians 9:9-11, "He has distributed freely, He has given to the poor, His righteousness endures forever. He who supplies seed to the sower and bread for food will supply and multiply your seed for sowing and increase the harvest of your righteousness. You will be enriched in every way, which through us will produce thanksgiving to God."

*It's not about what I want, need, and earn. He will supply our need as we ask and receive with thanksgiving. Lord, give us this day our daily bread (Matthew 6:11). Amen and Amen*

# DAY 200

Good morning. Funny how time changes for us as we move through life. It all begins with anticipation for the arrival of the main character. A budding star is born! Then it's all about feeding time and time for the dreaded diaper change. On to walking, talking, nap time, bed time then play time and maybe even our first "time out." The first school time brought on Mom's tears, followed by several years of learning time with its recess times. Along the way came family time, vacation time, church time, dating, driving, and our very first job time. We could always look forward to Christmas time, summer time, fun times and graduation time. Mom may have cried once more when it was college, military or leaving home time. For many it became jobs, marriage, babies, growing kids, moving time and eventually empty nest time. I found him available all the time, even during the hardest of times, even when I had less time for him. Finally, retirement time and more time to share with the Lord. That time has become my favorite time, just the Lord and me. I look around and ask myself now, where has all the time gone? I am not sad at all, for now I can look at it all quite differently. I have time to watch the sun rise and set, to enjoy the snow and rain, the clouds, the sounds of birds and flowers that weren't there yesterday. I even enjoy the thought of mowing grass! What I have learned along the way is that it is all in God's time and there is no time like the present.

*It has taken me a long time to tell what time it is in my lifetime, but I'm glad to have learned. Today, it is your time. Go and make the most of it. Amen and Amen*

# DAY 201

Good morning. Anticipation is a visualization of a future event. We have all probably been advised not to count our chickens before they are hatched, or that we can't spend money that we haven't earned. The admonitions are true, but we do it anyway, don't we? Mind you, there is nothing inherently wrong with looking forward or planning ahead. Just know that things don't always turn out as planned. Here are a few examples. "I'm going to take geography because it will be easy." Not. "Let's have a picnic, it's not going to rain." Oh, yea? "Ohio State is sure to win the championship." Really? "Everyone knows who is going to win the election." Hah! "No one cares about me!" Wrong! God does! Now here is something you can always anticipate and count on: "The faithful love of the Lord never ends. His mercies never cease. Great is his faithfulness, His mercies begin afresh each morning. I say to myself, the Lord is my inheritance, therefore I will hope in him!" (Lamentations 3:22-24). Go ahead, anticipate His promises. He will not disappoint you.

*This I believe, this I anticipate. When I reach the end of the road, I will still look to the Lord and will see He has built for me a highway. Funny how even with all the turns I have made in my lifetime, it will lead me home to him. Amen and Amen*

Mattanah

Gift

# DAY 202

Good morning. These are times of turmoil, distrust, even terror nearly everywhere we look. It's undeniable, evil exists. In fact, it has been here nearly as long as man himself. So we surrender, "What can I possibly do about it? I am just an ordinary person." But history is filled with ordinary folks like Noah, Abraham, Joseph, Ruth, David, Martin Luther, John Wesley, Washington, Lincoln, Billy Graham to name a few. Acts 4:13 says "When they saw the courage of Peter and John and realized that they were unschooled, ordinary men, they were astonished and they took note that these men had been with Jesus." Are you ready to join forces with Jesus? He will stamp you with the Holy Spirit and arm you with the armor of God described in Ephesians 6:10-18 "…with the belt of truth…the breastplate of righteousness… feet fitted with the readiness that comes from the gospel of peace…the shield of faith…the helmet of salvation and the sword of the Spirit, which is the word of God…so that you can take your stand against the devil's schemes. For our struggle is not against flesh and blood, but against the rulers, against the authorities, against the powers of this dark world and against the spiritual forces of evil in the heavenly realms." Without it we are hopeless and defenseless. Jesus said "I am the way!" Do you believe it? Tell him so! Romans 8:38-39 promises that "Neither death nor life, angels nor demons, neither our fears for today nor our worries for tomorrow, nor even the power of hell can separate us from God's love."

*As for me, I'm glad to say I'm just an ordinary man who stands with Jesus. Amen and Amen*

# DAY 203

Good morning. "If only I had another chance." Have you ever found yourself saying something like that? While watching the Olympic Games I observed two relay teams suffering disqualification; one for a false start and the other for dropping the baton. Barring a successful protest there will not be a second chance, at least at this year's venue. Thank goodness many of life's ventures do offer a second chance. When Peter came to Jesus and asked "How often shall my brother sin against me, and I forgive him? Till seven times?" Jesus responded not seven times but until seventy times seven. Boy, that leaves the brother a lot of wiggle room, doesn't it? The simple truth is that the Lord has offered us many chances. Have you ever experienced the loss of a job, rejection at a school or from a university, separation or divorce, a major error in judgement? Have you sinned against another or the Lord, himself? Remember the price He paid so we might be given another chance. If it requires atonement, repent. If it requires a do-over, do it. If it means taking a new or different route, take it.

*I offer sincere thanks, praise and honor to my Lord and Savior who made second chances possible for each of us. It's more than we deserve. Amen and Amen*

# DAY 204

Good morning. I have been studying a book and DVD entitled Five Things God Uses to Grow Your Faith with a group of Christian friends. It is written by an Atlanta pastor, Andy Stanley of North Point Ministries, where more than 20,000 adults attend regularly. In this upside down world it is imperative that we come to know and understand our "Big God." Two of the five areas to develop this "Big Faith" are discussed in this study: practical teaching (Biblical knowledge) and providential relationships. Relationships? Who are the people in your life who have helped you grow in your spiritual awareness? Your mentors. Identify them and thank them! Now, here is a challenge for you. Can you be the mentor who is there for another person as they seek to know the Lord? The person could be a child or grandchild. What a valuable gift you can offer them! As I was studying the Word, I came across this short reading written by Paul to the Romans (1:11-12) "I long to see you so that I may impart to you some spiritual gift to make you strong—that is, that you and I may be mutually encouraged by each other's faith." It is up to each of us to encourage one another and others in understanding scripture.

*Peter, Paul and other disciples offered their insights and guidance. Are you willing to offer as much for your children and their children? Amen and Amen*

# DAY 205

Good morning. For many years through Jeremiah and Ezekiel and other prophets the Sovereign Lord gave warning to His people. They would not listen, nor would they turn away from their sinful behavior. They worshiped idols and turned their backs on the Lord. They thought themselves above it all. No need to listen to him! They broke the Old Covenant. Then He made a New Covenant with His people. We broke it. We think we are independently indestructible as did Israel, Babylon, Assyria, Egypt, Greece, Rome and all those who faltered and fell before us. Are we next? Do we control the mountains and the seas? Is our power over the sun and the stars? What armor do we possess over earthquakes, floods and fire? Can we make it rain where there is none? He offered us His earth-garden to tend and care for. Why is it that we choose to desecrate it? Repeatedly, He told us to mend our ways and stop our sinful behaviors. "Obey my plans for you and I will forgive you," He said. Will His warnings continue to go unheeded? Do you believe we are any different than all those who preceded us? The time is coming, it is very near, when we must make a crucial personal decision. We broke the Covenant, not him! Will we repent and obey God's will and do it His way? Or will we, too, feel the justified reprimand of the destruction of our nation? It is up to each one of us!

*The Lord, one more time, is saying to His people, "If only I can find just one who will be righteous, I will spare them." (Genesis 18) Are you the one He is searching for? Amen and Amen*

# DAY 206

Good morning. I am reading *I'm Second,* written by Doug Bender and Dave Seasett. In it they ask "are you a 'me first' person?" As I'm reading, I'm asking myself, do you try to be the first in line? Do you take the last jelly donut? Are you only satisfied if you lead the pack? Or maybe you're the one who is willing to give up your seat on the bus? How would you feel if you could take the seat next to Jesus at His last supper? (Luke 22:24-27) I see that it would be valuable for all of us to review Jesus' parable of the workers in the field. (Matthew 20:13-16) "But He answered one of them, 'I am not being unfair to you, friend. Didn't you agree to work for a denarius? Take your pay and go. I want to give to one who was hired last the same as I gave you. Don't I have the right to do what I want with my own money? Or are you envious because I am generous? So the last will be first, and the first will be last."

*Just a little something to think about as we all begin our day: We need to re-evaluate being first! Amen and Amen*

# DAY 207

Good morning. I've just retreated from our covered patio, watching the peaceful summer rain. I wonder if anyone has ever counted the raindrops falling during a summer shower. It's true that we count virtually everything. We count the seconds, minutes, hours, days and years. How quickly they pass! I remember a long time ago when I first learned to count. How proud I was, but not nearly as much as my parents. Then at four it seemed like an eternity until I could go to "real" school. Later on I counted the days until summer break. Everyone has counted the days until Santa comes once again! Oh, the counting we have done, let me count the ways: how many days to graduation, to marriage; nine months of anticipation for the baby's arrival; baseball season's scores, the balance in our savings accounts, the number of car and house payments, the next day off, the dates of vacation, the amount of income taxes, the circled dates of children leaving home, the number of grandkids. What's left to count? Try counting the stars, wild flowers in the meadow, lightning bugs on a mid-summer evening, cardinals at the winter bird feeder, and on and on. As for love, let me count the ways. Something we should count every day is our blessings.

*Then there is that One that I am counting on the very most, my Lord and Savior, Jesus Christ, the first and the last. How does one count the number of days in eternity? Only God knows. Amen and Amen*

# DAY 208

Good morning. “Give us this day our daily bread.” Can we be satisfied with that? If so, why is it that we chase after so much more than we need? We love “free, sale, credit, lottery, bigger, better, best.” We forget “satisfied, content, enough, blessed.” We need persuasion to pay attention to “love, joy, peace, patience, kindness, goodness, faithfulness, gentleness and self-control.” Why is it that enough never seems to be enough? We want more! We get more and overlook “thanks” and “giving.” In Ezekiel 34:2-4 we read these words about such ingratitude: "What sorrow awaits you shepherds who feed yourselves instead of your flocks. Shouldn't shepherds feed their sheep? You drink the milk, wear the wool, and butcher the best animals, but you let your flocks starve. You have not taken care of the weak. You have not tended the sick or bound up the injured. You have not gone looking for those who have wandered away and are lost." Six hundred years would pass and Jesus would reiterate Ezekiel’s message another way in Matthew 25:44-46: “‘You heard me right’...then they will reply, ‘Lord, when did we ever see you hungry or thirsty or a stranger or naked or sick or in prison and not help you?’ And He will answer, ‘I tell you the truth, when you refused the least of these my brothers and sisters you were refusing to help me.’ And they will go away into eternal punishment, but the righteous into eternal life."

*Matthew 6:33 advises us: “First and foremost seek His kingdom and His righteousness and all these things will be given to you also.” Amen and Amen*

Aleph Tav

First Last

# DAY 209

Good morning. It seems we live in a very fast paced world. Nearly everyone is in a hurry to get somewhere. Super highways have replaced our byways as byways replaced the trails of our forefathers. Restaurants and fast food service have taken the place of home cooked meals and TV dinners. Communication through Face Book, Twitter, and computer e-mails have made handwritten letters and newspapers obsolete. Jet planes, 200 mph cars and express trains take us from here to there at breakneck speed. We even have difficulty sitting through a one minute commercial without searching for another channel. Tell me, what's the hurry? Whatever happened to a relaxing road trip through the countryside or sitting quietly beside a mountain stream? Can you find the time to read a good book or to meditate about God's message from the Good Book? Is there time to get to know your kids, to teach them how to tie a fish hook or to hold a baseball bat? Will you take the time to stop and pet your neighbor's dog? When was the last time you paused to gaze at your reflection in a lake? Is there time in your life to find constellations in the night sky or wait for the full moon to rise? Too busy? Wait a second! What's your name? Oh, you have to go? I'm sorry to hear that as I was hoping to get to know you.

*There is no time like the present to slow the pace of your life. Make the most of it. Take a deep breath, let it out and smile. Rocking chairs, swings, and sunsets were made for those who are not in such a hurry. Amen and Amen*

# DAY 210

Good morning. So which will it be, happy days or joy to the world? Actually, I like them both in their right places. Happiness for me is having a great meal, catching a big fish, watching my favorite team play, seeing a really good movie, buying a new car. The Bible says in Psalm 144:15, "Happy are the people whose God is the Lord". Ecclesiastes 2:26 advises, “To the person who pleases him, God gives wisdom, knowledge and happiness. Matthew 25:21-23 tells us, “His master replied, ‘Well done, good and faithful servant! You have been faithful with a few things; I will put you in charge of many things. Come and share your master’s happiness.’” So how do I see joy? For me, joy begins by having Christ as an integral part of my very being. Joy is walking hand in hand with the woman I love. Joy is dancing with my daughter at her wedding. Joy is watching the birth of my son and daughters. Joy is serving God wherever He calls me. The Bible says joy is a fruit of the spirit in Galatians 5:22-23. Prov 10:28 notes, “The prospect of the righteous is joy.” The joy of the Lord is your strength” says Neh 8:10. Did you know that the word “joy” appears in Philippians sixteen times in just four short chapters? Look them up!

*It doesn’t have to be happiness or joy. We can have them both, praise God! Happiness is the Lord! Joy to the world! Amen and Amen*

# DAY 211

Good morning. Our waitress at Cracker Barrel asked, "What are you going to have today?" I responded, "How about the Old Timers Scrambled eggs, bacon, potato casserole, grits and biscuits with gravy and of course countless cups of coffee." Not a breakfast for the faint hearted. Actually quite a challenge for many "Old Timers," too! Every Friday morning at 6:00 finds us at our special table, being served by our special waitress. Just who are "us?" This morning it was ten of Jesus' disciples who share the Emmaus experience through weekly reunion. Note I did not imply God's angels or saints, just ten men who strive to keep Jesus and God central in our lives. For some of us it has been many years and for others just a few, but the blessing is the same. It's true that the breakfast feast is filling, but what transpires around that table is a feast of the Holy Spirit. This morning we began by laying hands on a waitress whose husband recently committed suicide. We prayed healing for others, gave testimony about the blessing of giving and offered fellowship to one another. It is much more than just the food that keeps us coming back week after week, month after month, year after year.

*There's something mighty satisfying about ordering a hearty breakfast, but Lord, when I'm at your filling station all I have to say is "fill 'er up!" Amen and Amen*

# DAY 212

Good morning. Most of us have been taught to sing "The Star Spangled Banner" and recite "The Lords Prayer." But how many of us are committed to learning the Word of God, the Bible? The author gave it to us "for teaching, rebuking, correcting and training in righteousness so the servant of God may be thoroughly equipped for every good work."(2 Timothy 3:16-17) Have we paid attention? What do we know about the Commandments, the Fruits of the Spirit or the Beatitudes? For many of us it is like admiring the cover of a book but never opening it. Dust it off, read it, study it, obey what it says to do. When Jesus taught the disciples and the crowds who came from far off places, did he consider His words idle conversation? Get serious! He is. The Ten Commandments (Exodus 20:1-17) have never been rescinded. The Nine Fruits of the Spirit (Galatians 5:22-23) are still available. The Eight Beatitudes (Matthew 5:3-12) are as comforting today as they were when Jesus first taught them to a crowd hungering for words from God.

*Pick up your Bible, sit down and read The Ten Commandments, The Nine Fruits of the Spirit and the Eight Beatitudes. You will soon learn them and be exclaiming with the psalmist, "Thy Word is a lamp unto my feet, and a light unto my path (Psalm 119:105). Have a blessed day! Amen and Amen*

# DAY 213

Good morning. The Message! Early this morning, as I began to awaken from my slumber, I received The Message—not from my cell phone—but from deep within my mind. The Message was words to ponder. Specifically two words dropped into my mind. What was their meaning, and why were they given to me? I urged myself, "Get up and write them down before you forget them!" I let the two words roll off my tongue, I failed to record them on paper—and now they are gone! Just a silly dream? Purposeless words? Or perhaps a message? I'll never know. Now I wonder how many thoughts I haven't heeded: warnings, prayer requests, and promptings to do something. Was I being called into action and did not respond? Will The Message return or is it too late to retrieve it? There are those who would confidently tell me, "If you can't remember it, it couldn't be very important." I don't agree. Perhaps that is why I've felt compelled to write down my thoughts, to keep journals. If The Message comes to me again, I am prepared to receive it and record it to share.

*"And it shall be in the Last Days," God says, "that I will pour forth My Spirit on all mankind; and your sons and your daughters shall prophesy, and your young men shall see visions, and your old men shall dream dreams." (Acts 2:17) I believe we are in the Last Days. Amen and Amen*

# DAY 214

Good morning. I was once a history teacher. Since I was a small boy I have been intrigued by the people and events that came before me. By the second or third grade I read extensively about men and women who changed our world. I dreamed that I might even be one someday. From our very earliest times it became evident that if we were going to live in small civilized groups, we needed to develop a language and a numbering system. Mankind agreed clothes would be nice, too. Humans weren't opposed to farming, hunting, gathering and taming animals to ease their burden. So much for that early stuff, now let's think about the ideas and inventions that have had an enormous effect on modern civilization. Many would cast votes for the printing press as greatest (not bad, Johannes Gutenberg). Others would elect electricity and the light bulb, or prize the automobile and plane as first place; telephones, nuclear energy, computers and cellular devices would be included by many. I am personally advocating for the eraser. Yep, from our earliest age we teach our children it's possible to erase our mistakes. What inventions do you know that were made without first experiencing failure? I often wonder why God did not create us with an eraser attached. If only we could erase some of the things we have said and done! After all, no one has never made a mistake.

*Here is the good news: God did give us an eraser! He offered his only Son so we can be forgiven for all our mistakes, large and small. I vote for Jesus Christ, the eraser of our sins. Amen and Amen*

# DAY 215

Good morning. Picture this. God has offered us a history, a storybook and an accounting that allows us to walk the journey not only with him, but with all those he has called throughout the ages. Indeed, there are pictures in my mind as I read his Holy work. I have seen Adam and Eve's creation, Noah, Jonah and the arduous journey of Abraham. I have walked alongside Joseph, Moses, David and Solomon. I've trekked with the Israelites to Babylon and back again. I celebrated with the shepherds at the birth of the baby Jesus. It seems that we sort of grew up together; just as He chose those who were to follow him, He has also chosen me. I wept at the sight of the cross, his bloodstained hands and feet, and I celebrated when I saw that the stone had been rolled away. I rejoiced when I saw him walking on the road to Emmaus. I can hardly wait to see him return as promised by his very own Word. The ages that followed, though often blurred, have brought us to today. The historical and spiritual picture that will be seen by those who follow us is left to us to help create. It won't be a blank canvas.

*Someday, perhaps like Peter, John and James, I too may climb to the mountaintop and once again see Moses, Elijah and Jesus painted in the most dazzling white we have ever seen. Can you picture that? Amen and Amen*

Stop and Listen

Selah

# DAY 216

Good morning. Are you worried, upset, angry, distressed, just plain mad at the world? That and $4.99 will get you a cup of coffee. You say you didn't sleep last night?  Gone forever, so what about today? Are you worried a Stop and Listen bout hurricanes or tornadoes? What good will that do? Your term paper is nearly due. Get to work on it. You have a doctor's appointment on Friday. The car is making a funny noise. It's going to rain, it's hot. You say "I'm  out of coffee. I'm getting old, I'm too young. I think I'll go back to bed, take another Xanax or if worse comes to worse, maybe I'll just eat worms. All these things I've mentioned, can't, won't and don't change a thing. When you are throttled with the troubles of life and the world, don't you think it's time to turn them over to the Lord? Psalm 55:22: "Cast your cares on the Lord and He will sustain you; He will never let the righteous fall" and "Cast all your anxiety on him because He cares for you." (1st Peter 5:7) Ask him for the good gifts. (Matthew 7:11) Proverbs 3:5-6 offers this: "Trust in the Lord with all your heart and lean not on your own understanding; in all your ways acknowledge him, and He shall direct your paths." Indeed, God is bigger than all our problems, worries and anxiety.

*I love this thought: "Only God can turn a mess into a message, a test into a testimony, a trial into a triumph and a victim into a victory." Amen and Amen*

# DAY 217

Good morning. Do you suppose our Lord and Savior ever told a funny story or tripped over his own feet? When He was young, did He cry when there was no one to play with him? Did He wish that the day would end so that tomorrow might be better? Did He ever stub his toe or eat more than He should? Did He weep at injustice or get angry at the sight of greed? Was He ever disheartened or did He know the pain of falling short? I believe He may well have experienced all of these and more. His Father made it so, that He might know what it was like to be human. What made him so different was that He was made perfect, without sin! He came to know us, to teach us, to lead us, to forgive us and most of all to love us. He came, not as a god, not as a king, a general, or even a warrior. He is the Son of God but He came as the son of a simple carpenter in a small village hamlet, like many communities today. He came so that He might know us. Do you know him?

*My prayer is that you do. If not, you might meet him, maybe on the road to Emmaus, or any other road for that matter. I pray you will get to know him, believe him, love him and trust him. I know that if He comes to my door, I want to invite him in! Amen and Amen*

# DAY 218

Good morning. Promises, promises! I remember as a little boy I was constantly making a promise to my mother: "I promise I will be good." It never quite turned out that way. In fact, I was tempted to not be good as soon as Mama turned her back. That is, if it hadn't been for the eyes in the back of her head! The Bible refers to promises often, as do many of the old hymns, for example, “Standing on the Promises.” One that I heard recently touched me to the core, the “Hymn of Promise,” lyrics by Natalie Sleeth. “In the bulb there is a flower; in the seed, an apple tree; in cocoons, a hidden promise: butterflies will soon be free! In the cold and snow of winter there's a spring that waits to be, unrevealed until its season, something God alone can see. There's a song in every silence, seeking word and melody; there's a dawn in every darkness bringing hope to you and me. From the past will come the future; what it holds, a mystery, unrevealed until its season, something God alone can see. In our end is our beginning; in our time, infinity; in our doubt there is believing; in our life, eternity. In our death, a resurrection; at the last, a victory, unrevealed until its season, something God alone can see.” Praise God!

*God's Covenant is His promise to you and to me. He keeps His promises, we can be sure of that from what we see in nature, in what we experience and in the Living Word. Amen and Amen*

# DAY 219

Good morning. Is today going to be just another day in the life of you? It doesn't have to be. Wouldn't it be terrific to look back on this day and say, "I remember that day, it was great"! There are some of us, me not included, who believe things and events just happen, that we are just along for the ride. Is that you? I am well aware we have no control of events when the ground moves or gale winds blow. You may not be able to change the event, but there are things you can do to change the outcome. Take up the challenge! For example, if snow interferes with your plans for the day, you can go sledding instead of shopping; build the largest snow castle ever instead of building your career network. When something goes awry, make something better happen, don't just stall out and give up. It doesn't have to be monumental, you don't have to pole vault over the difficulty but you could be the one who jumps up and takes steps around it. If you wake up and think it's going to be a "bad" day, flip it to a good one, do something unexpected for somebody: an elderly neighbor, your kids, yourself. Make a batch of fudge, take the kids to a movie, start writing your family history; pick up doughnuts for the office, take time to tell someone thank you, lock in your vacation destination. You'll be glad you got up and took up the challenge.

*Male or female, young or old, there is a great memory just waiting to be created. Have a good day! Amen and Amen*

# DAY 220

Good Morning. Authority. Just who is in charge? Romans 13 says the powerful positions on earth are ordained by God. What authorities has God established? James MacDonald in Lord Change My Attitude offers these: Human Governments, Church Leadership, Husbands in Households, Bosses at our jobs, and the entire Criminal Justice and Court System. The Bible records rebellion against authority as far back as Adam and Eve. The penalty was banishment and eventually death. In Numbers 16 Korah and 250 of his followers rebelled against Moses and the Word of God. He shouted, "Are you trying to fool these men? We will not come." The penalty for their rebellion was death. Galatians 5:16-26 defines the rebellion that exists in all of us. "The sinful nature wants to do evil...the Spirit gives us desires that are the opposite of what the sinful nature wants...When you follow the desires of your sinful nature, the results are very clear: sexual immorality, impurity, lustful pleasures, idolatry, sorcery, hostility, quarreling, jealousy, outbursts of anger, selfish ambition, dissension, division, envy, drunkenness, wild parties and other sins like these...But the Holy Spirit produces this kind of fruit in our lives: love, joy, peace, patience, kindness, goodness, faithfulness, gentleness and self-control. There is no law against these things...Those who belong to Christ Jesus have nailed the passions and desires of their sinful nature to His cross and crucified them there."

*The penalty for rebellion against God is death, but for those who belong to Jesus It Is commuted to Life Everlasting! Praise God! Thank you Jesus! Amen and Amen*

# DAY 221

Good morning. Teacher, teacher, what shall I learn? Little student, you will learn to feed from mother's breast, but there's more than sustenance, you will learn her touch, her caress and the depths of a mother's love. You will find words, make known your thoughts and wants, communicate and understand. You will walk and open the window to the world beyond the cradle. School will start and you will learn how to get along with others than your brothers and sisters. You will learn counting, writing paragraphs, reading stories of Dick and Jane; math, science and English followed by Latin and maybe Spanish, biology and botany, history and government. Student, along the way did anyone teach you how to boil water or prepare a meal, take care of a baby, tend the sick, work the garden, read the Bible or pray to God? Did you learn to fish or catch a ball? Did anyone teach you to be honest and to tell the truth, to share what you have, to work and do your best, to care for the lonely and the destitute? Were you taught to love one another, to respect what is good and avoid what is evil, to know there is only one God and that He loves you more than you'll ever know? Yes, sir, and there is so much more I want to learn from you!

*Teacher, Teacher, I can't wait to become a part of your class, the one about living it to the fullest! Amen and Amen*

# DAY 222

Good morning. Are you an "if" or a "when" person? For example, if the sun shines tomorrow morning, I may take a walk; or tomorrow morning when I take a walk the sun may or may not be shining. When I was a young student it was if only I can pass my classes when it should have been, when I get A's in my classes I will be very pleased. It took a while but I finally figured it out. It has so much to do with attitude and sheer determination. By the way, a healthy portion of belief works nicely, too. Don't waste your time with if-only-I-had thinking. Believe me, it is counterproductive. Ifs, wishes and can'ts keep you running in place. Is that what you want? When you make up your mind to do something, do it! Don't be afraid to fail as failure is only temporary. When you were a small child when you fell down you got back up. What is so different today? Life is full of challenges. That is what makes it so interesting. When you are in doubt, unsure of your direction, meditate about it, turn it over to the One who guides you. After all, He has gotten you this far. I have always been a proponent of "reach for the stars." I haven't always gotten there, but it sure has been fun and often times exciting. Determine where you want to go in life and then be determined to get there. It is not too late!

*No ifs, ands or buts for you, and only one must-do: pray to the One who knows you best and loves you most, the One who will guide you all the way. Amen and Amen*

Go'el

# גֹּאֵל

Redeemer

# DAY 223

Good morning. It's been several decades since the singer Madonna released her hit record, “Material Girl.” In that regard she hasn't really changed very much. But neither have we. As I see it we live in an increasingly material world. Most all of us love things! Oh, they may differ but most of us would perjure ourselves if we denied that it is true. We like big cars, little cars, fast cars, sporty cars. We like TV's, cell phones, computers and all kinds of playthings. We like diamonds, rubies, necklaces, watches, rings. When it comes to clothes, whoever heard of a single pair of anything? And as for toys, how many dolls and matchbox cars can little girls and little boys play with? How did we ever get along without fit bits, golf buddies and GPS? We've got three kinds of cologne, four kinds of perfume and deodorizers for every room. Not just men like tools, mowers, fishing poles; and I have enough screw drivers for the mechanics class in a high school. You count ‘em! So, my friends, I am going to become a better steward of the many blessings that the Lord has granted me. I can pare down what I keep for myself.

*The Bible quotes Jesus saying it is easier for a camel to go through “the eye of a needle” than for a rich man to enter heaven. “The Eye of the Needle” was a very narrow gateway into Jerusalem. Perhaps after a while I may find that the “eye of the needle” is becoming a better fit. Amen and Amen*

# DAY 224

Good morning. Where you goin'? I mean, where are you going? Everybody is going somewhere. It's a question most mothers tire of asking, especially when the response is "nowhere." Abraham and Sarah traveled to the Land of Milk and Honey. Joseph took an unplanned trip to Egypt. Moses and the Israelites took a forty year detour to the Promised Land. Paul was going to persecute Christians when he met Someone who changed his life forever. Don't forget the Pilgrims and the American Pioneers who were also looking for a promised land. Jack Kerouac was "On the Road" traveling across the USA. Astronaut John Glenn circled the globe three times and Neil Armstrong went to the moon and back. Where are you goin'?

*I know where I'm going. Jesus, the greatest trip I'll ever take will be with You!  This refrain by Eliza Hewitt says it well. "When we all get to Heaven, what a day of rejoicing that will be! When we all see Jesus we'll sing and shout the victory." Amen and Amen*

# DAY 225

Good morning. This morning there were some trivial matters that did not go the way I wanted them to go. My response was to become agitated. My coffee got cold while my patience wore thin. It was past time for an attitude adjustment so I opened my Bible to the New Testament, looking for the good news of the gospel. I read in Matthew 4 about the forty days Jesus spent in the wilderness where He fasted and became weak, then was tempted by Satan. Do you suppose Satan tempts us as we wallow in our wilderness times? Satan was not finished with Jesus. Luke 4:13 states it clearly, "When the devil had finished tempting Jesus, he left him until the next opportunity came." In my mind I heard, "Don't think that he is finished with you either!" That wasn't the Good News I was looking for. I know Satan attacks when he thinks it's to his advantage, when we are vulnerable either physically or spiritually. He also likes to attack when we are alone. Christians, I know, must always be on guard, but that's more easily said than done. I don't always recognize who is behind what is happening. Ah ha! The Good News light bulb just came on! It wasn't *what* made me so agitated that mattered this morning. It was *who.* Now I knew what to do. "Resist him, standing firm in your faith" (1 Peter 5:9). "Greater is He who is in you, than he that is in the world" (1 John 4:4). And here it is again, "Put on the full armor of God..." (Ephesians 6:11-17).

*The Lord will rescue me from every evil attack and save me for His heavenly kingdom. To him be the glory forever and ever (2 Timothy 4:18). Amen and Amen*

# DAY 226

Good morning. What challenges are you willing to accept? Can you recall those days when you were young and impetuous and willing to accept almost any dare? We would never have reached the moon, found a cure for polio or cancers, invented the airplane, overcome slavery, or found the strength to overcome debilitating circumstances without accepting challenges to reach higher or stretch farther. The Bible has challenges for everyone. "Love your neighbor as much as you love yourself. Give and it will be given to you in good measure, overflowing. In everything give thanks. Forgive and you will be forgiven. Whatsoever things are of good report, think on these things. Come to the aid of widows and orphans. Do unto others as you would have them do unto you. If you want wisdom, ask God and He will give it to you without reproach. Cast your anxieties on him because He cares about you. Trust the Lord with all your heart and lean not on your own understanding. In all you ways acknowledge him and He will direct your path. Keep your life free from love of money, and be content with what you have. Let every person be quick to hear, slow to speak, slow to anger. Love one another. Love even your enemies. Walk by faith and not by sight. Rejoice in hope, be patient in tribulation, be constant in prayer. Count it all joy when you meet trials of various kinds"—and many more examples if you look for them.

*Have you accepted your challenge from this list? Reach higher, stretch farther, I dare you! Amen and Amen*

# DAY 227

Good morning. I was lost but now I am found. "Lost," what an earth shattering word. It's a word that we all experience some time in our life. We do know the meaning of lost, as did the shepherd who lost one of his sheep and the widow who lost one small coin. How have your losses affected or shaped you? Just yesterday I lost my wallet and I can't begin to count the times my house key or my car keys have turned up missing. There have been so many times I've been lost as I traveled the highways and the byways! I've been from California to New York Island and everywhere in between. I was lost with calculus and trigonometry as well as Latin. I lost a few games, then a few opportunities and jobs. When it comes to anything mechanical, I assure you I am lost. But then there was a precious baby boy my oldest daughter lost at full term birth. Lost had a whole new meaning. The loss of family, parents, friends, all tear at the edges of my heart. But then comes that Amazing Grace. "I was lost but now I'm found." If you are lost, He can find you, no matter what you've lost or where you are, my friend.

*I have lost my way, lost my interest, lost things and lost precious people in my life. But I have never been so far lost that the Lord was not with me, offering Amazing Grace. Amen and Amen*

# DAY 228

Good morning. Dollar Stores have recently become the cat's meow for a great many people. Why do you suppose that is? Everything is "cheap" and that's a good start. Sometimes, it's the little things that make us feel better. For seven or eight dollars you can fill up a grocery cart with things that you wouldn't ordinarily think about; an ornament for the refrigerator, artificial flowers for the kitchen table, a tiny screw driver for your eyeglasses, a colorful tea cup, spice drops or a million other possibilities. You know, there are a lot of other places just like the Dollar Store where the little things make all the difference. A dab of cheese on my scrambled eggs works wonders. Just a pinch of salt and pepper can make a world of difference. Earrings or a simple necklace can brighten up a woman's outfit. Flowers on the kitchen table make the start of a day nicer. A night light in the bathroom is perfect at three o'clock in the morning. A kiss or a hug can work for almost any relationship. Nail polish or after shave lotion do wonders for one's psyche.

*I have found one more "little thing" that makes my day, every day: fifteen minutes spent reading my Bible and talking with the Lord first thing every morning. It's way better than icing on the cake! Amen and Amen*

# DAY 229

Good morning. Does size make a difference? I was reading this morning in Mark 12:41-44: "Jesus sat down opposite the place where the offerings were put and watched the crowd putting their money into the temple treasury. Many rich people threw in large amounts. But a poor widow came and put two small copper coins, worth only a fraction of a penny. Calling His disciples to him, Jesus said, I tell you the truth, this poor widow has put more into the treasury than all the others. They all gave out of their wealth; but she gave out of her poverty, putting in everything—all she had to live on." Size wasn't what made the difference. Another example: if you walk in the weeds, and encounter those minuscule critters called chiggers, you'll understand first hand that size can be quite deceptive. Their size is not in proportion to the intense itching they cause. Do you recall Jesus' parable of the sowing of the seeds? In Matthew 17:20, "He (Jesus) said to them...truly I say to you, if you have faith like a grain of mustard seed, you will say to this mountain, 'move from here to there' and it will move and nothing will be impossible for you." He compares the power of a mountain and a mustard seed! Does size matter? One more example: A stick of dynamite is about eight inches long and weighs maybe a half pound. It packs a powerful wallop when ignited.

*We are like dynamite, just a static stick until detonated by the fire of the Holy Spirit. My friends, is your faith ready to explode? Amen and Amen*

Todah

Thanks

# DAY 230

Good morning. It has been written that Genesis Chapter Three is the saddest chapter in the entire Bible, for it is here that God banished Adam and Eve from the Garden of Eden. Genesis 3:23-24 explains: "So the Lord God banished them from the Garden of Eden, and He sent Adam out to cultivate the ground from which he had been made. After sending them out, the Lord God stationed mighty cherubim to the east of the Garden of Eden, and He placed a flaming sword that flashed back and forth to guard the way to the Tree of Life." Here is the Good News. The last chapter in the last book of the Bible, Revelation 22, is the happiest chapter in the Bible. Revelation 22:3-5 explains: "And there shall no longer be any curse; and the throne of God and of the Lamb shall be in it, and His bond-servants shall serve Him and they shall see His face and His name shall be on their foreheads and there shall no longer be any night; and they shall not have need of the light of a lamp nor the light of the sun, because the Lord God shall illumine them; and they shall reign forever and ever." We live between Genesis and Revelation, leaning closer to Revelation all the time. The hope of the Old Testament was The Messiah will come. The hope of the New Testament is The Messiah will come again.

*Rev 22:16-17, 20 "I Jesus have sent my angel to testify to you these things for the churches. I am the root and the offspring of David, the bright morning star. And the Spirit and the bride say 'Come,' and let the one who hears say 'Come' and let the one who is thirsty Come, let the one who wishes take the water of life without cost. He who testifies to these things says, 'Yes, I am coming quickly.' Come, Lord Jesus!" Amen and Amen*

# DAY 231

Good morning. Be Prepared. That is the Scout motto. Some confuse preparation and organization. They are not the same. Mind you, there is nothing wrong with setting up structure to keep your life in order, as in Organization. On the other hand being prepared, Preparation, requires us to be aware of the plan. If you have no plan, there is nothing to prepare for. People often moan, "If I had known what my job, my marriage, my family, my faith expected of me, I would have tried a little harder, studied more, paid closer attention, prayed about it more fervently." If God called on you today would you be prepared? If you understand the requirements, the instructions, the recipe, the preparation becomes much easier. God does have a plan for you, for me, for all mankind. You can get a good introduction by reading the Bible. It's all in there, the requirements, instructions, recipe, and preparation. You have to read it, study it, learn part of it by heart, keep it close for reference, and trust the Source of its information. Then you, too, will be prepared.

*My question is, have you asked him what He wants and expects from you personally? Or are you afraid that He might actually tell you? Amen and Amen*

# DAY 232

Good morning. Who would choose to do something they really do not like doing? Nobody. If that is true, then why do we find ourselves embroiled in places and things that we find distasteful? Who would work in a job they do not like or even despise? Who would seek to be mistreated or abused? Who would take on more responsibilities than they could handle? Who would knowingly destroy healthy relationships? Who would avoid physical or mental activity? Who would eat so much that they were uncomfortable? Who would smoke knowing that it might cause lung disease or cancer? Who would avoid spiritual growth? Who would choose to become dependent on alcohol or drugs? Who? Me? You? Too often we don't do what we want to, but we do what we don't want to. We are an uncommon lot, aren't we? We're in good company though. Paul said, "I do not understand what I do. For what I want to do I do not do, but what I hate, I do. So I find this law at work: Although I want to do good, evil is right there with me. For in my inner being I delight in God's law; but I see another law at work in me, waging war against the law of my mind and making me a prisoner of the law of sin at work within me. What a wretched man I am! Who will rescue me from this body that is subject to death? Thanks be to God, who delivers me through Jesus Christ our Lord!" (Rom. 7:15-24) Isn't it funny, we choose gratification over good health. We covet wealth over happiness. We crave entertainment over knowledge. We need help!

*Choose to "seek first His kingdom and His righteousness, and all these things (the good life) will be given to you as well." (Matt 6:33) It's a win win situation. Amen and Amen*

# DAY 233

Good morning. How safe do you feel? As I tune in and listen to the television I am appalled at the news of terrorists in Barcelona. Danger seems to bring devastation all around the world: Spain, North Korea, Turkey, Africa, Iraq, Syria, Charlottesville, inner cities everywhere. Is your neighborhood safe? Do you lock your doors at night? Can you feel safe browsing the Internet? Is your bank account secure? Do you need to change passwords often to prevent hackers? Do you worry about the safety of your children? Do you trust the police, your local and national leadership, your schools, your neighbors, your brothers and sisters? Don't you think it's past time that we start purposely putting our trust where it matters most? Our currency clearly states "In God We Trust." The first time the motto appeared on our coins was in 1864 on the new two cent coin, and by 1909 it was included on most of the other coins. During the height of the cold war, on July 11, 1955, President Dwight D. Eisenhower signed Public Law 140 making it mandatory that all coinage and paper currency display the motto. What can God do, you ask? The Lord Our God has given us Jesus, the Hope of the World, the One who intercedes for us with the Father, the only One who can make the world safe.

*It's time for change. Look at yours, from the pennies to a half dollar, our currency reminds us every day to put our trust in God. Amen and Amen*

# DAY 234

Good morning. Sometimes it is difficult to be optimistic, let alone be a cockeyed optimist, and yet this morning I spoke with a young woman from a third world country. "Do you know what they call America in my country?" she asked. "Heaven," she announced. Why is it so difficult for us to recognize our own blessings? But then, the Israelites failed to realize what God had offered them even as they escaped slavery from the Egyptians millenniums ago. Where is our vision, the vision of our forefathers? Come on republicans, democrats, ethnic groups, religions, young and old, we are one nation "under God, indivisible, with liberty and justice for all!" Under God? Yes, we are! Without him we are lost, without purpose, hope, optimism. Jesus summed it up in Matthew 11:16: "To what can I compare this generation? It is like children playing a game in the public square. They complain to their friends, 'We played wedding songs and you didn't dance, so we played funeral songs and you didn't mourn.'" Nothing was right, everyone was tired of the lives they lived, no one was optimistic. Then Jesus said, "Come to me, all of you who are weary and heavy laden, and I will give you rest. Take my yoke upon you. Let me teach you, because I am humble and gentle at heart, and you will find rest for your souls. For my yoke is easy to bear, and the burden I give you is light."

*Optimists anticipate the best possible outcome. Cockeyed optimists believe something that doesn't make sense is the best possible outcome. Can you be one? Are you ready to carry His yoke? It's the best possible outcome ever! Amen and Amen*

# DAY 235

Good morning. Get out! The Lord told Abraham to pack up his entire family and all of his belongings and move. As for Noah, he had to get out of the ark that had saved him and his family. David was called to get out of Bethlehem to go slay a giant and become a king. Joseph got out of prison to become second only to the Pharaoh of Egypt. Moses got out of Goshen leading all the Israelites to freedom from slavery in Egypt. Three wise men followed a star out of the Orient to Bethlehem to see the child born King of the Jews. Jesus got out of Nazareth, trading his hammer for a cross and nails to redeem a broken world. Peter and Andrew, James and John got out of their boats, left their nets and followed Jesus. Jesus told his disciples to get out! "Go and train everyone you meet, far and near, how to live this way of life, baptizing them in the name of the Father, Son, and Holy Spirit. Then instruct them in the practice of all I have commanded you. I'll be with you as you do this, day after day after day, right up to the end of the age." Matthew 28:18-20.

*Are you prepared to get out of your comfort zone? You might be surprised where the Lord will lead you, if you will only get started. Follow your heart, as long as you are following him. Amen and Amen*

# DAY 236

Good morning. How much time are you spending on spiritual well-being? Stretching is a form of exercise in which a specific muscle group is deliberately flexed in order to achieve muscle tone. Do you stretch your spiritual muscles daily? Exercising faith and prayer builds spiritual strength. Do you run or walk every day? Regular "Walking in the Word" can help prevent various undesirable conditions from developing in your life. The farther and more frequently you walk, the greater the benefits. Have you been watching "Everybody Loves Raymond" reruns on TV? How much time have you spent loving your neighbors? Do you even know who they are? Two hours on the Internet yesterday— how many in intercessory prayer for our President, other national, state and local leaders; the homeless, the persecuted abroad, and for Israel? You can train alone to reach your physical health goals, but going to the gym will enhance the effectiveness of your workouts. You don't have to attend a church to stretch your spiritual muscles, but going gives you more options for exercise and ultimate success.

*Take a look at your medicine cabinet. If you are nervous or depressed you are advised to take a pill; overweight, take a pill; can't sleep, take a pill. Your best medicine is in The Good Book. Take another look In there and you'll feel much better.*
*Amen and Amen*

Sandra Fischer

And when He finds it, He joyfully puts it on his shoulders and goes home. Then He calls his friends and neighbors and says, "Rejoice with me, I have found my lost sheep."

Luke 15:5-6

# DAY 237

Good morning. What a beautiful day it promises to be. When I looked in the mirror, what did I see? A man with a smile who looked just like me! There's a cup of coffee, its aroma enticing, and a sweet roll all covered with delicious icing. I walked outside and took a big breath of fresh air; I admired the orange-pink sky in the east shining there. What a beautiful day it promises to be, a day God my Father has provided for me! Today, I'm sure I'll pursue making a new friend or two. I'll sing "Jesus loves me this I know, for the Bible tells me so," I'll pray for myself, it's true, but mostly I will pray for you.

*It promises to be a beautiful day because I know He loves me and He loves you too! Amen and Amen*

# DAY 238

Good morning. From time to time it's time to get out your bucket list—and your MAD list—and take inventory. You may find that some things have changed for you. There may be deletions and/or additions. Don't tell me that you don't have a bucket list! It's a list of things you would really like to accomplish or experience before it's too late. As for a MAD list, you probably aren't acquainted with what that means. Let's identify the acronym: Make A Difference. I am not speaking about self-serving things, but instead ways you can help those in need. You might eagerly want to know, "When do I start?" or you might say, "I don't have time." I suggest you try four hours a month. Twelve of us could account for nearly six hundred hours a year. What could a thousand or a million of us do? As for your money, five dollars a week would create over three thousand dollars; multiply that by ten-thousand or more. By the way, that amounts to seventy-one cents a day. So get a small drink or fries at McDonalds instead of the large size. Here are just a few examples of those in need for you think about: Alzheimer's patients, folks in nursing homes, those in homeless shelters, and people needing food supplies at care centers; local organizations like Habitat, Salvation Army, and Bread of Life. It doesn't have to be either/or. You can do both!

*Add a MAD item to your bucket list and whatever you do, don't let your bucket get a hole in it! Amen and Amen*

# DAY 239

Good morning. As a young person can you remember sitting around an open fire on a starlit night singing, “Tell Me Why?” Even before that do you recall answering everything anyone told you with “Why?” That question is the catalyst that continues to move us forward as we mature. I highly recommend it to everyone! What if everybody took a few minutes (or more) every day to meditate (think), read, study, dream? We don't think twice about spending countless hours on Twitter (does that make one a twit?), on Facebook or watching mind numbing television shows. Some of my very best "thinking" occurs as I pause for a few moments before I settle in at bedtime or when I awake early in the morning. To capture times when we come across a “why” we’ve never wondered about before, keep a notebook and pen handy. (Be sure your pen has ink.) If you wonder why a golf ball has dimples, or why you capitalize some words and not others, the internet has lots of information waiting at your fingertips. But if you wonder why a Mockingbird mocks you’ll have to look somewhere else.

*The Internet is a good place to find answers for lots of things, but when it comes to wondering why the sky is so blue, the stars shine, the ivy twines, or just why I love you—not so much. Do you suppose God has anything to do with it? Just wondering. Amen and Amen*

# DAY 240

Good morning. When God created man and woman, He created one of the great anomalies of the universe. Synonyms for "anomaly" are "oddity," "peculiarity," "abnormality," "inconsistency," and "rarity." We certainly are all of that and much more! There are more than six billion of us humans and we are each and every one different, and yet we are all the same, even though we deviate from what is normal, standard or expected. Think of it this way: you are one of a kind. When He finished making you, He broke the mold. What a diverse, interesting, vibrant family we could be. One thing we all are, and that's God's creation. We can all become His children. Wouldn't that be wonderful?!

*All we have to do is declare with our mouth, "Jesus is Lord," and believe in our heart that God raised him from the dead, and we will all be saved—still the unique individuals God created, but now part of His forever family. Amen and Amen*

# DAY 241

Good morning. As a kid, did you ever get caught with your hand in the cookie jar? Didn't have a cookie jar? So what was it that tempted you when you knew it wasn't the right thing to do? Would you have picked the fruit from the Tree of Knowledge? Would you have looked back at Sodom and Gomorrah? Temptation abounds everywhere; why else would Jesus have spoken of it in the prayer that he taught us to pray? (Matthew 6:13) In 1 James 1:13-14 it says, "When tempted, no one should say, 'God is tempting me.' For God cannot be tempted by evil, nor does He tempt anyone, but each person is tempted when they are dragged away by their own evil desire and enticed." The writers of scripture found temptation important enough to mention it no less than twenty-eight times. Even Jesus was tempted by Satan in the desert before He began his ministry. Here are a couple more examples. Luke 22:40 records, "On reaching the place He said to them, 'Pray that you will not fall into temptation.'" 1 Timothy 6:9 relates "Those who wish to get rich fall into temptation and a trap and into many foolish and harmful desires that plunge people into ruin and destruction." In three words—don't go there!

*In the 1970's comedian Flip Wilson made these five words famous: "The devil made me do it." Truth be told, we make the choice within ourselves by saying either "Yes" or "No." Amen and Amen*

# DAY 242

Good morning. Can you imagine fitting sixteen men around a table for eight at breakfast? We did it! At six o'clock on a Friday morning, our Emmaus group succeeded, no shoehorn necessary. Can you imagine the lift one receives when breaking bread with thirteen Christian men devoted to Jesus Christ, meeting to pray and share with one another? You know, it could be said that we are the Fifth Gospel in a world that needs Jesus so very much. It does become our responsibility to "pass it on" by sharing our thoughts, prayers and more importantly our actions. That is the Gospel in real life! As we were praying and sharing, one of our Emmaus brothers offered this additional insight: "You know, we are the Twenty-Ninth Chapter of the Book of Acts." What would it be like if the whole world decided that we really can be the living Gospel? I can only imagine.

*Bart Millard wrote these inspired lyrics: "I Can Only Imagine what it will be like when I walk by your side. I can only imagine what my eyes will see, when your face is looking at me. Surrounded by your glory, what will my heart feel? Will I dance for you Jesus or in awe of you be still?...I can only imagine!" Amen and Amen*

# DAY 243

Good morning. Bible Study, Prayer, Church, what difference does it make? If you ask me, I say, "All the difference!" It is in the Word that we come to realize that God is speaking to us! Our enemy is not flesh and blood. Don't give place to Satan. It is so important for you to know that you are accepted by Jesus Christ. He has paid the price for you and for me. He has won the victory! We who believe are empowered to stand in His authority. Put on the whole armor of God. Everyone has a call to stand. Where have you been called to stand? There exist many gates of influence: courts, politics, media, education, church. Israelites returning from captivity in Babylon were asked to stand at the gate in Jerusalem. Where do you need to stand?

*A friend of mine recites this prayer every morning: "Good morning Lord, I don't know what you're going to do today, but I want to be a part of it." Can we stand in the gap? Amen and Amen*

Yahweh Yireh

The Lord Will Provide

# DAY 244

Good morning. How courageous do you think you are? Does the word "courage" make you think of Biblical and historical figures larger than life? David, Mahatma Gandhi, Anne Franke, Mother Teresa, Audie Murphy, the marines at Iwo Jima, or the firemen of 911? Maybe it brings up childhood memories of the cowardly lion in the Wizard of Oz who found his courage. You, too, can be courageous when it comes to protecting your children, family and neighbors; you, too, can stand up for your faith and your church and a nation. 1 Corinthians16:13-14 says, "Be on your guard, stand firm in the faith, be men (and women) of courage, be strong. Do everything in love." Hebrews 3:6 urges, "But Christ is faithful as a Son over God's house. And we are His house, if we hold on to our courage and the hope of which we boast." Large or small, strong or weak, young or old, we can all be of great courage when we join the Saints marching in. "We are traveling in the footsteps of those who have gone before, but if we stand reunited on a new and sunlit shore then a new world is in store...

*...O, Lord, I want to be in that number, when the Saints go marching in." Amen and Amen*

# DAY 245

Good morning. Humor and wisdom can go hand in hand. Many of the following assortment of phrases, proverbs, sayings and idioms, can be traced back to Poor Richard's Almanac written between 1732 and 1758, by none other than Benjamin Franklin. (1) There are no gains without pains. (2) Early to bed and early to rise makes a man healthy, wealthy and wise. (3) Plow deep while sluggards sleep and you shall have corn to sell and keep. (4) Have you something to do tomorrow? Do it today. (5) A watched pot never boils. The next ones have been handed down, some whimsical and some wise. (6) Beauty is only skin deep. (7) An apple a day keeps the doctor away. (8) Don't cry over spilled milk. (9) Don't put all your eggs in one basket. (10) You can't teach an old dog new tricks. (11) Never bite the hand that feeds you. (12) Time flies when you are having fun. (13) The early bird gets the worm. (14) He was born to fail. (15) Don't burn a candle at both ends. (16) The grass is always greener on the other side of the fence. (17) There is a pot of gold at the end of the rainbow.

*And here are three of my favorites: (18) Happiness is a warm puppy. (19) All things are possible with God and (20) Praise the Lord! Amen and Amen*

# DAY 246

Good morning. There are 2.2 billion Christians, the largest religion in the world. Nearly one-third of all living persons profess to believe in Jesus Christ. I used the word "profess" for an important reason. As of October 15, 2017 there are 325,127,159 of us living as "One Nation Under God" in America. So they say! I wonder what this world, and particularly this nation, would be like if we lived together in peace and solidarity. Caution. That is not to say that we must all think alike. Ancient Talmudic philosophy stated it like this: "Ask two Jews, you'll get three opinions." Thoughts and opinions that are different can be compared and even tested. The process hones our ability to think clearly and to avoid or overcome dogma. I am deeply concerned, even worried, especially about our nation, a people that are growing ever more unwilling to listen to the thoughts and views of others without becoming aggressive, belligerent, quarrelsome, and confrontational; a people with the mind set of I'm right and everyone who disagrees with me is bad, even evil. The very process of becoming "civilized" was born out of a philosophy of tolerance, of individuals learning to live together in harmony. The world, our nation, us – can we do it?

*Don't be as the Old Testament put it, "stiff-necked." What's that popular old saying? "Two heads are better than one." To make it work, the two heads don't have to agree on everything, but they do have to be agreeable. Amen and Amen*

# DAY 247

Good morning. What's in a name? My given name is James, but those who know me best call me Jim. I have been called lots of other things throughout my lifetime. As a young man, there were some who called me "Dubie." In Junior High it was "Speedy" and thanks to the radio, in high school it was "Duberry." In later years I became Teacher, Mr. DuBro, and Coach, but the name that I cherish the most is Daddy. Being Daddy or Dad takes a great deal of time and effort but there is nothing like being told, "I love you, Daddy." The disciple-fisherman was called Simon until Jesus said, "I tell you, you are Peter, and on this rock I will build my church..." The former Pharisee called Saul persecuted Christians but forsook his Jewish name and adopted the Greek name Paul after his conversion experience with Jesus on the road to Damascus. Women often change their names by adding the husband's surname to theirs. Lots of children are named for family members admired by their parents. Others are given nick names, affectionate substitutions for their real names. Names identify family affiliation, character, family history, and are used to show affection. God started the practice of changing names: He changed Abram and Sarai to Abraham and Sarah, and told their son Jacob his new name was Israel. Yeshua bar Yosef in Hebrew is Jesus son of Joseph, the name He was called as he grew up in Nazareth. Jesus is also named Emmanuel which means God With Us.

*One more significant name change is God's. He loves for His children to come to him and say, "I love you Abba, meaning Daddy. What's in a Name? Everything! Amen and Amen*

# DAY 248

Good morning. When was the last time you received presents? Was it an anniversary, birthday or maybe last Christmas? Some of us older folks proclaim that we don't need presents anymore. Some people say that there's no one to give them a present. How sad! There is a certain joy to be felt in giving and in receiving presents. It says somebody cares (or at least it should). I love to give my wife unexpected presents. It is amazing how a single rose can bring joy to her. For me, I am most appreciative of your presence. I am not a loner, I am a "people person." The gift of being present is far more important than you may realize. If you can't give a million dollars at least offer a hug or a warm smile! One of God's 95 years old princesses said she couldn't wait to receive one of my hugs. How good it made us both feel! I know that God's greatest present to us is His Son's presence in our lives. I can feel it every day. How? He opens my eyes to the beauty of the Father's world, especially to the variety of His children in it. He speaks to me through His Holy Spirit, sometimes in whispers, sometimes insistently, guiding my steps. I feel His response of love when I sing to him (it doesn't bother him if I mix up words or hit "wrong" notes) and when I talk to him (in prayer or meditation or journaling). The gift of His Presence makes me want to give presents of self to others.

*You don't have to wait for a special day to receive your present from our Father, the Presence of the Lord Jesus; He is there Sunday through Saturday, twenty four hours a day. Amen and Amen*

# DAY 249

Good morning. Have you ever argued with someone? Silly question, everyone argues at some time or another. According to Luke 22:24 even the Disciples argued about which of them was the greatest. Jesus settled that! I recall that as youngsters, my brother and I argued from dawn to dusk. Some say that debating and arguing are one and the same. I disagree. An argument is defined as opinions clashing, while a debate is a formal argument with evidence to support it. Isn't it funny that most arguments have very little to do with listening, and almost never with compromising? When it's my way or the highway, it might as well be the highway. Disagreement is inevitable, and in fact differing ideas are often the antecedent of change. Our government representatives in all offices could benefit by agreeing to disagree, being willing to listen and even to compromise. Don’t you suppose God knew what He was doing when he made us all different? It was for our own good. When dealing with our differences, start adopting some of the attributes He approves in us: forgiveness, patience, perseverance, self-control and kindness. While you are at it, why not rid yourself of these: dissension, discord, arrogance and jealousy.

*Make no mistake about it, God’s loving wisdom can take care of everything disagreeable between us just as thoroughly as Jesus settled the arguments of the Disciples. Amen and Amen*

# DAY 250

Good morning. When I'm tired and perhaps pensive, someone may ask me, "What's wrong?" Actually, I think being tired may well be a sign of something positive. Tiredness indicates that we've been doing something, being an active participant in life. So I've often replied, "It's a good tired." It is not like the exhaustion of those restless nights when we toss and turn. I'm pretty certain that we've all been there, too. But why is it that in many circumstances we tend to look at the negative side, the wrong side, the bad side of life? Granted, it's out there, that's undeniable. But then, so is the positive side, the right side, the good side of life. It never left, even for a moment. You see it with the rising of the morning's sun dispersing the darkness. You hear it in the Good News of the Gospel proclaiming Jesus' victory over death, the devil, and darkness.

*Where do you find the remedy for feeling tired and despondent? Sometimes we are just looking in all the wrong places. So instead of asking what's wrong, why not start looking for what's right! Amen and Amen*

Abba

Daddy

# DAY 251

Good morning. “Eat, drink and be merry!” This well-worn proclamation is one I receive with mixed feelings. It is actually a combination of two Biblical sayings. The earliest appears in Isaiah 22:13: "Let us eat and drink, for tomorrow we shall die." Also Ecclesiastes 8:15 says, "Then I commend mirth, because man hath no better thing under the sun, than to eat, and to drink, and to be merry." So I ask, “Is that it? Is eating, drinking and making merry the ultimate experience of life?” Unfortunately, it seems we do find greater joy in being entertained than we do in other facets of life. The Patriots, Buckeyes, Spartans, and Crimson Tide take a place ahead of Matthew, Mark, Luke and John. Outback, Red Lobster and Ruth Cris Steak win out over serving food at a local shelter for the homeless. The books in The Divergent series by New York Times bestselling author Veronica Roth hold a more prominent place on our bookshelves than the series of books in The Holy Bible.

*Test my hypothesis. Which of the following do you rate the highest in your experience: a bowl of pretzels, three beers and a rousing fist pump and cheer at the stadium or a piece of bread, a taste of wine and quiet reflection and prayer at the Communion Table? Just askin'. Amen and Amen*

# DAY 252

Good morning. Can you hear me now? Just about everyone is familiar with that catchy jingle made famous by Verizon. But if you think about it, it could have a totally different meaning for all of us as we travel through the forests, bayous and mountaintops of life. I can remember my early years when my mother often impatiently asked, "Are you listening?" Later, as a teacher I sometimes wondered, while grading exams, which of my students was listening. Did we listen when others offered us advice or direction? How many of us have confessed that we wish we had paid closer attention to it? There were those times in my life when I was in such a hurry I didn't even listen to myself! We've all been sure at times that we "knew it all." It took me decades to understand that all the praying I had done and would do was not a one way street. Why did it take me so long to learn that? Human nature is not always our friend! Take heed, even Peter had to be told three times about a rooster crowing and still didn't get it.

*As our Christian experience grows, Our Lord continues to ask us, "Do you hear me now?" Listen carefully. He really does know all the answers! Amen and Amen*

# DAY 253

Good morning. Cheerios or Raisin Brand? Vanilla or Chocolate? Red or Blue? Carpenter or Teacher? Even not making a choice is a decision that we choose to make! So how are things going with your choices? Are you where you hoped and dreamed that you would be? What's that? You didn't make it to the NFL, the Presidency or Miss America? You say that you chose a few alternate routes and even made a few wrong turns along the way. You explain, "I never planned it this way" or maybe you didn't have a plan at all. Guess what, that's quite alright, God has a plan for you, He always has. I love the promise of Romans 8:27-28, "And the Father who knows all hearts knows what the Spirit is saying, for the Spirit pleads for us believers in harmony with God's own will. And we know that God causes everything to work together for the good of those who love God and are called according to His purpose for them." It's really quite simple. Choose to love God with all your heart, mind and soul and He will give you more opportunities than you ever imagined possible.

*I may have difficulty choosing between chocolate and vanilla, but when it comes to God, that's a no brainer. Wealth, power, fame and success will all fall away; Jesus, the Father and the Holy Spirit are forever! Amen and Amen*

# DAY 254

Good morning. Would you take the time to read Matthew 25:31-44? It wouldn't hurt if you read it every day when you arise. Maybe we all ought to stencil it on the back of our hands or on the inside of our eyelids. A friend of mine exclaimed how inconvenient it was to volunteer at homeless shelters and the like. Another spoke of being retired and not doing that sort of thing anymore. I heard a church member proclaim he'd help, if it wasn't that all they wanted was a handout. Isn't that what social workers are for?" he questioned. Another commented, "If you are poor, sick or in jail, it's your own fault, it's all about the choices you make." Finally came the excuse, "I would have helped but nobody asked me." Jesus did!

*We truly are not worthy to ask it, Lord, but please forgive us, we have no valid excuses. How our attitude must sadden you. Help us to see the needs of others. Help us fill their cups to overflowing as you are so willing to fill ours. Never say to us, "Truly I tell you, whatever you did not do for one of the least of these, you did not do for me." Amen and Amen*

# DAY 255

Good morning. Dr. Seuss shared with his readers the story of the Star Bellied Sneetches. Do you recall them? There were the Star Bellied Sneetches and the Plain Bellied Sneetches. Oh, how the Plain Bellied Sneetches desired to have "stars on thars." Then there was the classical tale of Rudolph the Red Nosed Reindeer. He wasn't like all the others. How about that black lamb in the middle of the flock or what the albino goat that doesn't seem to belong. Isn't it strange how we adore that ugly little mutt, you know, the smallest one in the litter, or the pony with the speckled nose? Who cares what color cat you choose, unless of course it's entirely black. Do you know anybody that doesn't look like you? Tall or short, skinny or fat, black, yellow or white, or any other combination in between? Won't you love me just as I am? What if I am gay? "Happy to know you," I say. Little Boy Blue, the Jolly Green Giant, or the One Eyed, One Horned Flying Purple People Eater? "You're just fine with me! I really don't care if your IQ is 194 or 78; if you are the king of Siam or that cute little girl I taught in school named Kathy, long ago...if God made you that's good enough for me."

*You see, the real truth is that God made all mankind in His image, no matter what our perception of "the others" is. By the way, did you notice that elderly woman sitting all by herself, apart from the rest of "us"? Have you told her how good it is to see her? Amen and Amen*

# DAY 256

Good morning. As I was lying in bed last night, somewhere between slumbering and awake, thoughts were literally "whizzing" through my mind. I traveled from capons and turkeys to locating lost coins, back to childhood and Kool-aide and a thousand other innocuous thoughts. Have you ever experienced that place where things seemed to move by so quickly? That's kind of like life in a nutshell, isn't it? Where on earth did yesterday, a year, a decade, fifty years and more go so rapidly? One definition of "whiz" is "to pass by quickly." Another meaning is "someone who is very good at something." Can you remember the "Whiz Kids" from earlier television days? Here's a little advice from one who's whizzed through life for nearly three quarters of a century. Life is much like a roller coaster ride, with thrilling ups and frightening downs and plenty of curves thrown in at lightning pace—but what I wouldn't give to take another ride! We need to make each and every day count, to live life to the fullest, all of it. The good news is, we can start today, no matter what the first part of the ride was like for us, thrilling or chilling or in-between.

*Here is the really good news: God will be waiting to greet you with open arms when you get off the roller coaster and are finished with your ride. Hallelujah! Amen and Amen*

# DAY 257

Good morning. "A picture is worth a thousand words." So you might think that words are really not that important. I don't happen to think so. There are times when I have found that one word makes all the difference in the world. Mind you, I have never been known for my one word dialogues or prayers. A loving word, a caring word, a kind word, a wise word has been known to open many gateways and even to crack some very daunting doors. I've heard naysayers remark, “If you ask God to help you, He will treat you like a tube of toothpaste; He will squeeze everything right out of you.” Well, He has helped me and been squeezing me for years. It’s funny. It feels more like He's wrapping his loving arms around me.

*If a picture is worth a thousand words, do you think the reverse can be true? Can a word be worth a thousand pictures? A word like “love,” as in “God so loved the world,” John 3:16; “God is love,”1 John 4:8; and “There remains faith, hope, and love, but the greatest of these is love,” 1 Cor. 13:13. Amen and Amen*

Lev

לֵב

Heart

# DAY 258

Good morning. How do we measure our pain? When I have gone to the doctor or a hospital, one of the first things I am asked is, “Are you experiencing any pain?” If the answer is yes, the response is, "From one to ten, ten being the greatest, what are you feeling?” Sounds pretty simple, doesn't it? But if pain was new to me, how would I know its intensity? Believe me when I assure you that kidney stones had to have been a ten! But what about all those other pains we are sure to experience throughout our lives? Growing up, my brother was often a "pain” as was old Mrs. McCray who lived down the street. What of all the other pains of stress, anxiety, grief and loss, guilt, failure, deprivation, sinfulness, loneliness, depression; how do we quantify them? From one to ten is not sufficient for that task. The Bible is filled from the Garden to Revelation with pain. Tim Keller shares this thought about that: "One of the main ways we move from abstract knowledge about God to a personal encounter with him as a living reality is through the furnace of affliction." Could there be any pain greater than the pain that Jesus endured for us?

*If you are experiencing pain seek help and by all means find comfort from God and from His Word. This very moment, I pray a healing prayer for you that God's miraculous hand will touch you and begin to bind all your wounds and heal your pain. Amen and Amen*

# D A Y 259

Good morning. Have you ever been called to serve on a jury? First, your ability to judge fairly and impartially is evaluated. Then it becomes your responsibility to do just that. Still, there are some who seek ways to avoid the responsibility, although it is a reasonable obligation of citizenship. Most of us will be called as jurors only once or twice in our lifetimes, but what about our responsibility every day of our life? 1 Corinthians 4:4-5 puts it this way: "My conscience is clear, but that doesn't prove I'm right. It is the Lord himself who will examine me and decide. So don't make judgments about anyone ahead of time." Hmmm. What would your reaction be to a young girl with tattoos and piercings or a man huddled in the alleyway, asleep? How about the couple who arrived at your church in ill fitted clothes and somewhat unkempt hair? You don't like the way he looks at you? How do you look at him?! Yes, he appears different from the rest and isn't as clean. You have already found him guilty as charged! Don't you remember he and she are God's children? Imagine what a lot of love could bring to their situation and to them personally. You don't know that tattered soul was severely wounded in a war for your sake, and that his wife has given herself to helping him.

*Oh, I almost forgot to ask. How would you judge the man with long hair riding into town on a donkey? Amen and Amen*

# DAY 260

Good morning. I am so glad that you are here. Have you ever asked, "Who am I?" My guess is that most of us wouldn't dare. Why is that? I believe it is because we are afraid of what we might hear. Jesus Christ wasn't afraid. In Matthew 16:13 He asked Simon, soon to be named Peter, "Who do people say I am?" Others offered their answers, but Simon offered the right answer, "You are the Christ, the Son of the Living God." The long awaited Messiah! And so it began....Two thousand years later I am a disciple. I know who Jesus is. Who am I? I don't know, exactly, but I know who I aspire to be. I want to be that one piece of sand on the beach that glistens in the sunlight. I want to be the brightest diamond in the mine. I want to be a raindrop blessed to be a part of the rainbow. I want to be that golden nugget in the bottom of the sifters pan. I want to be the ray of sun that turns night into day. I want to be the light at the end of the tunnel. I want to be the first song of the birds opening the first spring day. I want to be unafraid of being me.

*I want to live today without worrying about yesterday or fretting about tomorrow. I want to thank my God who makes all things possible. I want to make the world a better place because I have yearned to be all that I can be. I want this so I might better serve my Lord and Savior, Jesus Christ, who was not afraid! Amen and Amen*

# DAY 261

Good morning. What are the words somebody could say that would make you happy or at least feel good? You probably know that there are lots of people that would cherish the thought that somebody, anybody would say something to them. There is nothing better than knowing that somebody cares. “Hello,” is a great start, but it's what follows that really matters. If Karen and I had not stopped to speak to a brand new couple in our community one evening, two of our very best friends would have been missed forever. So here are some words that I love to hear. I'll start simple. "Thank you," "I've missed you," "You look great (even if you are overweight, slightly wrinkled and over seventy)," “dinner’s ready," and two that I like best, "Lets pray together" and "I love you." "The kids are comin'" is awlfully good, too! Now here are a few names that always brighten my day: Catie, Cody, Olivia, Jack, Jacob and Trevor. What grandpa wouldn't be cheered by the names of his grandchildren? I've never been disappointed at hearing, "Can I help you," "It's been fun," or "Was that a birdie?"

*You know, don’t you, that someone doesn't have to sneeze for you to bless them? Sometimes, if you just hold hands, that's enough. I'm beginning to feel happy already! You, too? Amen and Amen*

# DAY 262

Good morning. There are literally millions around the world that have hanging somewhere in their homes or offices, one of the great masterpieces called The Praying Hands, by Albrecht Durer. For countless numbers this work of art holds deep spiritual meaning. Many believe they are the hands of Jesus. Albrecht was one of eighteen siblings who lived in a tiny village near Nuremberg, Germany during the fifteenth century. Two of those eighteen dreamed of pursuing a career in art. But it was not possible for the family to fund even one at the Academy in Nuremberg. Finally, Albrecht and his brother Albert devised a plan; they would toss a coin, and the loser would go down into the mines and support his brother's studies. Albrecht won the toss, while Albert spent the next four years in those dreadful mines. Albrecht became an immediate sensation and was soon earning substantial income for his art. There was a triumphant homecoming, with much love, laughter and celebration. Before the evening ended, Albrecht offered a toast. He blessed his brother, saying "Now it's your turn; I will financially take care of you." Albert, tears streaming, replied, "It's too late. Look at my hands. The bones in every finger have been smashed and I am suffering from arthritis so that I can't even hold a glass to return your toast...for me it's too late."

*To pay homage to Albert, Albrecht Durer painstakingly drew his brothers worn and withered praying hands. So when you view "The Praying Hands," let it remind you that no one ever makes it alone. And yes, without a doubt, they are the hands of Jesus! Amen and Amen*

# DAY 263

Good morning. It seems that we look everywhere under the sun for answers to life's questions. We seek others to solve our problems and to take care of our needs. We elect political leaders to direct our government, and hire intelligent, trained leaders to address problems. Then why is it that the world always seems to be turned upside down? Could we be looking in all the wrong places? Maybe it's not what's under the sun at all. 1 Corinthians 1:18-21 suggest something else. "The message of the cross is foolish to those who are headed for destruction! But we who are being saved know it is the very power of God. As the scriptures say, 'I will destroy the wisdom of the wise and discard the intelligence of the intelligent.' So where does this leave the philosophers, the scholars and the world's brilliant debaters? God has made the wisdom of this world look foolish. Since God in his wisdom saw to it that the world would never know him through human wisdom, He has used our foolish preaching to save those who believe." It continues in verse twenty-five: "This foolish plan of God's is wiser than the wisest human plans, and God's weakness (if there is such a thing) is stronger than the greatest human strength." Those of us who trust in the Lord realize that it's not the rulers of this world, but God himself, who has the answers. That is good to know!

*"No eye has seen, no ear has heard, and no mind has imagined what God has prepared for those who love him." 1 Corinthians 2:9  Amen and Amen*

# DAY 264

Good morning. Why can't I be like everybody else? Actually, I am—an imperfect human being. Why am I so judgmental of my brothers and sisters? What is it that makes me angry and even hate filled and deceitful? How come I second guess my own actions? Does it always have to be me first? Why are my thoughts impure at times? Do I overlook those who have real needs? Is "Love your enemy," just something printed in a book? Why is it so difficult to forgive, to say, "I am sorry?" Do these things make me a sinner? Yep, without a doubt! Here's the Good News: Jesus Christ took all this and more away on the Cross. Lord, you are a mighty God. Psalm 71:16-21 offers testimony of what God has done for us. "I will come and proclaim your mighty acts, O Sovereign Lord; I will proclaim your righteousness, you alone. Since my youth, O God, you have taught me, and to this day I believe your marvelous deeds. Even when I am old and gray, do not forsake me, O God, till I declare your power to the next generation, your might for all who are to come. Your righteousness reaches to the skies, O God, you who have done great things. Who, O God, is like you? Though you have made me see troubles, many and bitter, you will restore my life again, from the depths of the earth you will again bring me up. You will increase my honor and comfort me once again."

*David believed this, and so do I. Do you? Amen and Amen*

Berakah

Blessing

# DAY 265

Good morning. Several years ago I read a book written by Rick Warren, a well-known Christian evangelical pastor, entitled The Purpose Driven Life. In it he writes that since life is about bringing glory to God, the question to be answered is "How can I bring glory to God?" The answer is by worshiping him, loving other believers, becoming like Christ, serving others with our gifts, and telling others about him. Just as I firmly believe that there are no coincidences in life, I also willingly concede that all life is purposeful. God has created an amazing balance that allows His creation, Earth, to exist. (I must admit that I still struggle with spiders and mosquitoes.) There are, however, some actions that seem to detract from our purpose, to bring glory to God, as they are self-deprecating and often challenge the human spirit. In my mind they are worry, anxiety, depression and anger. I can't count how many "butterflies" have anxiously fluttered in my stomach, or how often sweaty palms from needless worry have afflicted me. Occasionally depression has darkened even the sunniest day, and why, oh why, have I allowed anger to flare and enflame my actions. Warren reminds me that worship is not about what pleases us, but about what makes God smile. God smiles when we love, trust, obey, and praise him, and when we use our abilities for His glory.

*How can I bring glory to God? Jesus says it even better than Pastor Warren. "Love the lord your God with all your heart, with all your soul and with all your mind, and your neighbor as yourself." Amen and Amen*

# DAY 266

Good morning. Somebody said to me a day or so ago, "I love your hugs." Was it just the hug, or was there something different about it? I treat hugs as a contact sport. If you are not into hugs, you'd better steer clear of me. Now mind you, I do try to respect the folks made uncomfortable by hugs, but if you need one, I'm the guy you are looking for. I feel the same way about my journaling. You are not going to be forced to read what I write, nor are you expected to respond unless you feel called to do so. I do, however, feel very blessed to know that what I write may at times be meaningful to you. God has called me into a relationship with him, and I feel compelled to share His and my thoughts, as far as I comprehend them. There are times that He challenges me, convicts me, and covers me in his unparalleled love. When I write, I literally feel his arms hugging me, holding me, confirming for me that He indeed is Lord and I belong to him, for better or for worse.

*If you need a friend, I'm here. If you need an ear, mine is open. Some days I might show my tears, other times my smiles or laughs, now and then even my fears, but I am always ready to show my love and especially share my hugs with God first, and then you! Amen and Amen*

# DAY 267

Good morning. Did you know that "fear" is one of the most common words used in the Bible? It, or something derived from it, appears over eighty times. It seems that we have always lived in a world filled with danger and fear. The world we live in today is surely no exception. There are wars, terror, crime, disease, hate, prejudice, distrust, poverty; that doesn't even count the many things like the unknown, darkness, heights, spiders, snakes and scary clowns. For many of us fear even follows us into our slumber to become nightmares. Do you wake up fearful of what the day might bring? Take heart, fear touched even Peter “The Rock,” and Paul on the road to Damascus. David feared his many enemies and Abraham was fearful at the altar on the mountain. The Bible furnishes us with no less than sixty-four thoughts about "courage" and "encouragement." Isaiah declared God’s words to Israel, "So do not fear, for I am with you; I will uphold you with my righteous right hand. All who rage against you will surely be ashamed and disgraced; those who oppose you will be as nothing and perish. Though you search for your enemies, you will not find them. Those who wage war against you will be as nothing at all. For I am the Lord, your God, who takes hold of your right hand and says to you, do not fear; I will help you." (Isaiah 41:10-13).

*Hold out your right hand! Reach for him, He is right there with you, waiting to allay all your fears. Amen and Amen*

# DAY 268

Good morning. We should be thoughtful and careful when selecting words to label another person's character. An example: there is a great difference between saying I judge him by his character and joking that he's known to be quite the character. An actor might play a character from a novel or in a movie, but his character is part of him. Personality and character are related, but a bit different. A person could be friendly, funny and eccentric, but be careful that you don't speak of those as his character traits—they are personality traits. His character and reputation could be described as exemplary and kind. When someone talks about your "character," what do you hope they might be saying? You might select from trustworthy, honest, faithful, dynamic, humble, creative, considerate, happy, or reverent. You certainly wouldn't want your reputation and character to be described as angry, hateful, dysfunctional, calculating, fickle, disrespectful, intolerant, or prejudiced.

*Many people today would like to possess wisdom, a character trait highly prized in the Bible. But James 1:5 says the best way to get it is to ask for it from God. "If any of you lacks wisdom, you should ask God, who gives generously to all without finding fault, and it will be given to you." What characteristics do you desire in yourself? Live it in your daily life. Make it so. You are in the driver's seat. Amen and Amen*

# DAY 269

Good morning. I have a really good friend who doesn't believe in God. I am well aware that he is not alone and I know that some of the "great" thinkers, scientists and philosophers disagree with the premise that there is a God. There is no empirical evidence, they say. I would ask them, "Can you conclusively disprove the existence of God?" Christians believe the Bible. Others say the Bible is one sided history and the rest fairy tale. I would ask them, "Have you read it, studied it, let its words sink in? Can you explain why believers tend to live longer, healthier lives, have fewer broken relationships, are less likely to be drug offenders, alcoholics and commit fewer crimes? Empirically, that's a fact! Some say, "If he is real, why doesn't he show himself?" The answer is right before our eyes. He shows himself every day. You are breathing His air, you woke up to His dawn display, saw His trees, flowers, bumblebees, rivers, oceans and mountains. If you understand the complexities of DNA, the formulation of our planet, or the technicalities of our ecosystem, how could you not believe God created and sustains our planet? As for my friend and many more, I will continue to pray for you all and let the Lord do the rest.

*Maybe when they least expect it they will have a God moment. He won't give up on them. Amen and Amen*

# DAY 270

Good morning. Have you ever felt compelled to write in BIG LETTERS to make a kind of parenthetical point? You know, the ( ) part that helps to clarify what someone is trying to say. Let me put it this way. It's like now, when I feel like SHOUTING, all caps! Why is that? I will tell you. There was a time in my life when I said, "I didn't see him coming." It came right out of the gospel song, "Amazing Grace," line eighteen, "I was blind but now I see." Have you ever rolled through a stop sign or entered a dark room without turning on the lights? That was me! I was much like Bartimaeus, the blind beggar from Jericho who cried out to Jesus. I have never been a beggar nor have I been blind, but I had to ask how many times had Jesus passed by me and I didn't see him? Thank goodness Jesus is always seeking to find the lost and the spiritually blind ones like me. I'm not really sure whether I found him or He found me, but it doesn't really matter. Let's just say He was right on time! My experience wasn't like the invitation offered Cephas (Peter) or the blinding light that stopped Saul (Paul) on the road to Damascus, but it was at a point in my life when I was more than ready to quit running and going nowhere. In the midst of a thundering crowd I STOPPED and cried out to him, "Help me! I'm lost!" and He said quietly, "Just follow me. I am the Way."

*Just like the song, I was blind but now I see. I was lost and now I'm found! May it be so for you. Amen and Amen*

# DAY 271

Good morning. How far are you willing to go to defend your faith? For most of us that challenge has never been issued, or has it? One only has to turn on their television or connect with the Internet to see how flawed we have become. We turn our heads as if there was nothing tearing at the fabric of what we believe and hold dear. We call it being politically correct then say we don't trust political figures. We let prayer become illegal, we accept that others find a crèche so offensive it must be removed, we all but disavow the Ten Commandments. We stop using the word Christmas when greeting one another in a public place. Not very important, you think? If our Bibles were taken away, would you resist? Would you even miss them? If our churches were closed or made illegal, would you stand up or stand down? We allow flags to be burned and Bibles to be desecrated in the name of freedom for all. What kind of freedom is that?!

*If God asked you to carry a cross, would you accept? None of this is new. Ask Peter, Paul, Stephen, Timothy or Apollos. Ask Lincoln, Kennedy or Martin Luther King. Would you give your life for Jesus? He gave his for you! Amen and Amen*

Chazaq

לְחַזֵּק

Strengthen

# DAY 272

Good morning. What makes you angry? It may be lots of things. Some of us even wake up angry! But it could be because 1. It's an ugly day, too cold, rainy, snowing, too hot...it's all bad. 2. The boss, teacher, landlord is a real blankety-blank. 3. My big brother, little brother is a mess. 4. The job, school, housework is just too difficult. 5. The baby won't stop crying or the kids won't stop arguing. 6. Traffic drives me crazy. 7. My husband/ wife never listens (mostly husbands). 8. The government never gets it right. 9. I can't trust anybody. 10. God just isn't fair. You get my point. What a waste of time. There is little or no value in being angry. My Dad used to tell me, "Bite your tongue." Somehow that never worked very well, but I understood what he meant. So, what's the antidote for a bout with anger? Good question. For starters, I have personally found that a strong dose of forgiveness works very well. When your temperature cools down, communication is recommended. Pray every morning and evening until your symptoms disappear. Patience is required if you want to receive the full benefit of the prescription.

*It is highly recommended that you exercise your smile and laughter muscles often during each day in order for them not to atrophy. Amen and Amen*

# DAY 273

Good morning. The daily news tells us that much of the world is waking up to devastation of one sort or another. I makes me pause to think what little a "good morning" greeting would mean if I was suddenly a displaced person. If you were faced with having to give up nearly everything, what would you select to keep with you? That brand new suit or fancy dress would serve no purpose. Microwaves and televisions wouldn't make the cut. Extra this or extra that? Not on your life. No fine china or sterling, but perhaps a sharp knife, a spoon and a fork in hopes you would find food.  You would be faced with leaving your bed, your couch, grandmother's rocking chair and the pictures that hang on the wall. You couldn't carry fresh clothes for each day of the week, but might pull on a pair of sturdy jeans, a sweat shirt, woolen socks and shoes that will last. You mustn't be without a coat for cold weather along with bottled water tucked in every pocket and rolled up in the bedding. You'll want to grab your Bible, a photo or two, a toothbrush, a cup and a skillet. With no idea of where you are going or how long it will take to get there, your burden will be heavy indeed. What should you do?

*Jesus said to trust him, because He will always be with us. He said that His yoke is easy and His burden is light. If I am ever faced with all those choices, I choose him first. Amen and Amen*

# DAY 274

Good morning. How many "what ifs" or "if onlys" do you have in your possession? If only I had gone to college, joined the navy, taken that job, married that guy or girl. What if I had saved more for retirement, had treated my kids differently? If only I had told her how much I really cared. Why didn't I follow the directions? Let's see, was it one cup of cream and two cups of flour or two cups of cream and one cup of flour or was it water? Did you say turn left, then right or was it turn right then left? What if Pinocchio never told a lie or Humpty Dumpty never fell off the wall? What if Abraham had never heard the Lord at the altar or Moses decided not to return to Egypt? What if Jesus decided to accept Satan's offer or what if He said, “I can't do this” in the garden? Don't waste your time looking backward, what is done is done. Empty your pockets! Look for that street called, "No Regrets.”

*Turn your eyes toward Jesus. Look for the stepping stones or maybe even the corner stone that lies just ahead. Won't you accept His invitation to follow him? He came just for you! Amen and Amen*

# DA Y 275

Good morning. We have all overlooked something one time or another. Let's talk about a song that does the opposite: it calls attention to some things we usually don't give much attention. It's a 1927 Irish melody made famous by Emmy Rossum and Willy Nelson. The lyrics begin, "I'm looking over a four leaf clover that I overlooked before. First is the sunshine, the second is rain. Third is the roses that grow in the lane. No need explaining, the one remaining is somebody I adore. I'm looking over a four leaf clover I overlooked before..." Pretty simple little ditty, isn't it? Michael W. Smith reminds us of yet another essential in our daily lives that most often goes without mention: "This is the air I breathe. Your holy Presence living in me. This is my daily bread, your very word spoken to me, and I'm desperate for you and I'm lost without you..." Instead of sunshine, rain and roses it may be mountains and streams or many other things we overlook, but always remember the ones you love and never overlook the One who always loves you, through rain and shine, thick and thin, now and forever.

*Oh! Lord, I adore you, I'm desperate for you! Amen and Amen*

# DAY 276

Good morning. Are you on the brink? Who has not thought "I just can't take it anymore," one time or another? When you have been betrayed, your cancer has returned, your son is in deep trouble or your daughter has turned to drugs, you have lost a child or a family member, your relationship is failing, your finances are in a shambles, and on and on...when you are at the end of your rope, where do you turn? When someone tries to tell you that God won't give you more than you can handle, don't believe it! The truth is, God will give you more than you can handle, but there is nothing that He can't handle! Offer him your pain and your tears. When David faced his worst fears, he wrote, "Lead me to the rock that is higher than I, for you have been my refuge, a strong tower against the enemy." (Psalm 61:2-3) Trust in the Lord with all your heart and your soul; He will never forsake you. When the road ahead seems too dark and too rugged to walk alone, He will walk right beside you and if necessary he will carry you, if only you let him.

*Now here is an opening prayer for you to repeat with David: "Hear my cry, O God, give heed to my prayer. From the end of the earth I call to you, when my heart is faint. Lead me to the rock that is higher than I." Now add your own words to him. He is listening for your voice. Amen and Amen*

# DAY 277

Good morning. The other day we were driving down the road and a majestic deer strolled out of the woods! I missed it. Then an American Bald Eagle soared over our nearby lake. I missed it. Movie openings, new stock options, job opportunities, chances of a lifetime; I've missed them, too. Most of us have. It's past time for us to be purposely seeing the opportunities God offers us each day. If you haven't had the occasion to see tall, snow covered mountain peaks or great ocean waves, you really haven't missed them. But if you haven't watched your child or grandchild play soccer or perform in the marching band or a recital, you've missed an appointment with a gift from God! If you haven't had the opportunity to visit Disney World, you really haven't missed it, but if you meet someone God has sent your way you've missed an appointment with a blessing from Our Father. Look at your life with your spiritual eyes wide open, don't miss the beautiful sights and sounds of God's creation, and don't miss the people He has appointed to interact with you.

*Don't miss the time that is given you to meet with the Son of God. Get to know him and you will have no regrets about the things you've missed and you will see more clearly what you've really been missing. Amen and Amen*

# DAY 278

Good morning. Are you a dreamer? I'm not really referring to scenes that appear in your head when you are in a state of slumber. When I attempted to define just what it means to be a dreamer, I checked what the dictionary has to say. This is what I found: "One that dreams (duh); one who lives in a world of fancy and imagination; one who has ideas or conceives projects regarded as impractical, speculative, visionary." Excuse me, Mr. Webster, but I take issue on that last one. When I was very young my teachers suggested that I was a day dreamer, that my mind was often somewhere else. And I must admit that they were right! As I grew older I continued to dream, in fact I still do. If dreams are so fanciful why do we speak of achieving our dreams? Why is it that I see my wife and family as my dreams come true? Why is it that the Bible refers to dreams and visions dozens and dozens of times in circumstances from Genesis to Revelation? One that cries out to me is Joel 2:28. "And it shall come to pass afterward that I will pour out my spirit upon all flesh, and your sons and daughters shall prophesy, your old men shall dream dreams, your young men shall see visions." I believe many song writers and poets are dreamers at heart and that seeking to achieve one's dreams is not fanciful or impractical at all.

*If God has made you a dreamer, don't be afraid to follow your dreams...and may all your dreams come true! Amen and Amen*

Immanuel

עִמָּנוּ אֵל

The Lord With Us

# DAY 279

Good morning. When I was a very young boy I was a bit of a challenge to my teachers. You could say with certainty that I was not a motivated learner. It was a very long time before I recognized the value of education. It was the teachers who never gave up on me that made the difference, thank goodness, and there was a lesson to be learned: it is never too late. Consequently, as a teacher, coach, and even as a father, I recognized the value of persistence. I never gave up on a student. As I look back on my favorite teachers, I recognize they were the ones who cared about me. The subject matter was often secondary. I have long since forgotten many of their names, but a few remain firmly implanted in my waning memory bank. But let me tell you about my greatest teacher and friend. The lessons I have learned from him have changed my life forever. He was a young man, but wise beyond his years. He taught me words I never understood before. He taught me how to use my hands and my feet. He taught me how to fish and to stand on my own two feet. It was through him that I learned to trust and learned to love. Have you guessed his name by now? Praise God, my favorite teacher was, and still is, Jesus!

*Thank you, Jesus, for showing me how to get out of the boat. (Matthew 14:22-33) Amen and Amen*

# DAY 280

Good morning. Priere, Gebet, Oracao; just practicing. How many languages can you speak or understand? Are you like me, utterly challenged? From my earliest childhood days, my best friend's parents were deaf, but I never did get a handle on sign language. Latin in high school was a disaster and Spanish in college was not much better. Nanako lived with us for an entire year yet Japanese totally eluded me, as did German when Gunter lived in our home. Thank God, I've picked up marginal English and I'm still working on Tennessean. There is, however, one universal language that we can all speak because the spelling and the words matter little, and that is the language of prayer. The words differ from person to person, sometimes spoken aloud, sometimes not, but always received by our Father, through Jesus. I haven't mastered prayer yet, but I am giving it my all. I know that if I practice it every day I am sure to improve. God will surely understand my imperfections and yours. Prayer is truly the language of Love between us and God.

*Talk to him right now. Tell him you love him. Give him your requests. Listen to His response. God is patiently waiting to hear from you. Amen and Amen*

# DAY 281

Good morning. Back in time, nearly prehistoric, 1962 to be exact, in a college class I was introduced to a children's book written by Charles W. Schulz titled Happiness is a Warm Puppy. As I think back to that time in my life I become aware that this little 64 page book would have a profound effect upon my life and who I would become. Perhaps I had been taking the good things in my life for granted. A child's book, yes, but I soon discovered it to be a diamond in the rough for me. I realized that if you take good for granted you may well filter out that which is good. Life in its simplest form is made up of a microcosm of small things that make us happy, bring us joy. Every blessing we receive is actually a gift from God. Did we deserve them? No more than we deserved the grace offered by His only Son. So what might it be that brings you happiness? What is your warm puppy? Maybe it really is a warm puppy, or it could be countless other small, simple things: that old swing in the backyard, the smell of pumpkin pie fresh from the oven, the purring of a kitten in your lap; a roaring fireplace in the quiet hours of the night, watching your family as they grow, praying in your secret place, long walks early in the morning, or maybe a hot shower after an intense workout or at the end of a long day. Feel the satisfaction that they can bring. Remember what Lucy said, "Happiness is a warm puppy," but know for Sally, "Happiness is having your own library card." Call them by any name, but whatever you call them don't take your "warm puppies" for granted!

*Find your happy places wherever they exist. Grab onto these moments, cherish them, know that they are indeed a gift from God. Amen and Amen*

# DAY 282

Good morning. Glory be to God in the highest! That should be the place we find ourselves each and every morning as we rise up. Without him we are nothing. Everything that I am is because of him, everything I do comes from what He has bestowed on me. I possess no gifts, talents or accomplishments that are not directly derived from him. Don't you remember? “Thine is the Kingdom, the Power and the Glory, forever....” But so often we get all puffed up about who we are and what great things we have accomplished. Keep in mind that we are no more than the wisp of the wind or seed pods of a blown dandelion. We spend a lifetime seeking discernment of our purpose. It becomes much clearer when we recognize that it's not ours at all, but His purpose designed for each one of us. Our strengths, our intelligence, talents or wisdom are but His doing; we had absolutely nothing to do with creating any of it.

*Lord, when I recognize that you are indeed the Holy of Holies, the Glory of Glories, truly the Alpha and the Omega, I offer my thanks, Oh Lord, just to be a part of your Kingdom. May all that I say and do be done to honor Your Name now and forever more! Amen and Amen*

# DAY 283

Good morning. I often struggle with the effort to say something that is bright or at least intelligible, able to be clearly understood. It has been said that wisdom comes with age. I guess I am still awaiting that time. There are plenty of theologians, philosophers, people of superior intellect, who have spent years offering their best observations. How could I possibly do anything of the sort, sitting at our kitchen table with a cup of coffee clutched in my hand, awaiting enlightenment? What is it that is important for us to know about life—or anything, for that matter? Is it the secrets of black holes or knowledge of objects in the solar system, Mars and the dark side of the moon? Or just understanding E=MC2? Maybe it's business dynamics or the process of the socialization of civilization. Then out of the blue, suddenly it came to me; my answers are right here on the table in the Word. It offers us all the answers that we truly need. He can take good care of all the rest! Do you need any primers to understand what I am suggesting? John 16:33 says, "These things I have spoken to you, that in Me you may have peace. In the world you will have tribulation, but be of good cheer, I have overcome the world." Would you consider doing Matthew 22:37-40? “Jesus said unto him, Thou shall love the Lord thy God with all thy heart, and with all thy soul, and with all thy mind. And the second is like unto it, Thou shall love thy neighbor as thyself. On these two commandments hang all the law and the prophets." Luke 1:37 puts it all together in a neat little package. "For nothing will be impossible with God.

*"As I see It, I don't have to reInvent the wheel. HIs Word Is quite enough for me and thee. Amen and Amen*

# DAY 284

Good morning. Have you gone "sour" on life? Do you wonder whatever happened to the "good old days" when you could run like the wind or climb the tallest trees? Now does it seem to take an extra thrust or two just to get out of bed in the mornings, and don't even speak about getting on bended knees. When someone suggests, "Why don't we run to the store," you respond, "You've got to be kidding me!" I used to dream about completing the Appalachian Trail, now I'm perfectly satisfied to sit down and consume a bowl of trail mix. A pickup game is no longer a basketball game, now it is more like Pick Up Stix or Trivial Pursuit. I used to laugh when grown men spoke of taking an afternoon nap; now it's don't mess with my naps! Size thirty-two has been replaced with a size forty-two and a brush now serves the purpose of a comb. Barbers laugh when I say "just trim around the edges." I go more often for prescriptions than I do to for groceries and my doctor is among my closest friends. I used to think I was a stallion, now it is more like the old gray mare. Oh, I know that I am not half the man I used to be—but I am certainly blessed with the half that God has allowed me to be. You see, I know more than ever before about love and friendships. I appreciate my time more than ever before. The Lord and I speak every day and I never miss an opportunity to laugh. I am surely happier with who I am. Do I miss those bygone days? I can truly say, only a little bit. I am pleased to call them memories.

*I call today "special" as it is the day the Lord has made and is pleased to offer to me. Now if I could only figure out how to put on matching socks in the morning. Amen and Amen*

# DAY 285

Good morning. “To each his own.” Have you ever stopped to examine what that means? It means that we are all entitled to our own thoughts and preferences: "I wouldn't choose that color" or 'I'd rather do it my way." Is that how it is in “real” life? I remember the efforts my teacher made to teach me how to write with the right hand (with emphasis upon "right"). My stubbornness won out! But teachers weren't through with me yet. I was instructed to catch a baseball with a right-handed glove and to hit a golf ball in an awkward way for me. And still they wouldn't give up, as in my college days I was a "failure" at handwriting, not because it couldn't be read, but because it wasn't slanted to the right. I struggled to fit in, so after fourteen weeks I passed their test. On the fifteenth week I returned to my normal slant. Today I write my numbers and my letters "backward" and tie my shoes differently from others, but guess what? To each his own! I don't think God created us all to be the same. My eyes are blue and yours are brown. You are tall and I am short. I love to write and you love to draw. My fingerprints and DNA are unique. God likes it that way! We used to be a butcher, a baker, or a candlestick maker; we may now be an astronaut, computer guru or part of a production crew. Here is the bottom line; don't be afraid to be you, God made you just as you are and He said, "It is good." So when anyone tells you, "that's the wrong color," just remember what I did in the second grade: I chose to color my elephant bright blue! *Now here is the one striking concession that must not be forgotten. It’s always best to do it His way. After all, He created us In HIs own image. Amen and Amen*

Channum

חנון

Gracious

# DAY 286

Good morning. I can never pass a Salvation Army bell ringer without dropping something in the kettle. Why do you suppose that is? They offer food for the hungry, shelter for the homeless, and hope for the desperate. God has offered me ears that I might hear the calling of the bells. Can you hear any bells ringing out to you? I can hear the mother of three young children asking if I know of any place she can get some decorations for an empty Christmas tree. I hear a great grandmother who has just inherited three babies because their mother has abandoned them. I hear a young mother who has just lost her leg because of diabetes. I hear the voice of a middle aged man giving sincere thanks for the food received at a mountain care center, saying he doesn't know how he would have made it without help. I hear the homeless at a Bread of Life shelter praying that the year ahead will be better than the last. I hear a rural school requesting shoes and underwear for kids who are without them. I hear the cries of the young who are hopelessly addicted. I hear my friend asking that I pray for her. I hear the haunting pleas of our wounded warriors. God has given us ears to hear, can you hear the bells of need ringing in your ears?

*Every time I hear those bells ringing, this is what I hear: "They will answer, Lord, when did I see you hungry or thirsty or a stranger or needing clothes or sick or in prison, and did not help you?' And "He will reply, truly I tell you, whatever you did not do for one of the least of these, you did not do for me." Matthew 25: 45-46. Amen and Amen*

# DAY 287

Good morning. Today, have you prayed the prayer that our Lord Jesus taught us? Why not? You could explain, I just didn't have time. To tell you the truth, I didn't think about it. It's not Sunday. Does it really matter or make any difference? We only repeat the words, we never really think about what we are saying. Are any of these you? Funny how we can pray for rain or for sun, for improved health, for a promotion or a victory, but His prayer all too often passes through our lips without much real thought. I have to ask, is his name really hallowed? Do you believe his Kingdom will come? Do you really believe you have trespasses to be forgiven and are you ready to forgive others their trespasses against you? Do you really believe that his is the Kingdom, the Power and the Glory forever and ever? Just asking. If you say yes to this prayer let's hear what Israel had to say about over four thousand years ago in Deuteronomy 6:4-9: "Hear, O Israel; the Lord our God, the Lord is One alone. Love the Lord your God with all your heart, with all your soul and with all your strength. Those commandments that I give you today are to be on your hearts. Impress them on your children. Talk about them when you sit at home and when you walk along the road, when you lie down and when you get up. Tie them as symbols on your hands and bind them on your foreheads. Write them on the door frames of your houses and on your gates."

*So let me ask you again, today did you pray the prayer the Lord taught us? It's not too late! Amen and Amen*

# DAY 288

Good morning. Are you a weight lifter? I think we all are or have been at one time or another. No, I am not referring to the barbell variety; I am talking about the kind that we carry upon our shoulders. Though I may disagree with those charged with the awesome and sometimes terrifying responsibility of making decisions for our country and our world, I hold a deep respect for what they have to do. There is no one who can honestly say they have no responsibilities. Let's view a few weights: a job in jeopardy, no work, children doing poorly in school, worries about the failing health of parents, a mate, a child; more days in the month than there is money, depression, concern about community, country, the world, frustration. Anything sound familiar? What's the answer? When our burdens seem heavier than we can bear, turn them all over to the One who handles heaven and earth. He will not only carry your heavy burden, he will also lift you up. In Psalm 145:13-20 King David writes, "The Lord is faithful to all his promises and loving to all He has made. The Lord upholds all those who fall and lifts up all who are bowed down. The eyes of all look to you, and you give them their food at the proper time. You open your hand and satisfy the desires of every living thing. The Lord is righteous in all his ways and loving toward all He has made. The Lord is near to all who call on him, to all who call on him in truth. He fulfills the desire of those who fear him, He hears their cry and saves them. The Lord watches over all who love him."

*I cannot begin to tell you how many times He has lifted the weight laid upon my shoulders. With Just a prayer to him and my burdens are lighter. Amen and Amen*

# DAY 289

Good morning. I have been lamenting about the fact that I have not been communicating with the Lord throughout the day, and that I haven't been in the Word as I should be. I am frustrated at being too busy. Just what is "too busy?" It's busy doing good things, helping others, donating time to ministries, traveling, speaking, teaching; but some of my busyness includes an exorbitant amount of time in often repetitious and sometimes mind numbing activity and entertainment. I feel drawn to do for my country what Ezekiel Chapter 22 called standing in the gap: "I looked for someone among them who would build up the wall and stand before me in the gap on behalf of the land so I would not have to destroy it, but I found no one." God could not find one person willing to stand there. Am I willing? Yes. What is my call to action? To quit wasting the time that has been allotted to me. Millions of us scream and cheer for our favorite team or entertainer, but few of us cry out, persistently pleading for God's mercy on our nation. God is not looking for part time help. He needs twenty-four-seven people, those who seek to serve him and who care about this nation and its people. He's asking, "Is anybody out there? Anybody?"

*Quit finding fault with others, there is enough blame to go around. Pray for a clean heart and a right spirit. It is His desire to save us. Stand in the gap. Pray for revival. Pray to reclaim this land for God. Make a difference. The maker of heaven and earth will always be there, looking for us, listening to us. He is never too busy. Amen and Amen*

# DAY 290

Good morning. Do you believe in second chances? Do you believe in miracles? Do you believe in heaven and eternity? Do you believe in Jesus Christ, our One and only Savior? Just what is it that you believe? My friends, I believe in all of the above, simply because it all begins with him! Why else would the Lord have created us? I can only know that which I know. When I was in my mother's womb, I only knew darkness and the beat of her heart, but I yearned for more! Lord, you gave me eyes to see, ears to hear, a mouth to speak, hands to feel, feet to walk, a mind to think and a heart to love. From the very beginning I was destined to be given a second chance! There would be more, far more. As for miracles, this world of your creation is in itself a miracle. Every breath I take, every thought I possess are miracles in themselves. When we were in the womb we did not know of things beyond us, of flowers and trees, sunsets, turtles and singing birds, of rainbows and promises of tomorrow. You provided my second chance to know you. Yet there is more. Much more!

*Jonathan Cahn speaks these bold words of belief in a second chance. "When you hear of Heaven, you're hearing of it as a child in the womb. You've never seen it or touched it. And yet everything within you was made to know this world, the world of Heaven...with a heart made for love... a soul yearning for that which is eternal, a spirit longing to dwell in a place of no death, no fear, no darkness, no evil." Yes, Lord, yes! A second chance! That is what I want to believe and because of you, I can! Amen and Amen*

# DAY 291

Good morning. You are not just any old somebody. God made you to be somebody. You will always be special in His eyes, but how about in your own eyes? Open them to this: the world is full of somebodies just waiting to meet you! Somebody is very proud of you. Somebody is thinking about you. Somebody misses you. Somebody wants to talk with you. Somebody wants to be your friend. Somebody hopes you are not in trouble. Somebody is thankful for your help. Somebody would like to hold your hand. Somebody hopes everything turns out alright. Somebody wants you to be happy. Somebody hopes you will find him/her. Somebody wants to gift you. Somebody thinks you are a gift. Somebody wants to hug you. Somebody admires your strength. Somebody is smiling at you. Somebody wants to protect you. Somebody can't wait to see you. Somebody loves you for who you are. Somebody treasures your spirit. Somebody is glad you are their friend. Somebody wants to get to know you. Somebody wants to be near you. Somebody wants you to know they are there for you. Somebody would do anything for you. Somebody wants to share their dreams with you. Somebody is alive because of you. Somebody needs your support. Somebody needs you to have faith in them. Somebody trusts you. Somebody hears a song that reminds them of you. Somebody loves you!

*The world is full of somebodies waiting for somebody just like you. Because you are really somebody! Amen and Amen*

# DAY 292

Good morning. I just can't do it! Please don't ask me. Don't call on me. Some things in life seem just too difficult. Does any of this sound familiar to you? Don't despair, you are not alone. History bears me out: Moses, Gideon, Amos, George Washington, and Sgt Alvin C York all responded in similar fashion. I have been reading, The Power of Yes, from the Chicken Soup for the Soul series of books. In this edition there are examples of individuals overcoming their fears and perceived inadequacies to say yes to challenges. What will you respond when God challenges you to teach Sunday School to a group of junior high kids or to lead a men's breakfast group? How will you respond to the homeless shelter that calls out for help or the Ugandan orphan who just wants a pair of shoes or to go to school? Is that new Bible Study just too much for you? Did you know that hospitals, hospice and the Salvation Army always need volunteers? Can you step up and take care of a dying mother or father?

*If the calling that you receive seems too big, God will see that you grow into it. He wants to help you become more than you already are. Believe it and God will make it so! Amen and Amen*

Rachum

Merciful

# DAY 293

Good morning. I love the song, “Amazing Grace,” especially where the refrain says "I was lost but now I'm found.” It came to mind again as I was searching through a Lost and Found column recently, and I couldn't help relating the lost and founds on the page to thoughts about what has been lost and what has been found in my life. My thoughts went this way: What is it that you have lost? There are those earthly possessions like car keys, glasses, cell phones, golf balls, fishing lures. Who hasn't lost their directions on the road, or lost a recipe for a favorite cake or casserole? And what person hasn't lost a board game or a ball game? There are the really big losses, too; losing a loved one, a job, your way—because of addiction, divorce, depression, stubbornness, or illness. That's why I find “Amazing Grace” so comforting. In my Lost and Found musing about life, I found that it was never about me and my gains or my losses; it has always been about him, my Lord and Savior.

*I didn't find him; it was Jesus who found me and offered me the grace that I could never earn on my own. It turns out I haven't lost anything and I've gained everything. Amen and Amen*

# DAY 294

Good Morning. What is it that you have stopped saying? "Good morning," "I love you," "God Bless America," "Thank you, Jesus," "Can I help you?" When did you stop believing in God's promise? In a better tomorrow? Whatever became of compassion, caring and forgiveness? Why is it so difficult to believe that all of us can live together peacefully even with our differences? In truth and in fact we can actually flourish if we are willing to just let go and let God. Let go what? Let God what? Let go, turn everything over to him: the dislikes, the anger, the offense; we are His you know! Our very selves, and their very selves, belong to him. Let God. Let God work in all our lives. Quit looking for what is wrong and start working for what is right. "His divine power has given us everything we need for life and godliness through our knowledge of him who called us by his own glory and goodness." 2 Peter 1:3. Let go and Let God bring our reconciliation.

*And you might like to try using words like I spoke of at the beginning. You may be amazed at how good they make you, feel! Amen and Amen*

# DAY 295

Good morning. What is important to you? Do you consider a good night's sleep or cream in your coffee important? How about rooting for the Yankees or the Warriors? Would you call a good education or a significant job important? Do you consider important the color of socks you wear with a dark suit or the brand of golf balls you use? Do you believe your financial status or your marriage is important? Your family or your physical health? Philippians 3:7-10 is a reminder of what is really important for us to realize. "I once thought all these things were so very important, but now I consider them worthless because of what Christ has done. Yes, everything else is worthless when compared with the priceless gain of knowing Christ Jesus, my Lord. I have discarded everything else, counting it all as garbage, so that I may have Christ and become one with him. I no longer count on my own goodness or my ability to obey God's law, but I trust Christ to save me, for God's way of making us right with himself depends on faith...."

*Nothing on this earth should get in the way of, or come ahead of, our trust in Jesus Christ, our Lord and Savior. We don't need to be blinded as Paul was on the Damascus Road to see this. It's there, right before our very eyes. Amen and Amen*

# DAY 296

Good morning. Can you remember when you opened your first savings account? For many it was probably a small piggy bank or something similar. I can barely remember that little pink bank, but how I cherished it. Did I comprehend why I was saving my change? Probably not! Then came my first savings account at a neighborhood bank. I can still remember how very proud I was to put in ten dollars straight from my paper route earnings. I thought I was really rich when my earnings swelled to a hundred dollars. From eleven years old until I was preparing for college I managed to save enough to purchase all my own clothes and basic needs for beginning the college life. After marriage and three children, savings became a real challenge. It was then that a new kind of "savings" began to develop: planning for the future—education, a house, a church for our children to grow up in. There weren't a lot of dollars being saved but I sure thought of it as "lifesaving." Later, the savings plan grew when retirement funds and IRA's were added to the mix. Then the greatest savings of all emerged; accepting Jesus Christ as my "lifesaving" Savior, my true savings account kept safe in him. He taught me how to use my savings to be a hand up for others. He taught me how to put all my trust in him. They say, "You can't take it with you." Don't believe it even for a minute. What's really important, eternally valuable, will stay in your account forever and ever.

*Don't you want to invest in God's savings plan? It's far superior to any other. You can never empty it; the more you pour out the more you will receive. Is all this really true? You can bank on it! Amen and Amen*

# DAY 297

Good morning. Do you have things you'd like to know? I am not speaking of wishes as in a wishing well or for the bottle that contains a genie. In the grand scheme of things there is much to know and as it is, we actually know very little. In school we learn about letters and words. They teach us how to count, add and subtract. We learn about the past and how a flower grows. We learn to play ball and how to draw. We learn when to stand up and when to sit down. We are taught the "rules of the game." But all too often we are taught that memorizing is good and little effort is given to thinking on your own. So, I would like to know why music or a hot shower makes me feel good. When do we get old? What makes the rivers flow and why do birds sing so beautifully in the early morning? What makes something beautiful? Or not so much? It is good to know I can ask my Heavenly Father some things I want to know. O God, why did Jesus love me so much that He would die on a cross for me? Where is the end of the universe? Can you really hear my thoughts? Can you hear me now? What does tomorrow look like? Are my yesterday's all that I can expect or can I hope for much more? These are just a sampling of things I would like to know! Most of all I want to know You, Father God, and Jesus and The Holy Spirit.

*Heavenly Father, what purpose do You have in store for me? Show me how to love even more. Can I learn to be more like Jesus? And won't you tell me why I am follicle challenged? One more thing. I would still like to know why you created mosquitos. Amen and Amen*

# DAY 298

Good morning. It doesn't take much to throw us off track, does it? Some of us might refer to it as a "bad hair day." Isn't it ironic that I would refer to anything as being bad for hair. Mine is absent! Let's say you get up a half hour late or the engine in your car won't start. The milk is sour and you're out of coffee. You have a serious hangnail on your little toe and your contact lens has disappeared down the drain. The printer doesn't work and the computer says you are "offline." You completely forgot about yearbook pictures and you wore your blue jeans with holes in them. Isn't this the day you are scheduled to have a wisdom tooth removed or is it a colonoscopy? It's Monday morning already! It's Tuesday and you thought for sure it was Friday. You forgot your anniversary. They are serving Brussels sprouts for lunch and your new puppy reminded you that he is not housebroken yet. You don't have hot water. Is that all that is bothering you? Here is the Bible's answer to all that and more: "For our present troubles are quite small and won't last very long. Yet they produce for us an immensely great glory that will last forever. So we don't look at the troubles we see right now; rather we look forward to what we have not yet seen. For the troubles we see will soon be over, but the joys to come will last forever." 2 Corinthians 4:17-18.

*So if you don't mind seeing me without my broken upper plate, I won't let it bother me either. Amen and Amen*

# DAY 299

Good morning. I love what Mother Teresa is quoted as saying: “I alone cannot change the world, but I can cast a stone across the waters, to create many ripples." Through her deep faith and trust in God, her "Missionaries of Charity" has grown nearly four-hundred times, all over the world, without the aid of politicians, kings, armies or federal mandates. What ripples are we creating? There are far too many in this nation and the world who have chosen to throw stones rather than casting them on the water for the betterment of our communities, our nations, and our world. There is much danger in all the unwarranted criticism and harsh condemnation heard everywhere. As it says in Romans 14:10-11, "So why do you condemn another? Why do you look down on another? Remember each of us will stand personally before the judgment seat of God. For the Scriptures say “As surely as I live, says the Lord, every knee will bow before me and every tongue will confess allegiance to God." Are we throwing rocks to hurt and harm or skipping stones across the waters to create ripples of mercy and goodness?

*I say we are aligned with God or against him. Some may say “What does God have to do with it?” The answer is Everything!!!” So where will you pledge you allegiance? Amen and Amen*

Nefesh

Soul

# DAY 300

Good morning. “There is only so much I can do.” Yes, but there is so much that you can do. Your only limitations are those given to you by God and they can be stretched far beyond our Earthly notions. Too often we succumb to "I just can't do it." We say it is just too difficult or I tried and I failed. Soooo..... failure is never final. Quitting is. Interestingly enough there is always a chance to start over either way. How lucky we are to have a God who says, "All things are possible." What if Abraham and Sarah thought they were too old and the trail was too far? What if David thought he was only meant to be a shepherd? What if Martin Luther resisted nailing the Ninety-five Theses on the wall? What if Abraham Lincoln said I have already lost too many times? What if Thomas Edison gave up on the light bulb after 25-50 attempts? What if Jonas Salk quit believing in a cure for Polio? What if Martin Luther King had said we can never overcome? And what if Jesus had said anything but the Cross?

*So what's stopping you? Dare to dream big dreams. Never give up on your visions. Believe in yourself even when everyone else doesn't. God gave you a lifetime to get there. Trust in the Lord. There is so much that you can do. Once you get rid of the 't, you can do anything! Amen and Amen.*

# DAY 301

Good morning. What direction are you headed? If you answered north, south, east or west, that is the wrong answer. Many of us wait until somebody else gives us directions. “Tell me what to do, tell me what I need.” What ever happened to making decisions? We ask “What am I going to do today, next week, next year, in my lifetime?” Too often the answer is “I haven't a clue.” Why is it that some know just what they want, while others wander aimlessly as if in the black of night? Because vision isn't about seeing 20/20, it’s about seeing the vision. Look for the light, don't be afraid to make a decision; don't back down from exploring your visions and by all means don't be wary of learning who you are or what you were meant to be. Every one of us was born endowed with a purpose. Whatever it is that you do, do it with exuberance. Be the best you can be. You don't have to be the best, you only have to do your best.

*Don't spend your life trying to be or do. That is like walking on a treadmill, lots of effort gets you nowhere. Most importantly, pray every day, for God knows your direction, and He will unerringly guide you if only you are willing to trust in him. Amen and Amen*

# DAY 302

Good morning. It has been said that we are a product of our environment. We are, indeed, a microcosm of everything that surrounds us; our relationships, our families, our society. Some say we are what we eat. Boy, that's a scary thought. Others say our values are often directly derived from what our checkbook tells us. (Be careful of overdrafts). More often we identify with our credit cards. As I search myself in the mirror, am I satisfied with what I see there? (It's always better from a distance.) But then, that is what mirrors are for, to see yourself as you are, not as you perceive yourself to be. Time is a necessary element in who we are. A case in point is how we spend our time. Think about this for a nanosecond. If you watch television for three hours a day, in a year that's nearly eleven hundred hours, a decade is eleven thousand hours and in a lifetime nearly seventy-seven thousand hours. Let's add another four hundred hours on the Internet and two hundred on the cell phone. That will put us at about one hundred and twenty thousand hours in a single lifetime—and there are no nine lives for us. If we have sixteen usable hours per day that computes to approximately seventy five thousand days or twenty and a half years. How does that work in our value systems? How many books could we read? How many could have benefited from our care? Imagine, if we spent just thirty minutes per day with the Lord and the Word, in a lifetime we would share more than three and a half years together.

*Maybe It's time to look into the mirror of our lives and seriously assess what is truly important. Amen and Amen*

# DAY 303

Good morning. I was baptized by water many years ago, but it took considerably longer before I became baptized by His light. Let me explain. I often found myself walking through life all by myself. I completely forgot or ignored being a part of a much greater power. When it all began to fall apart, who could I blame but myself? I had ignored my Maker along the way, so guess what? I turned back to him, the One who gave me my abilities, intellect, creativity, strength and most of all His Spirit. Forgiven and prayerful, I asked for help and He guided me into the Word. First I found Isaiah 65:1-2, "I revealed myself to those who did not ask for me. I was found by those who did not seek me. To a nation that did not call my name. I said, here am I, here am I. All day long I held out my hands to an obstinate people who walk in ways not good, pursuing their own imaginations." He had been calling me but I hadn't listened! Next I came to Isaiah 29:15-16, "Woe to those who go to great depths to hide their plans from the Lord, who do their work in darkness and think, Who sees us? Who will know? You turn things upside down as if the potter were thought to be like the clay! Shall what is formed say to him who formed it, He did not make me? Can the pot say to the potter, He knows nothing?" Had I thought I could live life my way? I felt ashamed. And so I came to Isaiah 64:8, "Yet, O Lord, you are our Father. We are the clay, you are the potter, we are all the work of your hands." I realized that I was the clay and that God wasn't finished with me yet!

It *was at this point when, much like Saul on the road to Damascus, I finally saw the Light and became His and He became mine forever! Amen and Amen*

# DAY 304

Good morning. While lying comfortably in my warm bed earlier this morning, I came to the realization that I must be a time traveler. I don't recall any fancy time machines or a modified DeLorean car delivering me to the past and back before I even got out of bed, but it must be true. How do I know this? I distinctly remember using real silver coins to buy things and eating meals with real silver utensils. It was summer, and get this, we all opened our windows when the heat became unbearable, and we actually rolled down the windows in our cars. Folks hung their sheets and clothes outside on clotheslines to dry. Kids played outdoors and rode bicycles until called inside to eat with the family. The milk man delivered milk right to the door. I saw men shining their shoes and taking their clothes to a dry cleaners. There were people at the library reading. At bedtime children were reciting, “Now I lay me down to sleep, I pray the Lord my soul to keep. If I should die before I wake, I pray the Lord my soul to take."

*A couple more things stand out from my time travel into the past. School began with the Pledge of Allegiance and you could pray in school. And this I know for sure, there was a real Jesus listening then and He is very much alive today! Amen and Amen*

# DAY 305

Good morning. The love of my life sat across from me at the breakfast table this morning. It was difficult for me not to notice the colorful shirt she was wearing. On it were several buckets dripping paint with the inscription, "Creative minds are seldom tidy." Why, I must be one of the most creative minds that has ever lived! I thought. Tidiness is not my forte. My next thought was about God's unequaled creativity. Doubt my assessment? Consider this: He created the Heavens and the Earth, night and day, mountains and seas, grass and trees and of course the birds and the bees. How many flowers do you suppose He has created on this planet and how many bees and butterflies do you suppose it takes to germinate them? Does a rainbow make you whistle in appreciation? Could you dream up a platypus, elephant or zebra? He created humans and then there's this to wrap your head around: no two human fingerprints or DNA are alike! Does a mountain so high that you can barely see the top take your breath away? Not to mention the birth of a child.

*And how about this: God created a way to forever eliminate sin and death by sending his only Son to pay the price for it and save us for eternity. Yes, I would say He's the Master when it comes to creativity! Amen and Amen*

# DAY 306

Good morning. I love a quote from Ben Carson. "A father said to his son, 'Be careful where you walk.' The son responded, 'You be careful; I walk in your footsteps.'" How true that is in the world in which we live. Proverbs 22:6 put it like this: "Train up a child in the way he should go, and when he is old, he will not depart from it." How are we doing? Are we the examples we are called to be? You may not realize it, but you are their most profoundly important teacher. Love them. Introduce them to Jesus Christ and they will know the deepest meaning of love. We are not only teaching our sons and daughters by our actions, we are passing down a set of values. English, mathematics, science and geography are all important, but if you don't teach a strong work ethic, taking responsibility, and "Love your neighbor," they will be lost in a sea of doubt and confusion.

*And by all means teach them to pray for the answers you cannot give them. Amen and Amen*

Bara

Create

# DAY 307

Good morning. How's your memory? You might be thinking, "It ain't so good." As a teacher long ago, I remember countless young students trivializing their ability to remember. I recall many a young man who couldn't remember to tie his own shoes, but knew the batting average for every major league player; and my granddaughter who forgot things but could recite virtually every song on the radio. Aging can do that too. As for me, I struggle to remember which pills I have or have not taken or where I left my glasses and my keys. But remembering and memorizing are not the same, although both require some stretching, actually more like practicing. The more you do it, the better you get. So how do you do that? Begin by memorizing a scripture that's meaningful to you. Start small (as in short) and work your way up (as in longer). Here are three to try on for size, or find your own. Psalm 4:23 "Above all else, guard your heart, for it is the wellspring of life." Philippians 4:13 "I can do all things through Christ who strengthens me." Mark 16:15 "Go into the world and preach the Good News to everyone." Soon you will be ready to go long. Isaiah 43:1-3 "Fear not, for I have redeemed you; I have called you by your name; you are mine. When you pass through the waters, I will be with you, and through the rivers, they shall not overflow you. When you walk through the fire, you shall not be burned. Nor shall the flames scorch you. For I am the Lord, your God. The Holy One of Israel, your Savior."

*Who knows, maybe the entire Gospels await your memorization! Now I have got to go. I just remembered where I left my keys. Have a great day! Amen and Amen*

# DAY 308

Good morning. It's often stated that you can determine someone's values or what they deem important by simply searching their checkbook. That would never work in my case since my checkbook is seldom used and I maintain no log of entries. Do you suppose that means I am without values or that there is nothing I think is important in my life? I certainly hope that is not the case. It is also said that if you don't master what you do, it will master you. It is no wonder that the ancient biblical term for other gods was Baal, which translated "master." An alternant meaning was "owner." So what or who is your master, your owner? Perhaps it is money, success, power, pleasure, or even self-indulgence. Careful, they may become your master, your idol, your Baal. Take inventory, there is only one true Master, and that is the Lord our God. By allowing yourself to become his possession you will no longer be owned or mastered by anything but his love. That's what is called Freedom!

*Whatever you give the highest value to in your life will determine who or what owns you. In 1 Kings it says: "If the Lord is God, follow him!" That's good advice. Amen and Amen*

# DAY 309

Good morning. Have you ever said something like this? "I would die for a hot fudge sundae." Or perhaps, "I am dying to see the World Series." It seems that we are sometimes pretty flippant about what we would die for. Our military is deadly serious about being willing to die for our country. Jesus didn't take dying on the cross lightly, either. Neither did his disciples. Remember who it was that gave us the gift of life in the first place. Genesis 2:7: "And the Lord formed a man's body from the dust of the ground and breathed into it the breath of life... And man became a living person." Our lives are precious. Just how precious? John 10:10: "My purpose is to give life in all its fullness." God himself made us on purpose and for His purpose. Examine what Psalm 139 says about life, "Thank you for making me so wonderfully complex! Your workmanship is marvelous." The apostle Paul explained what living meant to him in Philippians 1:21-22. "For to me, living is for Christ and dying is even better. Yet I live, and that means I have fruitful service to give to Christ."

*So what is it that is worth giving up the most precious thing we have, life itself? Would you die for Country? Family? Friends? Would you become a martyr for your love of Jesus, if necessary? He died for you! You are that precious to him! Amen and Amen.*

# DAY 310

Good morning. They say if you are feeling bad or low, just begin to think about a few of your favorite things. In fact there is a song about favorite things. Julie Andrews performed it in The Sound of Music many years ago. The things weren't the big things in life like cars, boats, houses, and other possessions, but many of the simple things that cross our paths over time. Do you remember how the song begins? "Raindrops on roses and whiskers on kittens, bright copper kettles and warm woolen mittens, brown paper packages tied up with strings...." There were plenty more: cream colored ponies, snowflakes and blue satin sashes..... Here are a few of the things that keep me smiling: raindrops on tin roofs, kittens purring, slices of coconut cream pie, mountain streams rushing downhill and big puffy clouds floating high in the sky. I love red sunsets and lightning bugs glowing, bright smiling faces, sloppy joes and big fluffy pillows. I enjoy fireplaces and steaks on the grill, mountains all around and flowers galore, the smell of fresh popcorn and pumpkin pies in the oven; spice drops and Reese cups, thick down blankets and the singing of Celine Dion.

*What about your favorite things? Make a mental list and you'll begin to smile. There are so-o-o-many favorite things I could name, and that's why I seldom feel sad. Oh, and there is always a place for hugs and feeling Jesus nearby. Hope that works for you as well. Amen and Amen*

# DAY 311

Good morning. My morning readings brought me to this quote: "Never rest on what you have known or done, but come to him newly, each day, as for the first time." We so often look to what we know quite smugly, a "my way or the highway" kind of intellect. So what happens when the highway ends or comes to a fork in the road? You cannot possibly know all that any day holds. As you approach your day, keep these instructions in your mind, "You shall love the Lord your God with all your heart, with all your soul, and with all your mind. This is the first and greatest commandment and the second is like it; you shall love your neighbor as yourself." (Matthew 22:37-39) God's reminder to Paul was a humbling, unidentified affliction that kept him aware that he was like all other men. Don't become so absorbed in who you are or what you have done; the credit is really not yours at all. That is how the Pharisees failed, moving from righteousness to self-righteousness. You can see what that got them! You can become the fruit of His vine, but remember who the Vine is—the Lord Jesus.

*Lord Jesus, like a young child, I sit on the edge of my seat, a student excited to hear what you have in store for me to see and hear and feel and learn this day. Amen and Amen*

# DAY 312

Good morning. Have you ever started reading a book, but never finished it? Many a student has chosen Cliffs Notes over actually reading their assigned book, while there are a few others who choose to read only the ending. This is like seeing a picture of a beautiful flower garden without the colors or cooking an apple pie without the aroma it creates. Unfortunately, we leave more than books unfinished. Have you ever started a job you didn't finish or attended a school only to leave before you completed your course of study? How many friendships have never connected because you gave up too soon? It's much like attempting to complete a puzzle without all the pieces. There is much to be said about staying the course. Many a victory has been won by those who refused to give up. If you are feeling defeated or overwhelmed, don't turn away, turn around to the Bible. It can show you the way out of the darkest places. 2 Timothy says, “I have fought the good fight. I have finished the race. I have kept the faith." Or maybe you need Isaiah 40:29-31, “He gives strength to the weary and increases the power of the weak. Even youths grow tired and weary, and young men stumble and fall, but those who hope in the Lord will renew their strength. They will soar on wings like eagles, they will run and not grow weary, they will walk and not be faint."

*The one that I call on so often is Philippians 4:13, "I can do all things through him who gives me strength.” Now I can have confidence that I can finish the day well, whatever it brings. Amen and Amen*

# DAY 313

Good morning. I just heard someone say, "What a beautiful day!" What is it that makes the day beautiful? It could be the skies of blue, the majestic clouds with the sun shining through. Then it could be songbirds in the colorful trees and butterflies in the flower garden. Maybe it's the unseen but felt coolness of the morning dew or the whispering wind. Perhaps it is the miracle of God's light overcoming the darkness of the night. You have probably heard it said that everything is beautiful. Ray Stevens sang it out loud and clear, “Everything is beautiful in its own way, like a starry summer night or a snow covered winter's day. And everybody's beautiful in their own way. Under God's heaven the world's gonna find a way... We shouldn't care about the length of his hair, or the color of his skin. Don't worry about what shows from without, but the love that lives within...." God made you beautiful in His own way; you are a reflection of His love for you. He spoke of it in the Bible in Song of Songs 6:10: "Who is this they ask, arising like the dawn, as beautiful as the moon, as bright as the sun..." It’s you! If only you will forget about yourself and focus on the beauty of His radiance, then you too will shine with His marvelous light.

*It is His radiance reflected in us that removes the evidence of our imperfections and leaves us truly beautiful, so we can join in, forgiven and purified, singing and shouting, “Oh, what a beautiful day!” Amen and Amen*

Tahor

Pure

# DAY 314

Good morning. Is the dark cloud of long-gone yesterdays still hanging over you? Are you anxious about what lies ahead? Are you angry at the world, or maybe even at God himself? You need clouds dispersed, hope for the future, and peace. Through his Word, God has an answer for your every need. No excuses, now. Look up these helpful scriptures I have found. If you are frustrated, try Matthew 7:7-11 or James 3:13-18. Lonely? Psalm 22 or maybe John 10:14-16. If you need patience for what lies ahead, then 2 Thessalonians 1:3-5 or James 5:7-11 is for you. Maybe faith and hope are what you need. Read Matthew 15:21-28, Romans 10:5-13 or 1 Peter 1:3-7. Need to feel God's love? 1 Corinthians Chapter 13. Experiencing the loss of a loved one? Psalm 23, Isaiah 25:6-12 or John 3:16-17. Is being forgiven a burden that's holding you hostage? Psalm 32, Matthew 18:21-35 or Ephesians 4:32.

*Whatever the need, you will find the answer. If someone tells you that you can't get there from here, don't believe them for an instant! "And you will seek Me and find Me, when you search for Me with all your heart." Jeremiah 29:13 Amen and Amen*

# DAY 315

Good morning. Have you read Acts, chapter twenty nine? Have you lived chapter twenty nine? In the Bible there is no chapter twenty nine! That chapter is entirely left up to you and me. Not alone, mind you, but with and through all of God's children. What are you going to do about it? We have been given an awesome responsibility, not only to become his hands and feet, but to truly become his disciples to all the world. This is what Jesus has told the eleven disciples in Matthew 28:16-20, The Great Commission: "Then the eleven disciples went to Galilee, to the mountain where Jesus had told them to go. When they saw him, they worshiped him, but some doubted. (Which are you? Worshiper or Doubter?) Then Jesus came to them and said, "All authority in heaven and on earth has been given to me. Therefore go and make disciples of all nations, baptizing them in the name of the Father, and of the Son, and of the Holy Spirit, and teaching them to obey everything I have commanded you. And surely I am with you always to the end of the age."

*God in all His wisdom has picked you to be a part of His newest chapter. Are you ready to accept his invitation? "Behold what manner of love the Father has bestowed on us, that we should be called children of God! 1 John 3:1. Amen and Amen*

# DAY 316

Good morning. Psalm 9:10 says, "Those who know your name will put their trust in you, for you, Lord, have not forsaken those who seek you." And the truth shall set you free! Have you ever heard the ancient Hebrew word, "avanim?" It means weights and measures (balance). Even in those ancient times merchants and kings redefined measures to fit their will. This, from The Book of Mysteries, by Jonathan Cahn, suggests that things never change: "When a civilization redefines its values, when it changes meanings and definitions of reality away from the created order, when it alters the measures of morality, of right and wrong, to conform them to its will and desires...it is turning the objective into the subjective, and man into God. Never change the truth to fit your will. Change your will to fit the truth."

*Never bend the Word of God to fit your life. It is not yours to change! Proverbs 11:1 screams out "A false balance is an abomination to the Lord!" and Isaiah 5:20 makes it quite clear, "Woe to those who call evil good and good evil." Beware, America, for God is watching you! Amen and Amen*

# DAY 317

Good morning. I find myself hungrily reading from the Word. This morning I felt a very strong need, an urgency, to pray for our nation. In John 14:6 Jesus stated, "I am the way and the truth and the life." Are we listening? My eyes become teared as I am afraid that we are a nation that has lost its way; a nation of anger, fear, lies, deceit, distrust. What has happened to integrity, honesty, fairness, truthfulness? I grew up believing that we were one nation, under God, indivisible, with liberty and justice for all. Indivisible—not able to be separated. Under God. No other gods. It breaks my heart to see some of my former students spewing hatred, calling our leaders obscenities, rioting in the streets of our cities. Do you really think that any of this will heal our country of what ails it? I believe our forefathers would be ashamed to see what we have become. America the beautiful is becoming quite ugly! How much of that can be credited to you or your actions or lack of action? Where is your faith? You may not want to hear this, but it starts with you, with me, with every last one of us. This isn't what we want for our children and our children's children.

*Are you willing to get down on your knees and pray for a better nation? Not once, but until we make it so! The Lord stands ready to forgive our trespasses if we confess and turn from them and back to him. Amen and Amen*

# DAY 318

Good morning. I love the mornings. Maybe not getting up so much, but I really love the light of the early morn. There is a special freshness about it all. Everything seems to wake up and come alive (especially after I've had a cup or two of coffee). Just as we would never think to pull the curtains to keep out the beauty of the morning sunlight, the same applies to our lives. Why would we ever wish to remain in the darkness? Matthew 5:15 shares this thought with us: "Neither do people light a lamp and put it under a bushel (bowl), instead they put it on a stand, and it gives light to everyone in the house." Wouldn't you like to offer your light to everyone you meet? Isaiah 60:1 says, "Rise and shine for the light has come." Matthew 5:14 makes it clear that you are the light of the world.

*Take a little advice from the song "Open Up Your Heart." "If I forget to say my prayers the devil jumps with glee. But he feels so awful when he sees me on my knees. So if you are full of trouble and you never seem to win, just open up your heart and let the sunshine in... Smilers never lose, frowners never win. So let the sun shine in, face it with a grin. Open up your heart and let the sun shine in." Amen and Amen*

# DAY 319

Good morning. So often when we pray for or with someone, we pray for healing or their physical well-being. There is nothing wrong with praying in this manner, but there is much more required of us in our daily prayers. Don't overlook the need to forgive or to be forgiven. Remember the all-encompassing need for spiritual well-being and guidance. Offer up thanksgiving and blessings to the Lord and to his Son, Jesus Christ, for all they have done and continue to do in our lives. Don't be afraid to pray for the small things as well as those of great magnitude. He is capable of answering them all! Pray for discernment, wisdom, compassion and understanding. I find nothing wrong with praying for rain and for sunshine, flowers and ladybugs. Pray for peace on earth and goodwill toward mankind. Isaiah 53:4-5 says, "Surely He has born our griefs and carried our sorrows, yet we did esteem him stricken, smitten of God, and afflicted. But He was wounded for our transgressions, He was bruised for our inequities; the chastisement of our peace was upon him, and with his stripes we are healed."

*Praise God, thank you Jesus, come Holy Spirit! Just keep on praying my brothers and sisters! Pray without ceasing, praise without pause. Amen and Amen*

# DAY 320

Good morning. It doesn't take a math major to know that God is Number One. Capitalized. He is the first and foremost of all that we know. In math terms, the number two is prime. Two, as in you and one other. It's always important to understand the numbers. Mind you, I am no great mathematician, but I understand how important it is to do the math. Do you realize that if every person living in the United States recycled thirty pounds of paper per year that would amount to about a billion pounds a year? That is about 2 1/2 pounds a month or a little over an ounce a day. Multiply that by just one prime pair (you and one other) in the world's population, and we are looking at 60 billion pounds. Now try your multiplication tables for a decade or a century. How many of God's trees might we save? The same applies to water— just running the water when we are brushing our teeth or taking an extra five or ten minutes in the shower really adds up. Do you realize that if you alone just read eleven pages a day that would amount to four thousand pages a year or nearly fifty thousand in ten years? You could read the Bible from Genesis to Revelation nearly thirty times in a decade. Think what else you and one other could accomplish in a lifetime. Think about what if that other is none other than God!

*Never let it be said that you don't count, because I know in God's eyes you do and that God is counting on you! That is why I pray every day, but then who's counting? Amen and Amen*

Ahava

אהבה

Love

# DAY 321

Good morning. Are you in a hurry this morning? Most of you will say, "Of course, I am always in a hurry," or "I'm late for work," or "the kids will miss the bus, I've got to leave." Maybe it's "Gotta go pay the light bill," "Forgot I'm picking up Kathy," "My plane leaves in just three hours..." Whoa, take it easy. You say, "Hurry up Jim, I'm too busy to listen long, get to the point." Sit back in your chair and take a deep breath. Let it out very slowly. It'll take only a second or two. Now how about that little prayer you didn't have time for this morning because you felt out of control; it'll just take a few seconds more. Tell God thanks and ask for his guidance for the day. Don't make yourself a slave to time. If you don't control it, it will control you. Now, before the day is over, sit down in your favorite chair, maybe that outside chair. Take another deep breath. Look around, really look. See the things you love all around you and say, "Thank you, Lord." Look into the eyes of the special person in your life. Go ahead, tell them, "I love you." They'll probably ask what's wrong but that's OK.

*Now tomorrow when morning arrives, remember it is your time to manage your time. You can do It. With God, all things are possible! Amen and Amen*

# DAY 322

Good morning. Let's step back in time a little bit. Picture this scene. Jesus is walking along the shore of the Sea of Galilee, stepping around other groups of fishermen until he comes to the group He's looking for. Jesus calls out to Peter, John, Andrew and James, and unexpectedly invites then to join him. They were simple fishermen doing what they always had. What do you suppose He said to them that would entice them to leave their boats, their families, their village, all that was familiar to them? He told them that He would make them fishers of men. Not one of them declined the invitation. I don't think they had a choice, as I believe they were chosen and prepared to respond and follow Jesus. It was part of God's plan. These were the very men that God wanted. He wants you, too! He would not have allowed His Son to go to the cross to be crucified if He hadn't wanted each of us. You, too, have been chosen and prepared to follow Jesus.

*If you say, "I am not deserving," He says, "You are now, because I made it so!" Don't you hear him? He's calling to you, the very one God wants, "Come, follow me." Amen and Amen*

# DAY 323

Good morning. It has been said that we should put away our fears. That's easier said than done, to that I can give testimony. I used to think that I feared nothing, but as I've grow older I realize that fear intrudes into most of our lives. Yes, I have read the verses in the Bible referencing fear, all thirty-three to be exact. One verse that stands out to me is Isaiah 41:10, "Don't be afraid for I am with you. Don't be discouraged, for I am your God. I will strengthen you and help you. I will hold you up with my victorious right hand." Of course I also look to Psalm 23:4, "Even though I walk through the valley of the shadow of death, I will fear no evil for you are with me, your rod and your staff, they comfort me." Perhaps someday I will dismantle my earthly fears. I keep searching, climbing Jacob's ladder if you will, seeking more each day of my Lord.

*Speaking of ladders, heights remain one of my enduring fears. I'm not sure why, as I truly love the majesty of the mountains. Perhaps I just need to trust God more. So I'll rise and shine, give God the glory and I'll keep on climbing until I make It safely home. Amen and Amen*

# DAY 324

Good morning. Who is that in the room with you? As you look around I know a great many of you are answering “not a soul.” There are a number of us who may answer that we are surrounded by the ones that love us most. There may be a few, hopefully only a few, who may say they feel terribly alone and because of it they are afraid. So I am here to tell you, all of you, there is another Person in your presence. You can't see him. Close your eyes. Can you feel him right there next to you? Feel the Holy Spirit within you? Trust me when I say you are not alone. Take a deep breath. It comes from him, for He is the very air we breathe. He has asked me to sing you this song. Thank goodness you can't hear my voice, but only the words. The hymn I share with you is called "God Is In This Place" and it goes like this: "I need to say that God is in this place. And God is right by your side. You need to know that anywhere you go, just by faith His love will abide. The moment could be here and now when you need someone to be there. I'm telling you He is reaching out with love beyond compare and He knows your soul and He knows your heart, knows everything you are. Everybody stumbles, gets lost along the way, but His mercy comes raining down with His amazing grace, ‘cause all you need is just to believe He's waiting to set you free."

*So as we go our way today, let these lyrics remind you to "Put your hand in the hand of the man who stilled the water. Put your hand in the hand of the man who calmed the sea... Put your hand in the hand of the man from Galilee.” You aren’t alone. Amen and Amen*

# DAY 325

Good morning. I have a serious question for you this morning. When and where is it appropriate to hug someone? I am quite aware that it is more than a little awkward to hug someone you don't know. I've heard it said that everyone needs at least three hugs a day. Why is that? Research tells us that laughter and hugging are effective in healing sickness and disease, loneliness, depression, anxiety and stress. They tell us we can benefit from a hug in many different ways: 1 A hug builds a sense of safety and trust. 2 Hugs instantly boost ocytocin levels which serve to heal loneliness, isolation and anger. 3 An extended hug boosts serotonin levels which create a feeling of happiness and calm. 4 Hugs improve the immune system. 5 Hugs boost self-esteem. 6 Hugging relaxes muscles which releases tension and can take away pain. 7 Hugs balance out our nervous system. I won't get into the details of parasympathetic systems here. 8 Hugs serve much like meditation. Let go and be present in the moment. 9 Hugs teach us to give and receive. 10 Hugging becomes an investment in developing relationships. A well-known family therapist states, "We need four hugs a day for survival, eight hugs for maintenance and twelve hugs for growth." So that's why I weigh so much! There are some who need thousands of hugs just to catch up, and you can help. Have you hugged your wife, husband, children, friend, neighbor lately? The widow in the last row at church or someone you met recently probably needs a hug, too.

*So let's get to it. This world needs a whole lot of hugs and I want to be among the first to answer that call. Hugs, kisses and a bit of laughter, I offer to you all. Amen and* Amen

# DAY 326

Good morning. Magicians have fascinated me ever since I was a very young boy. They take us to a land of make believe. I marveled at how they made things appear and disappear. What they did so often seemed impossible. We watched in disbelief, and yet we believed because we saw it with our own eyes. But let's not forget that magicians are entertainers just like comedians, singers or gymnasts. What they do is to make us believe, or should I say, make believe? These magicians have been performing as far back as the time of the pharaohs. Do you remember the stories of Moses in the Pharaoh's court? Yes, the pharaoh's magicians could turn a walking stick into a snake and they even turned water into blood, but their magic was only make believe. Could Egyptian magicians create man from the dust of the earth or separate the waters of the Red Sea? Could they form stars in the sky or make the oceans? Which one could send their only son to a cross so that the sins of this world could be forgiven forever? Impossible.

*Sin isn't make believe and God is about real belief. Yes, to this day, I still love to watch magicians perform, but I love the Lord with all my heart and soul because with him, there is no make believe. He is the Truth. Amen and Amen*

# DAY 327

Good morning. When I was becoming a grown man, I often heard people refer to the patience of Job. I really never gave it much thought. Maybe that was because I have never been a very patient person myself, or maybe it was because I never really knew Job. I knew there are over forty chapters in the Bible that carry his name, but I paid little attention to their content. I could say the same for the twenty-two chapters of Revelation, but that is a topic for another day. As I have accepted my own personal challenge to read the Bible once more in its entirety, I have found myself looking at the chapters of Genesis and Job in a new and different way. Always before, it was much like skimming the surface. Sure I knew about creation, Adam and Eve, Abraham, Isaac, Jacob, Joseph and, yes, even Job; but they were only casual acquaintances. I never really understood their accomplishments and their failures. Most of all I never understood their indomitable faith in God. As I stop to ponder who the real Job was, I don't see a patient Job, I observe a man with unshakable faith that could never be shattered, even by Satan himself. His pain and suffering makes any that I have experienced pale in comparison.

*Lord forgive me for the shallowness of my belief. I want to personally know you just as Abraham, Joseph and Job did. I look forward to continuing my journey into your Word—no more skimming and a lot more praying. Amen and Amen*

Chaverim

Friend

# DAY 328

Good morning. What's on your agenda for today? Do you even have an agenda? Most of us don't have a written plan. I admit these days my plans are usually neatly tucked away in the little gray matter I still possess. I do find it helpful to write an occasional note just to keep me on track. My main problem with making lists is that I have trouble remembering where I put them. Sound familiar to anyone else? It doesn't matter much if the day is mostly a repeat of the day before it, but for many the repeating may be a weekly Monday through Friday pattern. This Friday is like last Friday and every other Friday. It isn't necessarily a bad thing, but a number of us will relate to TGIF. Some agendas are catch-ups to finish what didn't get done during the week. Having reviewed all that, there is one more agenda item to talk about. Have you considered whether your plans for the day-week-month are pleasing to God? Have you penciled in giving thanks for the blessings of each day? Have you asked him what He would like you to put on your to-do list? No? Then take a few minutes at the beginning of your day to talk it over. After all, he created you to be who you are and he is interested in your plans. God has you on his agenda and has just been waiting to hear from you.

*It may sound trite, but there is something to be said for periodically asking yourself WWJD (What Would Jesus Do). Amen and Amen*

# DAY 329

Good morning. I was watching several competitive events the other evening on television. There were the Olympic tryouts for swimming, diving, and gymnastics as well as the college baseball world series and the Ninja Warrior competitions. How hard the athletes must all train, working and sacrificing to reach the level of success they have achieved. Many have spent years honing their skills and talents. I cannot help but look with admiration at the zeal they exhibit. Not everyone feels the way I do. There are some who view them as "fanatics" just focused on achieving acclaim and winning awards. They dismiss anyone like them focused on their race to the finish line. But they haven't met my friend Stephen. He is a "fanatic" of another sort. His race is spiritual and his reward is not an earthly one. He has trained himself to remember Bible verses and uses them frequently in conversation; he faithfully attends church to practice worship; he praises the Lord throughout the day and prays without ceasing to keep his spiritual muscles fine tuned. He relentlessly pursues the goal of being good and doing good, loving his neighbors and helping the less fortunate.

*Paul encourages all of us to be disciplined disciples like Stephen in Hebrews 12:1-3. "Therefore, since we are surrounded by such a great cloud of witnesses, let us throw off everything that hinders and the sin that so easily entangles. And let us run with perseverance the race marked out for us." The race can be grueling but the prize is priceless. Amen and Amen*

# DAY 330

Good morning. Many years ago, while attending graduate school, I came across a book entitled Transactional Analysis or TA, written by Dr. Eric Byrne, a highly respected psychologist. He organized life into various circumstances and outcomes that we all encounter. It went something like this: "Win-Win, Win-Lose, Lose-Win, Lose-Lose. I have always considered myself a winner. Competitive is my middle name. Yours, too? As I have experienced a little (well, a lot more) about life, I have come to understand that you cannot win all the time. That's OK. Did I do my best? Did I give up or give in? That became important to me. In the tenth grade our first year wrestling squad faced Richmond High School, Indiana State Champions, in our first meet. We lost. We were embarrassed. Everyone on our team except one was pinned in the first round, the score 55-0! Did we quit, give up or give in? Not on your life! Hard workouts, weight programs, summer camp and lots of sweat would make a difference. Two years later we defeated that same team and won 33-17. Several years after that, when I applied to graduate school, I was told my undergraduate grades were insufficient and I would be admitted on probationary status for one semester. Two years later I received my master's degree with a perfect 4.0 grade point. I won! Amazing what a supportive family and a desire to achieve can help you accomplish.

*What is it that you and God want you to do? It really isn't all up to you. He will be there beside you all the way to the finish line so like Paul wrote to Timothy, you will also be able to say, "I have fought the good fight, I have finished the race, I have kept the faith." Amen and Amen*

# DAY 331

Good morning. I simply love to read. Since I was a young boy I have been enamored by what others have to say. I have found a degree of pleasure in reading a dictionary, thesaurus or even a phone book. It seems that there is something to be gleaned from almost anything! I was captivated by the biographies of men and women from the past. This led me to a genuine interest in history and it would become a saving grace for this immature rascal. For me, school was more about socializing than learning. I viewed class as a necessary nuisance; the result was mediocrity, but my love for reading never ceased. I once had a teacher who asked me if I was planning to go to college. When I responded in the affirmative, he smiled and said, "Take my advice and don't unpack your bags." My interest in history and reading, and involvement in sports, would define who I was to become. After marriage and starting a family I finally grew up. It wasn't until then that I found the only book that I could never put down. Every time I pick it up I learn something new. I recommend it to everyone. It's the Bible.

*Do you have a copy? Read it often and you'll be singing with me, "I love to tell the story, 'twill be my theme in glory, to tell the old, old story of Jesus and his love. I love to tell the story, more wonderful it seems of all the golden fancies of all our golden dreams. I love to tell the story, it did so much for me; and that is just the reason I tell it now to thee." Amen and Amen*

# DAY 332

Good morning. Are you prepared? Harvest time is nearing. What seeds have you planted along the way? Have you removed all the weeds, briars and brambles that can overrun what you have planted? Left untended they could even make your path impassable. When difficulties arose, did you seek sound advice or experienced assistance? Don't seek help from a butcher, baker or candlestick maker when a master gardener is needed. In Psalm 13:20 we read, "He who walks with the wise, grows wise, but a companion of fools suffers harm." Farmers are well aware that a single bad apple can spoil a barrel. Inspect your fruit as it matures. Be careful from whom you seek advice or help when needed. Have you prepared for the rain and the wind that will inevitably come? Have you mended fences and repaired the gateways that protect your garden? Remember that a quick fix is not always the best answer. Sometimes it takes sweat and tears. When your property is untended or in disrepair you are inviting trespassers, problems and difficulties. Report your progress, make requests and give thanks daily in conversation with the Master Gardener. Without God's help your fruit will never mature. Your fields will never produce. There will be no harvest.

*God doesn't care how big your field is, or how many fruits you tend, but he does care about the quality of your life and the size of your heart. If you are prepared, your harvest will be bountiful and you will celebrate at the Master's table. Amen and Amen*

# DAY 333

Good morning. I so love the sunshine. It has an almost magical way of brightening our days. It's not just the light and the warmth that I reference. It has the ability to wash away sadness and loneliness and a special way to make things new. A few months ago I wrote in my journal about a favorite song of mine from the movie Annie, called "Tomorrow." I love the words. "The sun will come out tomorrow..." What a beautiful message about hope and trust in something better. But my absolute favorite sunshine song has to be "Amazing Grace." I particularly love these two stanzas, "Through many dangers, toils and snares, I have already come. Tis grace that hath brought me safe thus far. And grace will lead me home. When we've been there ten thousand years Bright shining as the sun. We've no less days to sing God's praise than when we first begun." How uplifting to know that God has granted his wonderful grace for ten thousand years and more! We will be bright shining as the sun. Right now you know that others can see the light in you when you smile, and they can feel the warmth of your loving care. Doesn't it make you want to sing? It did David long ago as he wrote Psalm 59:16-17, "But I will sing of your strength in the morning. I will sing of your love, for you are my fortress, my refuge in times of trouble. O my strength (my sunshine), I sing praise to you, O God, you are my fortress, my loving God."

*With God's love in our hearts, we will feel his Son shine in us, even longer than 10,000 years. Forever. Amen and Amen*

# DAY 334

Good morning. Last night I was sitting at home minding my own business when out of the clear blue my stupor was interrupted. I wouldn't call it an epiphany, but my attention was demanded. There was no one there, just the television, the quiet of the night and me. No, I wasn't dreaming and I most assuredly was not drinking. So who was it? The unspoken voice asked, “Why is it you spend more time watching "Sex in the City" and "Modern Family" than you do studying my Word? Do the Kentucky Wildcats or the Denver Broncos mean more to you than my Son?” The words not spoken but clearly heard kept coming. "What comes before your God and your Lord Jesus? You know there is a big difference between wearing a cross and taking up the Cross. Where are you willing to follow Jesus? What price are you willing to pay? Is Jesus your friend or your Savior? Jim, you need to keep reading and learning Matthew 25.”

*Lord, you have my attention! I know I should do more than always thanking Jesus for my blessings. He is my blessing. And I understand Jesus doesn't want me to die today for him, He wants me to die to my selfish desires every day. I believe what He promises. “I am the resurrection and the life. He who believes in me will live even though he dies, and whoever lives and believes in me will never die,” John 11:25-26. Amen and Amen*

El Roi

# אֵל רֳאִי

God Sees Me

# DAY 335

Good morning. "It's not my fault!" I bet I recited that a million times while growing up. Come to think of it, I've made use of it a few times well after puberty. How many of you were blessed with a brother(s) or a sister(s)? So you know what I mean. Many years ago I found that this journal opened up an avenue for conversation with the Lord. There have been many occasions when we talked about faults; my faults, your faults, the world's faults. God always answered that He was not playing with anyone in the blame game. He just wanted to know what I was going to do about playing it myself. I've concluded that I've expended too much energy blaming someone else for my problems and heartaches. I know others have, too. I bet some of us have even blamed the Lord for a few of our failures, even attributing our sadness to him. Just like it is hard to be sad or angry when you're smiling, it's difficult to keep finding fault if you're willing to forgive. Every day we find fault with the president, Republicans, Democrats, the rich, the poor, our wives, our children and yes, even the Lord Almighty. It's all wasted energy. I find that when I stop, think and pray, whatever it was never seems quite as important as it did before. When the fault factor clouds my sight or distorts my hearing, I have to ask myself, in the whole scheme of things, is it worth even another moment of my time? And it never is! Jesus forgives us. We must forgive each other.

*Henry Ford said, "Don't find fault, find a remedy." Jesus said, "Why do you look at the speck of sawdust in your brother's eye and pay no attention to the plank in your own eye?" So...the remedy is in you...and in me. Amen and Amen*

# DAY 336

Good morning. Wouldn't it be wonderful if there was an inoculation for temptation? When you go to get your flu shot there would be a sign announcing that you can now get vaccinations for measles, mumps, pneumonia, the flu—and temptation! After all, it pervades our society. It's at Krispy Kreme when the red light is blinking in their window. Just one won't be enough! Jelly beans and spice drops in the cupboard at home will call to you until you succumb. That thirty mile per hour speed limit causes you to break the law because you're late. There are so many things that entice us: too much alcohol, drug abuse, infidelity, greed, pornography. The list is long. Have you ever laid in bed and said, "Just fifteen minutes more," only to suddenly realize "I'm going to miss my appointment!" Temptation. It's as common as coffee in the morning or tea at bedtime. "The devil made me do it" may be truer than we think. Do you think devil is just an innocuous word? You couldn't be more mistaken. Satan, his politically correct moniker, spreads the disease of Temptation wherever he can. Even Jesus was tempted for forty days in the wilderness. How did He manage? The Bible states that angels ministered to him there. At Gethsemane it says the angels strengthened him. So why not ask for the Lord's remedy and allow him to administer it to you? Receive the Holy Spirit and experience Philippians 4:13; "I can do all things through him who gives me strength."

*Know this. We are all exposed to temptation every day, everywhere. Praise God, we already have the only vaccination against temptation. If you haven't had yours yet, go get it! Amen and Amen*

# D A Y 337

Good morning. Yesterday evening as I was preparing for bed, I chose one of the many journals I had written years ago (1999 to be exact). It is quite amazing how much I had forgotten. I know this, my writings have changed significantly. Back then they were more about the here and the now, today they seem to be more reflective. Then I not only read from the Bible and the Upper Room on a regular basis, but I made every effort to interpret and report what I had read. It was more about historical significance than meaning for my life. Almost every writing brought forward prayers for many folks in my sphere of influence. I was more plugged into praying for others in my writing. Some days the list of those I was praying for was quite lengthy. I really need to do more of that. At fifty-five my life was much more in a state of flux than it is today. Our kids were in the beginning stages of starting their families. Our oldest grandchild is now twenty-four! We've crossed many bridges since that time in our lives. Someday our kids or grandchildren may cherish my writings, especially the ones that include them. Who would have guessed that twenty years later I would still be writing my journals? It is well worth knowing that there is much that has taken place in that long dash in time between then and now. It's been nearly seven thousand three hundred days since then, much has changed and through it all I have become truly aware of how blessed I have been and still am.

*Lord, you are indeed an awesome God to have "saved a wretch like me." I once was lost but now I am found! Amen and Amen*

# DAY 338

Good morning. If Jesus appeared to you today and inquired about your prayer life, how would you respond? I am not looking for the little boy's answer when he was asked if he prayed. It may represent me more than I would like to admit: "Well," he said, "sometimes I pray, but most of the time I just say my prayers." Many of our prayers are of the flesh: "Give me, help me, bless me, me, me." Jesus continually modeled selfless prayers. I wonder if I'm ready to be selfless instead of self-centered. Do I earnestly pray for people who are struck by violence, addiction, strife, hunger, poverty, racism, hatred? I need to pray intentionally with Jesus' example constantly in mind. How is your spiritual tank registering low? Time to "fill up!" When you pray do you think nothing happens? Is that a reason to quit praying? I don't think so! In Habakkuk 1:2 and 2:3 the prophet cried out, "O Lord, how long shall I cry for help, and thou wilt not hear?" God answered him, "It may take a while, but wait for it; it will surely come, it will not delay." What were the disciples were doing when Jesus approached them after praying to his Father? They were sleeping! Are we asleep? I want to always remember what Luke 22:41-44 records that He prayed that night. "Father, if you are willing, take this cup from me, yet not my will but yours be done."

*That is the ideal I must strive for. Jesus, please forgive my selfish lack of passion, the absence of patience, the apathy and sometimes even doubt that weaken my prayers. Thank you for never giving up on me. I ask the Holy Spirit's help as I strive to follow you and pray selflessly. Amen and Amen*

# DAY 339

Good morning. Yesterday I encountered a question that I can't get out of my mind: "What can Jesus do for me today?" We are so used to asking, "What can I do for Jesus?" that it confused me. He can do all things! Philippians 4:14 assures me that "I can do all things through Christ who strengthens me." To my surprise it is I who need Christ to strengthen me, What can Jesus do for me today? He can strengthen me. He is everything to me because I am nothing without him. Without his direction I don't know which way to go. So I said, "Jesus, here I am, I have all day to see what you are going to do." He said to me, "First, take up my cross." Gulp. "Now pray." I prayed, "O Lord, if I am going with you today I need you to uphold me." He answered, "I knew before you asked. Follow me. Rescue the man alone by the curb. Talk kindly to him. He is in trouble. Take him to the homeless shelter where I will begin his healing." I thought I must remember that I am not managing His affairs. He is managing mine. What can Jesus do for me today? He can give me compassion and love for that man! Jesus offers us everything—forgiveness, peace, joy, a love that passes all understanding and eternal life. This morning I read this: "I think if we read the New Testament with clarity and honesty we'll see it doesn't promise anything easier. We're not encouraged there to look for the prize in the package. We are not assured there of any exemption or immunity from life's hardships. We're not promised any cheap triumphs or smooth sailing because of our allegiance. There is only the call to go and care, and give, and serve, and endure and trust in His incredible ability to do something worthwhile with our commitment."

*That's what Jesus can do for us. Amen and Amen*

# D A Y 340

Good Morning. Lord, you are such an awesome God. What great plans do you have for me? Am I being molded like the potters clay? It feels as though the pieces of a puzzle are spread out on the table before me, just waiting to be put in their proper places. The beauty of this puzzle is that You have the authority and ability and I have the opportunity to arrange those pieces to produce a beautiful picture. Or a lovely piece of pottery. Is it a picture or piece of pottery formed from miracles and impossibilities? "All things are possible with God." It is unfortunate that we often spend most of our lives believing that they are limited, that we are not good enough, talented enough, aware enough, rich enough and on and on. We create parameters that result in walls around us that cannot be scaled. At least not by us. But "all things are possible with God." It is true—there is more than enough of everything we need because the Lord has made it so. He offers us a mustard seed of hope that grows faith enough to remove walls and move mountains.

*Today is the first day of the rest of my life and I know I am being molded into a vessel of service to the Lord while the puzzle of what my life will become is less puzzling. One day both vessel and puzzle will be completed and I will walk through an open door into the wonderful future my Lord has created for me. Thank you, Jesus. Amen and Amen*

# DAY 341

Good morning. God is not a sometimes God. He is an all the time God and He expects us to be all the time Christians. We cannot pick and choose when we want the Lord in our lives. How incredulous that we should place ourselves and our personal wants and desires above him! If we seek him to do our will we are on the wrong road to nowhere. Quit making excuses for what you are not. Instead, do something about your sin condition. A good place to start would be with a prayer asking for forgiveness. Then make some really important changes in your life. One step at a time would do for starters and then you can pick up the pace. He will be patient as long as you mean what you say in your prayers to him. He'll even carry you part of the way if you need him to be there for you. Just ask him – you'll see.

*Our prayers aren't something that we do only with our lips. Our prayers are what we do with our lives. Amen and Amen*

Or

אוֹר

Light

# DAY 342

Good morning. We are all called to be God's ambassadors. He has given us the task of reconciling people to him. In 2 Corinthians 5:5 it says, "God himself has prepared us for this, and as a guarantee he has given us his Holy Spirit." Some are uncomfortable with my mentioning receiving the Holy Spirit. Some have expressed their thoughts that wherever and whenever I preach or teach this I am being "pushy" about it. If that be the case then what about Peter saying in Acts 2:38, "Repent and be baptized every one of you in the name of Jesus Christ for the forgiveness of your sins, and you will receive the gift of the Holy Spirit." Paul wrote in Romans 5:5 that "God's love has been poured into our hearts through the Holy Spirit who has been given to us." Some argue that things have changed since then. Yes, some things change, but not the Word of God. I would also contend that the earth possesses the soil and water He created eons ago. I believe that humans are the same, too. We still eat and sleep, feel the heat of the sun and the cool breeze; we still seek to love and be loved; we still seek God. The Holy Spirit and the Lord Jesus were present with God in the beginning and God is never changing, the Creator of life and the foundation of the Universe.

*Importantly, we must always remember that God is the Father, Son and Holy Spirit. You cannot accept the Father without the Son, the Son without the Holy Spirit. Amen and Amen*

# DAY 343

Good morning. To me a believer's smile is like the smile of God. God created us in His image. The aura that a smile releases can be read even by a stranger in the night. In fact, a smile has more to say about who you are and who you belong to than any words you might say. All the years that Jacob felt fear and distance from his brother Esau were erased with a smile and an embrace. I've seen God's covenant, the rainbow that promises the sun will follow the storm. I can't gaze at it without smiling. I pray that the words of my mouth and the words I write will be pleasing to my God, and that they will be of value to others and have an impact on those who are seeking to serve him.

*Lord, I humbly ask you to allow me to be like a rainbow, representing your covenant to everyone I meet. Please let others see your smile on my face. Amen and Amen.*

# DAY 344

How shallow to think that the Bible is just a good book or simply recounts the history of Israel. Some say that the stories in the Bible are little more than fairy tales and imagination. It is so much more than that! Every time I read Proverbs I am amazed at Solomon's wisdom and his wit. His rules and laws for living are every bit as contemporary now as they were when he ruled as King in Israel. The basic pattern of life has not changed much, if at all. It is true that we have added comfortable frills and trappings in our culture, but what transpires within the center of our being remains the same. In the Bible we read about people like ourselves. We still love with the same passion, we continue to seek a better existence, we feel the same inadequacies.

*We need the Bible. It is the foundational document by which we live and die, the covenant of God's relationship to us. It presents the Alpha and Omega and explains our alpha and omega from Genesis to Revelation. Without it nothing else would matter very much. Amen and Amen*

# DAY 345

Good morning. Take pleasure in the riches that the Lord has already given to you. You want to know "what riches?" You think you are poor and have to do without? Nonsense. You have been given rest when you've been weary. You have food and drink available when you are hungry and thirsty. Whether or not your parents were loving and wise, your Lord nurtured you and helped and protected you. He brings loving companions into your life. He provides you with a body that grows from infancy to adulthood and becomes the temple of the Holy Spirit. That is awesomeness! He gives you intellect and wisdom to fulfill your purpose in life. He offers all this and much more (read about it in the New Testament of the Bible) and all you must do is turn from sin and invite him into your life. Accept him as Savior and King. You will be blessed. Partner with the Holy Spirit and you will bless others. Instead of hording your riches He will guide you in what to do with them. You may learn in whatsoever state you are to be content, whether you become the king or the pauper, the leader or the follower, the perceived winner or loser. You are always rich if you are kin to the King of Kings. You have a reserved seat at the table God the Father has set for a celebration feast for His beloved children.

*Remember that excuses are man-made and failure to do something is a choice. Make your decision to join the family of God today if you haven't already. It's the single most important thing you will ever do. As for me, I'm looking forward to feasting at that table with the Lord. Hope to see you there! Amen and Amen*

# DAY 346

Good morning. Rest is good for the weary. It restores us when we need it, but watch out when slumber becomes the objective whether it is needed or not. Use rest wisely and it will serve you well, misuse it and it will become your enemy. Sleeping too much is linked with many of the same health risks as sleeping too little, including heart disease, metabolic problems such as diabetes and obesity, and cognitive issues including difficulty with memory. Similar to people who sleep too little, people who sleep too much have higher overall mortality risks. Nothing material is accomplished when we sleep. We need the balance God created within us. Work without play is not a good recipe. Too much food and too little exercise creates unsatisfactory results. There are no shortcuts to right living but its benefits far outweigh any alternatives.

*The medical advice is to listen to your body and it will tell you what it needs. The spiritual advice is to listen to the Holy Spirit and He will tell you what you need. You just have to listen. Remember, listening is more than just hearing, it is paying attention to your senses, your thoughts and your emotions. As for me, I am "retired" but I don't crave sleep. I seek to be replenished. Amen and Amen*

# DAY 347

Good morning. Did you ever get sand in your shoes or your bathing suit? Have you ever changed a baby's dirty diaper? Ever spill mustard on your favorite shirt or have an ink pen leak in your good suit's coat pocket? Did you ever get a flat tire on the way to work? Have you ever been turned down for a date or a job? Ever lost a job? Ever lost possession of something you highly valued? Ever mourned a parent or a child? Did you fail a test? Were you told you aren't good enough? Did you ever distrust a friend or worse yet did a friend ever doubt you? Did you ever doubt God? Well, join the crowd. It is at these low points in our lives that we discover what we are really made of. We have instinct to fall back on or we reach deeper and make conscious choices. Do we instinctively strike back? Complain? Cry out in anger? Give in to pain? Blame God? Or do we seek the Holy Spirit, Our Comforter, Advocate, Intercessor, Counselor, and Strengthener? Life is not always easy, or as we would like it to be, but that is exactly how we truly come to appreciate the life God has given to us. We know that God is good when times are good. But it is in the hard times that we come to realize that God is better than good, He is love. That's exactly what we need in both the good times and the bad.

*So the phrase from the movie God Is Not Dead is verifiably true. "God is good all the time; all the time God is good." Best of all, without a doubt, God Is Love. Amen and Amen*

# DAY 348

Good morning. We all look at each day differently; some with anticipation and some with trepidation. We do tend to make life more difficult than it has to be, worrying about matters that we have no control over or that will never occur. Some of us are nearly traumatized at the dawning of a new day. Some of us wake up angry or without hope. Then there are those who simply want to get up just to eat or be entertained by television or telephone. That said, I say you can change the world by a simple act of kindness. Short of healing, there is no greater antidote for the sick or distressed than surprising them with unexpected acts of kindness. There is no prescription for doing this kind of good deed, but Jesus personified the idea long ago. When He unexpectedly told his disciples that loving friends was good, but loving strangers and enemies was better, He personally showed them, and us, how it works. Although there are many books about this topic, I want to offer you a few suggestions. When you pray for someone's need, hold their hand in yours. Smile at people you don't know. Hand out a flower or little bouquet in a nursing home or senior center, and hug at least one person. Welcome a newcomer into your neighborhood or your church and give them your phone number. Tell your wife and children that you really love them, a lot! Tip your waitress before she serves you. Give away a good book you really enjoyed to someone who needs it or wants a copy. Laugh at your mistakes and kindly accept those of others. Oh, and feed the birds when the weather is beastly.

*This could become what you work into your schedule every day. Amen and Amen.*

Kadosh

קָדוֹשׁ

Holy

# DAY 349

Good morning. It's almost like magic to our generation—the great accomplishments of mankind. We proudly talk of how far we have come. We are sure we are responsible for all the wonderful social, mechanical and scientific wonders of our world. We flippantly laugh, "Who needs God?" Well, for one, I surely do. His work isn't magic. It's for real. Who do you know who can turn night into day? Which one of us can make a seed into a glorious flower or turn a caterpillar into a royal butterfly? Can we claim to change the color of the leaves or turn the browning grass into green with just a few sprinkles from a spring shower? Who do you know that has piled earth and rock as high as Mt. Everest? Or scooped out anything as deep as an ocean? And just who do you think made us? He's the only one I know who can answer my prayers. And let's not forget He is the One who gave us the amazing capacity to love. He gave us the Word made flesh to dwell among us, Emmanuel. He gave us the Bible, so we could come to know him more completely. We need to know 1 Corinthians 1:31, "Therefore, as the Scriptures say, 'If you want to boast, boast only about the Lord,'" and Colossians 2:16-17, "Everything has been created through him and for him. He existed before everything else began and He holds all creation together."

*Today let us celebrate the Lord God and the wondrous creation He has made from nothing, and the men and women He gave life who have been inspired to develop our great social, mechanical and scientific wonders. Amen and Amen*

# DAY 350

Good morning. The world is full of nay-sayers. If you want to find something negative you won't have to search very far. They are in our government, in our churches, schools, our jobs, and yes, they even lurk within our families. Many great ideas have shriveled and died simply because of a dismissive word from a pessimist. Many dreams have turned to ashes because of a cynical comment. No one has the right to cut down your ideas or to crush your dreams. That's why God created stubborn minded thinkers and impossible dreamers, believers who just won't accept failure. Where would we be today if Noah had listened to the likes of the nay-sayers while he was building the Ark? Or what if Paul let scoffers wear him down as he preached the gospel to the Gentiles? What would our modern world be like without God's persistent dreamers and thinkers we call the Pilgrims and our Founding Fathers? There wouldn't be such a thing as space exploration and astronauts without resolute believers, thinkers and dreamers.

*Pessimists have not left much of a footprint on our history while we have been immeasurably enriched by optimists. God bless them all! Amen and Amen*

# DAY 351

Good morning. God in his grace has offered us all gifts. Our responsibility is to find them and use them for the purpose of serving him and others well. If you say, "I have no talents," you may be correct, though I doubt it's true. Be aware that each of us has been granted a gift from God. Let's begin with the most important and universal gift, love. Every last one of us has been blessed with this gift from our first breath. If you have been honored with the gift of prophesy, don't be afraid to speak out. God has also given you as much confidence as you need. If your gift is serving, then serve others humbly and well. If it is teaching, then teach with all your heart. If you have been offered the gift of encouragement, use it to the fullest for adults and especially children. Generosity is a gift that keeps on giving. If you have received the gift of leadership use it wisely and accept the responsibility that goes with it. The gift of courage can help in times of trial and tribulation. Kindness is a gift we can all hope to have. Never be afraid to work hard, to be patient, to persevere. Hospitality is an important gift; use it to welcome people to your home, your church, your Lord.

*Whatever your gift, you can be a prayer warrior when it is time for spiritual battles. My prayer is that you find your gift, use it faithfully, and pray powerfully. Amen and Amen*

# DAY 352

Good morning. How are you doing? Answers can vary: "Ok", "alright," "not bad," "pretty good I guess," "best I can," "so kind of you to ask." Nobody has responded to me with, "Why are you asking?" or "Do you really want to know?" If you're asking me, here is my litany: "My stomach is a little turbulent. My lower back hurts every morning when I get up. I have a sinus headache and allergies. Did you already know about my knee and hip pains? Yes, I really do have a pain in the neck but so far this morning I haven't had an anxiety attack. I could go on and on, but I'll just add I need a cup of coffee and let it go at that." I'm just being facetious. Aren't you glad! Actually, I feel blessed that these aging bones still raise me up and out of bed every morning so I can lift my hands and thank the Lord for the blessing of another day. It's amazing how sunshine, a little fresh air, and a refreshing drink from the Word of the Lord can make me feel good. If you really do ask me later how I'm doing, no matter what I say you already know the truth.

*I have the joy of the Lord because I was with him earlier this morning. Now I am fine as a frog's hair and if I was any better there would be two of me! Amen and Amen*

# DAY 353

Good morning. Don't you think God just loves sharing His creation with all who want to see it? Last evening there was the most magnificent sunset I think I have ever seen. I captured a representative of it digitally, but its extraordinary glory could not be transferred through my camera's lens. So it is with the lives we lead. Those special moments of splendor and beauty that happen to us can't be fully captured either. Recall "falling in love" for the first time? The initial explosion like fireworks, with aftershocks that rippled and sparkled through you for weeks, can't be seen or heard, only felt. I will never forget when my wife told me she was pregnant. A glow began somewhere near my heart, spreading throughout my body, filling and warming me head to toe. Nobody could see the sweet emotion; only what it produced—teary eyes and a big smile! And you can't explain the feeling of peace and joy that overcomes you when the Lord calls, "Follow me," and you unequivocally respond, "Yes Lord, yes, to your will and to your way. I will trust you and obey."

*Lord, you are in the early morning sunrise and in the sweetest emotions of our days. Now we see as in a glass, darkly, but one day we will see your glory face to face. Amen and Amen*

# DAY 354

Good morning. Wake up my friends, it's a brand new day filled with opportunities, with possibilities. This is not just a day—it's a miraculous day! Behold this day that has never shown itself before. It's time to stuff your troubles, difficulties, and sorrow into a bag and leave it behind. God is offering you a fresh start. Accept it. There is only one requirement and that is that you seek him first. "Oh, that we might know the Lord. Let us press on to know him. He will respond to us as surely as the arrival of dawn or the coming of rains in early spring." (Hosea 6:3) Michael Buble's song "Feeling Good" expresses the freedom of a new day with the Lord. "It's a new dawn. It's a new day. It's a new life for me and I'm feeling good. Dragonfly out in the sun, you know what I mean, don't you know. Butterflies all havin' fun, you know what I mean..."

*"...sleep in peace when the day is done, that's what I mean and this old world is a new world and a bold world, for me. I feel so good!" I know what you mean! Amen and Amen*

# DAY 355

Good morning. Have you praised the Lord this morning? Don't you think you should? Rejoice in being forgiven! Be grateful for the guidance of the Holy Spirit in understanding scripture. "Bless the Lord, O my soul, and all that is within me bless your holy name!" Praise God from whom all blessings flow; count your blessings, name them one by one. Do you still need encouragement to face the day ahead? Here is a suggestion. Pick up your Bible and begin reading the book of Romans, Chapter Eight. It's only thirty-nine verses long and it'll only take a few minutes of your time. Read it slowly, though, and stop if you must. Let the words flow into you to become a part of who you are. You are being invited to become a part of God's family, one of His beloved children. Only through him and with him can we overcome the sin and darkness that sometimes clouds our lives. It wouldn't hurt us to read this every day until we know without a doubt who we are in Christ Jesus.

*I am especially comforted by what He tells us in Romans 8:31: "If God is for us, who can ever be against us?" I particularly like the word "ever," as in forever and forever, God Is for us! Amen and Amen*

Shekinah

Dwelling Glory

# DAY 356

Good morning. "So the last will be first, and the first shall be last." Matthew 20:16. Let's look at firsts and lasts. Much of life centers on firsts. In fact we seldom consciously make a decision to be last. Let's see: first words, first walk, first day of school, first bicycle, first best friend, first girlfriend, first boyfriend, first football game, first dance, first time away from home, first job, first love, first child, first new car, first home. I bet there were a lot of terrific firsts. And the most important first of all, Jesus Christ, our one and only Savior. But then there are some firsts that aren't so good: first shot for going to first school, first death in the family, first death of a friend, first failure, first mistake. Even worse, there are the lasts. We don't feel very comfortable about "and the first shall be last." We don't like last words, the last time, last chance, last hope, last minute. Then there is this surprising last: "In the last days," God said, "I will pour out my Spirit upon all people. Your sons and daughters will prophesy, your young men will see visions and your old men will dream dreams. In those days I will pour out my Spirit upon all my servants, men and women alike, and they will prophesy. And I will cause wonders in the heavens above and signs on the earth below—blood and fire and clouds of smoke. The sun will be turned into darkness, and the moon will turn blood red, before the great and glorious day of the Lord arrives. And anyone who calls on the name of the Lord will be saved." Acts 2:17-21.

*And the most important last is the same as the most important first: Jesus Christ our Savior. He is the Alpha and Omega, the First and the Last. Amen and Amen*

# DAY 357

Good morning. Some of you may think you can "read" me (not referring to my writing). I guess that means I am pretty transparent. But I am much more sensitive than you might think. I cry openly at sad movies and when those who I care about are hurting. I can find humor in nearly anything, even though it sometimes causes a groan here and there. I love my family and friends deeply. I'm known for hugging almost everybody. I have been captured by the Holy Spirit, even though I foolishly attempt to escape His grasp from time to time. I am very inquisitive. Perhaps that is why I love history and is also the reason I love to read. I read something from the Bible every day, as well as daily passages from The Book of Mysteries by Jonathan Cahn. I have just begun a new book, The Power of Yes! the latest in the Chicken Soup for the Soul series. Did you know this series began twenty-five years ago? The books are written like grandma cooked, with some of most everything so there's something for most everybody.

*Did you know that much about the real me? I'd like to know more about the real you. Let's have a conversation soon! This short monologue has been brought to you by station WHOIAM, 3.16 on your dial. Amen and Amen*

# DAY 358

Good morning. Celebrating mothers on a single day is like trying to celebrate Jesus on a single day. Seriously, our mothers and Jesus are a lot alike and worthy of our praise. From day one they pledged total unselfish love for each one of us. Mother and Jesus carried us until we grew strong enough to walk alone, then she and He walked beside us. She held us cradled in her arms; He embraced us from the cross. She rocked us, He is our rock. She sang about Jesus to us, and nurtured us. She encouraged us, laughed with us, cried with us, taught us and yes she even disciplined us, just as Jesus did. She never gave up on us even when we fell short. Neither did He. Because of our mother's we were made ready to face a daunting and challenging world. Because of Jesus we can overcome the world.

*She gave us life. He gave His life. We trust her. We trust him. We love her. We adore him. Let's celebrate them often! Amen and Amen*

# DAY 359

Good morning. What is it that you are seeking? Trust in the Lord and He will show you the way. The pathway of your life is filled with mysteries and the unexpected. It is truly impossible to know what tomorrow holds in store for any of us. That is precisely why it is so important to trust in the Lord. He knows! And whatever else is on the road, with him there is happiness to be found, joy to be explored, contentment to be experienced, grace to be felt and oh, yes, His love that envelops us. How does that all sound to you? Sounds the best to me! Along the way we should all take some time to learn, to explore, to feel excitement and to be entertained by our world. Just remember, if you take too much time along the way picking the berries there may be no time to eat the pie!

*As for me, I love this adventure created for me by God. I'll gratefully turn the steering wheel over to him; after all, He knows the way home! Amen and Amen*

# DAY 360

Good morning. Pass it on! Have you ever considered how many possibilities we have to do just that? I hope it's not just passing along the common cold. There is so much to be gained when we share our abilities, our experiences and our unique knowledge. We certainly owe a debt of gratitude to our parents for all they have given to us. My mother showed me overwhelming support and love, helping me integrate into the world around me. Dad, the master of the positive, demonstrated courage, showing me how a man faces challenges. One thing that I will always cherish that my father passed on was to be the family prayer warrior. As far back as I can remember it was my dad that taught us to pray at bedtime and family meals would have been incomplete without his leading thanks from the head of the table. On Thanksgiving Day 1995, he told me, "Jim, you offer the prayer today." Dad joined hands with the Lord that very evening and I have been praying ever since. What would you like to pass on? Maybe the hymn "Pass It On" will get you thinking. "It only takes a spark to get a fire going and soon all those around can warm up its glowing. That's how it is with God's love. Once you've experienced it you spread his love to everyone. You want to pass it on..."

*..."I wish for you my friend this happiness that I have found. You can depend on him. It matters not where you are bound. I'll shout It from the mountain top. I want my world to know; the Lord of love has come to me. I want to pass it on," to you! Amen and Amen*

# DAY 361

Good morning. Even though everything in all creation emanates from our Lord, God sent him to dwell among us for a time as the Word made flesh, then He returned to heaven. God has also provided us a written Word, the Bible, that we might continue to learn and grow in faith and witness. And there's more! We have the ability to express our experiences as part of God's ultimate plan as we write to one another, write about one another, and write about God. I have been humbled and blessed to attend a writer's group in our small mountain community. Each and every one in attendance has a story to tell, aptly part of God's Great Story. There is always humor and laughter mixed with sadness and tears. They tell about a Navaho Indian girl, about chapters in their lives, and the chickens, corsages and classrooms that taught them life lessons. They share stories about pets and angels as we explore the gospel contained in everyday life.

*A picture is worth a thousand words, but a thousand words or more can tell the personal details of the story of God's love, guidance, grace and humor, from His children's point of view! Amen and Amen*

# D A Y 362

Good morning. I remember a my brief experience with scouting. We were taught a very important principle: Be prepared. Have we taken that bit of personal advice seriously enough? There are so many things in life that really do require preparation if we are to succeed. Some of us have been satisfied just to "get along." Most of my early education experiences were just that. I seemed to be more interested in everything other than that which was happening in the classroom. The result was mediocrity. My saving grace was my thirst for reading. How do you learn about axioms, postulates, nouns and verbs without preparation? Was I doing enough to prepare myself for college, a vocation or any other work? Thank goodness for athletics! It kept me in school. All of our God given talents can be wasted if we are not preparing the way to use them. We cannot blame our lack of success on anyone else if we are not ready and willing to prepare ourselves for the future encounters we all will face. Just as you prepare for bad weather, you need to be ready for life's challenges as they appear. Even squirrels prepare for the winter. Have you prepared yourself for a successful marriage and family? Are you prepared for the vocation that you really want? Are you prepared for retirement? You know Jesus has told us He is coming again. Are you prepared for that?

*If your life is out of order it's time to do something about it. I have a suggestion I know from experience is even better than the Boy Scout motto. It's easy to remember and you can start right away. It even rhymes. Be pre-prayered. Start with prayer and go from there. Jesus knows the way, even when we don't. Amen and Amen*

Olam

עוֹלָם

Eternity

# DAY 363

Good morning. Do you suppose Jesus cried when there was no one to play with when he was a child? Think He ever told a funny story or tripped over His own feet? Do you wonder if He ever stubbed his toe or ate more than He should? Did He weep at injustice or feel angry at the sight of greed? Was He ever disheartened; could He have experienced the pain of falling short? I believe He may well have experienced all of these and more. His Father made it so, that He might know what it was like to be "only human." What made him so different was that He was perfect, without sin! He came to know us, to teach us, to lead us, to forgive us and most of all to love us. He came not as a god, not as a king, a general or even a warrior. He came as the son of a simple carpenter in a small village hamlet, much like many we know today. He came so he could get to know us. Do you know him? When He comes to my doorway, I want to invite him in!

*I praise him, trust him, and love him with everything that is within me. My prayer is that you and I can walk with him on the road to Emmaus, or any other road for that matter. Amen and Amen*

# DAY 364

Good morning. I spoke with a woman yesterday evening who is training to become a foster grandparent. How cool is that? (Cool: a term old people use to attempt to be in sync with the now generation.) It got me to thinking about all those "out there" who need someone to love them. Could you or I become that special one? No one is expecting us to be another Mother Teresa! But on a smaller scale we could be like Greta Van Susteren (The Greta Home and Academy in Haiti) and Dolly Parton (The Imagination Library) or Lord Badon Powell (The Boy Scouts) and William Booth (The Salvation Army). With the Lord all things are possible. Just think about the need. Currently in the United States there are more than 400,000 children in foster care hoping for adoption. There are others in need of person to person love: children falling behind in school who need tutors, teens needing mentors. There are old folks and families needing food and friendship; widows and widowers grieving the loss of a lifelong mate. There are new residents to the community. How about welcoming and befriending them? Let's open our eyes and our hearts to those near us.

*Just think how we can love someone. We could make a difference. Then they could make a difference. On and on and on it could go! Amen and Amen*

# DAY 365

Good morning. All is quiet around me now as my thoughts trail on into the past. But as I was traveling home from a business venture in Knoxville one day, a hidden drawer below the passenger seat suddenly popped open and what did I see? One of my journals staring up at me! Funny, I had completely forgotten that it was even there. Now here it was, big as life, my first journal, April 10, 1996. So I soon found myself fingering through those beginning pages. I had long forgotten many of the names of places I had traversed. As I was leafing through those opening days and weeks, I came across this entry: "Wouldn't it be heavenly if we could make the most of every day? Remember, it is important to know what you want to do and where you want to go." This was followed by a wish list of things I'd really like to do: "Write some good poetry. Create a children's book. Re-learn how to draw. Plant pretty flowers. Go on long, slow rides. Play golf. Walk in the mornings. Use the grill. Spend time reading, both for fun and to learn. Pray with more purpose. Spend time with my stamp collection. Get rid of excess material things. Call and write to friends. Have a picnic. Go fishing. Fix what's broken. Learn about computers. Clean the garage. Spend at least one day without TV or radio. Learn to play the piano. Go to a good movie. Sit on the porch. Take a vacation. Take more pictures. Have a garage sale."

*So how'd I do? Not going to tell you! But there are five more things I have added to the list: love my wife more every day, know my Lord and Savior more completely, pray for peace in this troubled world, live life to its fullest daily, and publish a book of entries drawn from my journals. Amen and Amen*

Ah-mehn and Ah-mehn

Amen and Amen

CPSIA information can be obtained
at www.ICGtesting.com
Printed in the USA
LVHW020335180619
621530LV00003B/4/P

9 780578 511634